Tom Morton-Smith Plays 1

Tom Morton-Smith Plays 1

In Doggerland
Oppenheimer
The Earthworks
Ravens

TOM MORTON-SMITH

methuen | drama
LONDON · NEW YORK · OXFORD · NEW DELHI · SYDNEY

METHUEN DRAMA
Bloomsbury Publishing Plc
50 Bedford Square, London, WC1B 3DP, UK
1385 Broadway, New York, NY 10018, USA
29 Earlsfort Terrace, Dublin 2, Ireland

BLOOMSBURY, METHUEN DRAMA and the Methuen Drama logo are trademarks of Bloomsbury Publishing Plc

First published in this collection in Great Britain 2024

In Doggerland © Tom Morton-Smith, 2013
Oppenheimer © Tom Morton-Smith, 2015
The Earthworks © Tom Morton-Smith, 2017
Ravens © Tom Morton-Smith, 2019

Tom Morton-Smith has asserted his right under the Copyright, Designs and Patents Act, 1988, to be identified as author of this work.

Cover image: *The Reception* © Andrew Rovenko

All rights reserved. No part of this publication may be reproduced or transmitted in any form or by any means, electronic or mechanical, including photocopying, recording, or any information storage or retrieval system, without prior permission in writing from the publishers.

Bloomsbury Publishing Plc does not have any control over, or responsibility for, any third-party websites referred to or in this book. All internet addresses given in this book were correct at the time of going to press. The author and publisher regret any inconvenience caused if addresses have changed or sites have ceased to exist, but can accept no responsibility for any such changes.

No rights in incidental music or songs contained in the work are hereby granted and performance rights for any performance/presentation whatsoever must be obtained from the respective copyright owners.

All rights whatsoever in this play are strictly reserved and application for performance etc. should be made before rehearsals by professionals and by amateurs to Casarotto Ramsay & Associates Ltd, Waverley House, 7–12 Noel Street, London W1F 8GQ Mail to: agents@casarotto.co.uk. No performance may be given unless a licence has been obtained.

A catalogue record for this book is available from the British Library.

A catalog record for this book is available from the Library of Congress.

ISBN: PB: 978-1-3504-5388-3
ePDF: 978-1-3504-5390-6
eBook: 978-1-3504-5389-0

Series: Contemporary Dramatists

Typeset by Newgen KnowledgeWorks Pvt. Ltd., Chennai, India
Printed and bound in Great Britain

To find out more about our authors and books visit www.bloomsbury.com and sign up for our newsletters.

Contents

Introduction by Tom Morton-Smith vii
Foreword by Pippa Hill xi
In Doggerland 1
Oppenheimer 81
The Earthworks 203
Ravens 245

Introduction

This volume contains four plays – two plays about grief, two plays about physics and two about New York-born Jewish geniuses both called Robert.

The earliest of these, *In Doggerland*, was written on-spec after a stint as writer-in-residence with the Paines Plough theatre company. I have always enjoyed writing at scale – the thrill of large companies of actors taking up space on the biggest stages, big ideas and big politics – but it was whilst writing for Paines Plough that I learnt how to write in a more detailed and delicate way. I had started researching a play about transplant tourism and had originally intended for Marnie and Linus to travel abroad for Marnie's life-saving operation. But there were curious little details that I discovered during my research that pulled me away from a large-scale piece and towards something more delicate and human. I particularly remember listening to an interview with a transplant recipient who felt great unease at receiving someone else's heart and repeatedly made himself retch to vomit it out. To have your heart removed and incinerated – the heart being so symbolic of the self – must be an incredibly powerful type of bereavement, so what is the process of grief that someone in that situation would go through? What resulted is the play as published here – of four characters grieving for forms or parts of themselves, being moved and healed by each other.

In 2011 I was invited by the Royal Shakespeare Company (RSC) to attend a series of workshops designed to encourage playwrights to think about writing with a sense of the epic. There were six of us who were treated to sessions with the RSC's rhetoric coaches and voice department (and a trip to see *Matilda*) in the hope that it might inspire ideas that could fill those grand spaces in Stratford-upon-Avon. We were then invited to pitch 'the biggest thing you can think of'. I pitched an eight-play cycle on the history of physics in the twentieth century. It came from a desire to write something that might have the breadth and scale of Shakespeare's History Cycle, and the scope of twentieth-century physics – from the birth of quantum mechanics in the 1920s to the out-there ideas of Multiple World theory in the 1970s – seemed to be an obvious fit to me. Clearly the RSC did not commission all eight plays, but they did ask me to pick one that I might want to have a go at writing. I started work on *Oppenheimer*, about a man who traded his principles for power – a suitably Shakespearean story arc. I researched and wrote the play in the evenings whilst I continued in my day job working for Waterstones. This was a man who sacrificed and severed so many of his relationships and associations to create a weapon of as then unparalleled force. He shed his friendships and his lovers just as the atoms of heavy elements eject particles to become more stable – a suitable metaphor for someone who dehumanized himself to such an extent that he 'became Death, the destroyer of worlds'. The success of *Oppenheimer* meant that I was able to support myself as a writer, wave goodbye to the life of a bookseller and finally feel comfortable in calling myself a playwright.

The Earthworks began life as a short play commissioned for a music festival. I have returned to it time and again, expanding and rewriting it until it became the piece that you find in this volume. I think the reason that I keep coming back to the piece is that I simply enjoy spending time with the characters. The play toys with the conventions of romcoms at the start but evolves into a character piece where two strangers – one overflowing and drowning, and one hollow and alone – meet and are immeasurably changed in a single night. I very much had Richard Linklater's *Before Sunrise* in mind as I wrote – with characters unpacking ideas and philosophies, and verbalizing them maybe for the first time, in a way that can happen with someone you've only just met. I have returned to the play again recently – it has been optioned as a screenplay and is getting its first revival next year (at the Young Vic) – so it goes on evolving, and Fritjof and Clare's relationship continues to develop.

Ravens feels like the obvious response to the success of *Oppenheimer* – another mid-twentieth-century bioplay, another genius, another Robert – but it was never written with the intention of being a 'Bobby Fischer play'. Fundamentally the story is one of populism and that of a revered institution struggling to enforce its guidelines so as to contain and exploit the appeal of a disruptive outlier. Rules are bent and petulance is tolerated because the world of chess was seduced by Fischer's popularity. In a political landscape inhabited by Tr*mp and J*hns*n, it felt like an aptly absurd period of recent history to revisit. The intention was to have two very different worlds existing together on stage. The Russian team and their fumbling was to have something of the workplace comedy about it, as though Spassky and his colleagues existed in the world of *The Thick of It*. Whereas the Bobby Fischer scenes were to be paranoid and shifting, a series of duologues with few returning characters. I had imagined Kissinger stalking the stage like one of Scrooge's ghosts.

I am thrilled that this anthology has been published – it brings together plays that cover a significant and meaningful period of my career. I have always tried to write plays that were as entertaining as they were thoughtful. Theatre is at its best when it provides a safe place for your heart to break – it allows for deep emotion and deep contemplation and has the power to support audiences through difficult times and with difficult questions. I hope you enjoy the plays contained within these pages – they are little bits of myself that I have poked and prodded and nurtured into being, and I give them to you.

Tom Morton-Smith
October 2023

Foreword

Tom sent me his first play in 2003 when I was running Hampstead Theatre's Start Night for emerging writers. It was an extraordinary piece of writing: wildly imaginative, formally inventive, deeply heartfelt, beautifully observed, utterly gripping. It lit up the page and ignited a working relationship between us that has spanned twenty years.

Tom wrote *In Doggerland* at the same time as he was writing *Oppenheimer* for me at the Royal Shakespeare Company. The two plays sum up for me Tom's extraordinary range: they are both epic but in totally different ways, they both skewer what it means and what it feels like to make world-changing decisions. Tom delivered a first draft of *Oppenheimer* in November 2011. It was well over a hundred pages long and was titled *Part One*. We worked together on the play through a series of dramaturgical sessions and workshops with director Angus Jackson and the play became the first new play to be programmed by Erica Whyman at the RSC, opening in January 2015. *Oppenheimer* transferred to the Vaudeville Theatre in London in 2015. We worked together on *My Neighbour Totoro* and *The Earthworks* while *Ravens* was in development and production at Hampstead Theatre. *The Earthworks* premiered at The Other Place in Stratford-upon-Avon in 2017 directed by Erica Whyman.

Tom writes with an exquisite economy that's both weighted and devastating. He writes on a scale that is both rare and exceptionally difficult, yet he makes it look effortless. He writes with heart and generosity – in a way that looks into the very essence of people and examines them with precision and empathy. He's an exceptional, fearless playwright and a dear friend.

Pippa Hill
Head of New Work
Royal Shakespeare Company
26 October 2023

In Doggerland

a play by

Tom Morton-Smith

In Doggerland

For JMS and GMS, with love and thanks.

Special thanks to Réjane Collard, Elly Green and Derek Bond for their support and dramaturgy, and to Paul Robinson and the team at Theatre503.

In Doggerland was first performed by Box of Tricks at The Lowry Studio, Salford Quays, on 7 November 2013.

Linus	Benjamin Blyth
Kelly	Natalie Grady
Simon	Clive Moore
Marnie	Jennifer Tan

Director	Hannah Tyrrell-Pinder
Designer	Rachel Wingate
Lighting Designer	Jack Dale
Sound Designer	Chris James
Composer	Chris Hope
Producer	Adam Quayle
Casting Director	Rebecca Jenner

Characters

Simon, *father*
Kelly, *daughter*
Linus, *brother*
Marnie, *sister*

1.

A hospital corridor.

Simon *and* **Kelly** *Lowe sit on plastic chairs.*

Simon *has a lot of blood on his shirt. He looks a little beaten up. Two of his fingers have been splinted and a cut on his face has steri-strips holding it together. He has been in a car accident. He can't look at* **Kelly**.

Kelly *dressed in a hurry; she threw on some tracky-bottoms and a jumper when she heard of the accident.*

Nothing but the sound of fluorescent tubes.

Kelly *stands and exits.*

Simon *barely moves. He stares at the floor.*

Long silence.

Kelly *returns, two plastic cups of water in her hands.*

Kelly *offers* **Simon** *a water.*

Simon *doesn't look up.*

Kelly Water.

Simon *takes it without looking – he doesn't drink, he just holds it.*

Kelly *sits.*

Silence.

Kelly If she needs anything ... any blood or ... or anything ... (*Beat.*) Have you let them know that?

Simon *silence.*

Kelly Do they know that?

Simon I'm sure that they do.

Silence.

Kelly Dad ...?

4   In Doggerland

Simon I'm sorry but I can't ...

Kelly That's completely ... yes ... no ... fine.

Simon Just don't say anything.

Kelly Yes ... course ... it's fine ... it's fine.

Silence.

2.

A cheap B&B.

A small handbasin to one side. Two single beds. Tea and coffee making facilities.

Linus *is at the basin wanting to brush his teeth, but there is no water in the taps.*

Marnie *is sat on one of the beds, eating biscuits, a bottle of Coke between her knees. A large, professional-looking digital camera is sat on the bed next to her.*

Linus *turns the taps. A loud groaning of pipes.*

Linus Nothing.

Marnie Brush them dry.

Linus How is that good for the gums?

Marnie You'll survive one night.

Linus *brushes his teeth.*

Marnie Does the kettle work?

Linus No water for my teeth ... no water for your kettle.

Marnie Go down and ask.

Linus Tomorrow.

Marnie Go down and talk to the lady.

Linus Tomorrow. (*Spits in the basin.*) This is no good.

Marnie *offers him her Coke.*

Linus *takes it and rinses his mouth out.*

Marnie *takes a picture of him with her camera.*

Linus Brushing my teeth? Why do you want a picture of me brushing my teeth?

Marnie *shrugs.*

Linus Let me see. (*Takes the camera and starts cycling through the photos on the tiny screen on the back.*)

Marnie What do you think? Do you like them?

Linus You took these today?

Marnie What do you think?

Linus Do you want criticism or praise?

Marnie Praise.

Linus The composition is very strong.

Marnie Thank you.

Linus The light … the contrast of the light and shadow … and these …

Marnie Which ones?

Linus … these … the old woman … the way she stands … the way she stands … you capture something very …

Marnie Very …?

Linus I don't know. Very ordinary … very moving … I guess.

Marnie You like them?

Linus Yes.

Marnie Good.

Linus You know I like your pictures.

Marnie Yes.

Linus You've got talent.

Marnie Talent is common. You need skill.

Linus You have that too.

Marnie Thanks. (*Beat.*) Now the criticism, please.

Linus I want to lie down.

Marnie Criticism.

Linus I'm tired.

Marnie You have some though?

Linus You know I do.

Marnie Say it.

Linus It's not constructive.

Marnie Say it.

Linus When did you take these?

Marnie Which ones?

Linus The old woman.

Marnie This afternoon.

Linus When?

Marnie You were looking for road signs … you were looking for street names. You told me to wait.

Linus These at the bus-stop …

Marnie Yeah?

Linus You ask their permission?

Marnie No.

Linus People don't want to be photographed at a bus-stop.

Marnie They don't know.

Linus   The old woman is hanging out her laundry.

Marnie   Yeah.

Linus   How old is she?

Marnie   Granny-age … great-granny-age.

Linus   She's hanging out her laundry … on a line. Where were you when you took this?

Marnie   Nearby.

Linus   There's some of her doing her washing up … through her kitchen window … taken through her kitchen window.

Marnie   I was fascinated by her.

Linus   You were stalking her. In her own home.

Marnie   I thought she was beautiful.

Linus   You slink around in her back garden – what if she had seen you?

Marnie   She didn't.

Linus   She would've been terrified.

Marnie   I wasn't doing anything mean.

Linus   You need a person's permission … it's an invasion of –

Marnie   It's nothing … it's … people are photographed all the time … are on camera all the time.

Linus   People expect … their own home … washing up … laundry … without … without … nosey … nosiness. Understand what is yours and what is other people's.

Marnie   Right.

Linus   Because … because this comes across as … you're a stalker.

Marnie   Am not.

Linus   Are too.

Marnie This is not stalking. Three minutes in someone's back garden is not stalking. Stalking requires months of patience and dedication – I don't have that kind of work ethic.

Linus I leave you alone for all of five minutes –

Marnie You were gone twenty.

Linus I got turned around.

Marnie Maybe you should've tried harder.

Linus Still … twenty minutes and this is … this is what you …?

Marnie I'm a terror, aren't I?

Linus You don't even acknowledge that it's wrong.

Marnie I shouldn't've shown you.

Linus Yeah, but … who else have you got?

Marnie Meanie.

Linus Bitch-face.

Marnie Idiot-hole.

Linus Cow-bag.

Marnie Biscuit?

Linus Don't do it again.

Marnie I was making a study of her … of old age and … and …

Linus Well, that all sounds marvellous, but don't do it again.

Marnie Alright.

Linus Do I have to make you promise?

Marnie Seriously?

Linus You're a nightmare.

Marnie And you are a knobber.

Linus (*laughs*) A 'knobber'?

Marnie Complete and total.

Linus And that's a legitimate insult?

Marnie It is.

Linus I am deeply offended.

Marnie Good.

Linus This is the thanks I get?

Marnie It's what you deserve.

Linus After I bought you a gift.

Marnie What gift?

Linus (*pulls out a pack of glittery stickers*) Found a shop, didn't I ... bought you some stickers. You want a sticker? (*Peels off a sticker and sticks it to* **Marnie***'s face.*) You want a sticker? (*The same again.*)

Marnie (*laughing and chasing* **Linus** *around the room*) You want a sticker? (*Peels one off and sticks it to* **Linus***' face.*) You want a sticker? (*The same again.*)

Linus You want a sticker?

Marnie You want a sticker?

Linus You want a sticker?

Marnie You want a sticker?

They're rolling around on the floor laughing; covering each other in stickers.

Marnie *tires out quickly.*

Linus Okay?

Marnie Fine.

Linus Sure?

Marnie Fine.

Linus You want a sticker? (*Peels a sticker from its backing and places it gently on the tip of* **Marnie**'s *nose.*)

Marnie Did you find him?

Linus He was out with a client.

Marnie I don't like this place.

Linus We can afford it … couple of nights.

Marnie If there's no water in the taps, does that mean there's no water in the shower?

Linus I haven't tried it. It's down the hall.

Marnie Communal.

Linus I haven't seen any other guests.

Marnie I will want to wash my hair at some point.

Linus Extravagance.

Marnie I want to look nice.

Linus I'll talk to the lady tomorrow.

Marnie Okay.

Linus It's all I can do.

Marnie I'm not having a pop.

Linus Maybe there's some showers at the station … or a local swimming pool …

Marnie I want him to see me as suitable … as a suitable …

Linus Tomorrow. I'll speak to him tomorrow.

Marnie Do that.

Linus And we'll find somewhere to shower … and we'll get you some new clothes … and all will be well with the world.

Marnie Promise?

Linus Stick a needle in my eye.

3.

A small estate agent's.

Simon, *in a suit, at a desk.*

Linus　She wants to meet with you.

Simon　Yeah? Why? What does she hope to get out of …?

Linus　She just wants to meet. Share the same air for a while.

Simon　Right. (*Beat.*) Yeah … I don't get it.

Linus　Is that what I'm going to tell her?

Simon　Tell her whatever you like.

Linus　Can I tell her you want to meet?

Simon　But that would be a lie, so I'd advise not.

Linus　She'll be heartbroken.

Simon　That's not a nice thing to say.

Linus　I didn't mean it. I'm sorry.

Simon　I think you're about to leave.

Linus　You could meet … if it's just proximity … a couple of minutes standing next to each other … in a public place. Talk … if you want.

Simon　I have nothing to say.

Linus　Well, that would be fine too.

Simon　Would you be there?

Linus　I'm all she has … so … so I probably would.

Simon　You're all she has?

Linus　It's been enough.

Simon　So far.

Linus　As with anything.

Simon Through the surgery?

Linus Yes.

Simon Just you?

Linus It is what it is.

Simon Family?

Linus She wants to meet. How does that sound to you?

Simon I'm not prepared to …

Linus What sort of preparation do you think you'd need?

Simon I'd need time.

Linus How much? Because I'm on a budget …

Simon I don't know … I need to think about … can't we just leave it at that?

Linus Okay … right … that's fine … time is fine … but if you're stalling … if this is treading-water … if this is an indefinite putting-off … if you've no intention of ever actually … then … (*Pause.*) Haven't you ever thought of her? Haven't you ever considered?

Simon You're asking if there's a curiosity?

Linus Yes.

Simon Is curiosity enough of a reason?

Linus You think something stronger would be appropriate?

Simon I have nothing stronger.

Linus Then, I would say, curiosity is as good a reason as any.

Silence.

Simon Where are you staying?

Linus I want to tell her you're a nice guy.

Simon You can do that.

Linus I don't want to blackmail you with her disappointment.

Simon Why should I care?

Linus I'm taking a gamble that you're not a dickhead.

Simon I do want to see her …

Linus I'll tell her that.

Simon … but it's only curiosity.

Linus Good enough for me. (*Beat.*) Do you have a photo of her?

Simon A photo? No. Why would I …?

Linus Sorry … no … of your daughter.

Simon Right … okay … right.

Linus Do you?

Simon Yes. Yes I have.

Linus On you?

Simon In my wallet.

Linus Can I see it?

Simon *uncertain.*

Linus What harm can I do by seeing a photo?

Simon *brings out his wallet and takes out a photo, holds it up to show* **Linus**.

Linus This is her?

Simon This is her. Okay?

Linus She looks nice. She looks like a nice person.

Simon Your opinion means nothing to me.

Linus Can I take this?

Simon No. Why?

Linus To show my sister. She'll want to see.

Simon This photo is never leaving my wallet.

Linus I could take your wallet. (*Beat.*) That was a joke, not a threat.

Simon Sure. (*Puts the photo and the wallet away.*)

Linus I'll tell her you're happy to meet.

Simon Do that.

Linus She'll be very excited.

Simon Right.

Linus No ... excited is the wrong word.

Simon She'll be pleased?

Linus She'll be grateful.

Simon A meeting is all it is. I don't want to be a part of her life.

Linus Yeah ... that's absolutely ...

Simon And there's no money ... there will be no money ... no matter what you ask or what you say.

Linus It's not about ...

Simon Don't pretend to be offended.

Linus Okay.

Simon You could be anyone.

Linus We're not out to scam you.

Simon My eyes are wide open.

Linus In truth ... if you were to offer ... if there was talk of money ... we would not turn it down ... things being what they are ... but there's no expectation and no asking. That isn't what this is about.

Simon She just wants to meet?

Linus Yes.

Simon   Okay … okay …

Linus   This afternoon?

Simon   Okay, yes … but it's just curiosity and my eyes are open.

4.

High street.

Marnie   I'm not clean.

Linus   We'll find you a … a …

Marnie   There's no leisure centre.

Linus   No?

Marnie   Not nearby. I asked someone.

Linus   Who did you ask?

Marnie   A traffic warden.

Linus   What about the railway … what about on the concourse? Sometimes train stations have showers.

Marnie   I feel grimy.

Linus   We'll get you some wet-wipes … we'll find a McDonald's.

Marnie   I can't wash my hair at a McDonald's.

Linus   I'll get you some bottled water.

Marnie   When does he want to meet?

Linus   Two o'clock. You'll be fine. (*Beat.*) No one's making you do this.

Marnie   I am. I am making me do this.

Linus   Okay.

Marnie   Do I smell?

Linus You don't smell.

Marnie Do I smell of sweat and nerves and dirt?

Linus You don't smell.

Marnie *shows him a photograph on the back of her camera.*

Linus That's good.

Marnie What was he like?

Linus I don't know.

Marnie Anything.

Linus He's middle-aged ... bit flabby ... greying ...

Marnie Would you say he was nice?

Linus Yeah ... he seemed ... yeah ... I don't know.

Marnie Would you say he was –?

Linus Marnie – you'll see for yourself.

Marnie *shows him another photograph.*

Linus Good ... that is good.

Marnie Public places ... different people ... street scenes. Not a stalker.

Linus Excellent work. Well done.

Marnie What should I say?

Linus You're asking me?

Marnie Yeah.

Linus Haven't you been thinking about this?

Marnie Yeah.

Linus I don't know.

Marnie *shows him another photograph.*

Linus Good.

Marnie *shows him another one.*

Linus Excellent.

Marnie *and another.*

Linus Brilliant.

Marnie *and another.*

Linus Excellent.

Marnie You've already said 'excellent'.

Linus Well, they're both … they're all … uniformly excellent.

Marnie 'Uniformly'?

Linus They've of a standard.

Marnie Right.

Linus You've reached a … a level … where everything's going to be of a certain … because it has been taken by you … and you're good … good at … pictures … okay?

Marnie A plateau.

Linus I'm sure others could criticise. My knowledge of the subject is limited.

Marnie It's not your field.

Linus I like looking at them though.

Marnie *and another … and another*.

Linus More through windows.

Marnie Shop windows. Not a private residence.

Linus It's a step up.

Marnie In the right direction.

Linus Yep.

Marnie I don't know … I like … I like … people when they're not aware … pictures of people when they're not aware …

18   In Doggerland

Linus   Shopping?

Marnie   Shopping. Or drinking coffee.

Linus (*recognising someone in a photo*)   When they're drinking coffee?

Marnie   Yeah.

Linus   Where did you take this … and when?

Marnie   Down there … on the left … five minutes before you came back.

Linus   Down there on the left?

Marnie   Yeah. Why?

Linus   Why?

Marnie   Yeah – why?

Linus   I fancy a macchiato.

Marnie   A what?

Linus (*gets out wallet*)   Go and get clothes.

Marnie   Really?

Linus   At least your clothes will smell clean.

Marnie   I do smell.

Linus   I didn't mean …

Marnie   Help me pick.

Linus   I'm no use to you in a Primark. How much is enough?

Marnie   How much is left?

Linus (*gives her money*)   You need to look nice.

Marnie   Meet you back here?

Linus   How long will you take?

Marnie   I can be ten minutes.

Linus Take as long as you like. If I'm not here …

Marnie Why wouldn't you be here?

Linus I'm not going to stand out in the possible rain. Here … you take the key.

Marnie The key?

Linus The B&B key.

Marnie Why? Where you going?

Linus Just in case we get separated.

Marnie Come with me.

Linus (*pulls out a pen and writes on Marnie's hand*) This is where you're meeting him. Two o'clock.

Marnie It's one o'clock now.

Linus Then you better hurry up and buy some clothes.

Marnie Enjoy your coffee.

Linus (*kisses her on the head*) You'll be good. I'll see you later. (*Exits.*)

Marnie *alone with wet ink on her hand.*

5.

A coffee shop.

Kelly *is sat at a table, working on a laptop and drinking coffee.*

Linus *stands at a near distance. He looks intently at* **Kelly**. *He has just bought himself a bottle of water.*

Kelly *feels him looking at her.*

Kelly Can I help you?

Linus No.

Kelly It's just you were …

Linus I was … what?

Kelly … staring. You were staring.

Linus I'm sorry.

Kelly Don't be sorry. Don't stare.

Linus You … you look like …

Kelly Impolite.

Linus You look like someone.

Kelly Everyone looks like someone else.

Linus I thought I recognised you. You know how it is when you see someone you think you might possibly know … and you're not sure … not sure whether you should approach or … (*Beat.*) Perhaps I'm mistaken. (*Beat.*) Linus.

Kelly I'd remember a Linus.

Linus Sure.

Kelly And I have a good memory for faces.

Linus I did that once … on the street … passing on the street … saw a guy … recognised him … said hello … had a little chat … like he was a friend or a long-lost relative … someone I hadn't seen for years, but always meant to call … stood on the street trying to engage this guy in conversation … turns out I didn't know him … didn't know him at all … turns out he presents *Countryfile*.

Kelly I'm not off the telly.

Linus I'm sorry. I've turned round too many times today. Seeing faces I think I know. Sorry. (*Beat.*) Is this seat taken?

Kelly Are you chatting me up?

Linus No.

Kelly It's a unique approach. (*Beat.*) If you want the seat, you can take the seat.

Linus (*sits*) Is this alright?

Kelly It's alright.

Linus Linus.

Kelly You said.

Linus Right.

Kelly Kelly.

Linus Hello, Kelly. What are you working on, Kelly?

Kelly Lesson plans.

Linus You're a teacher?

Kelly Yes.

Linus Teachers …

Kelly You don't like teachers?

Linus Shouldn't you be in school?

Kelly Half-term.

Linus What are you drinking … in your coffee-cup … what are you drinking?

Kelly Coffee.

Linus I've just bought a bottle of water.

Kelly Well done.

Linus I was going to get a … but I changed my mind. I'll buy you another.

Kelly No.

Linus I'll buy you another one.

Kelly I don't think so.

Linus I've got money … money for coffee.

Kelly I was just leaving.

Linus Because of me?

Kelly Because I've finished.

Linus But you could stay … you're not rushing off? We could talk a little. They won't mind … the coffee-shop folk … you did make a purchase … you have the dirty cup … it's not like they're busy … and I've got my water.

Kelly Why are you talking to me?

Linus I thought that I …

Kelly … recognised.

Linus Yes.

Kelly It's pretty apparent that we don't know each other.

Linus Yes.

Kelly So, why …?

Linus I must be chatting you up.

Linus' mobile phone rings.

Linus If I answer that, are you going to leave?

Kelly Probably.

Linus (*declines the call*) How many faces are there in the world?

Kelly What are we doing?

Linus We're playing a game. How many faces are there in the world?

Kelly How many people are there?

Linus Entirely separate question.

Kelly Okay.

Linus There are only one billion possible variations of the human face.

Kelly That's not true.

Linus Distance between your eyes ... size and shape of your mouth and lips ... bone structure ... muscle structure. There are only a billion combinations you can have and still claim to wear a human face.

Kelly I don't believe it.

Linus You want to believe you're unique.

Kelly I know I'm not.

Linus Seven billion people in the world, out of which six have your exact same face.

Linus' *mobile rings again.*

Kelly Girlfriend?

Linus Sister.

Kelly Could be important.

Linus Could be. (*Declines the call.*)

Kelly Do you smoke?

Linus No.

Kelly Do you drink?

Linus No.

Kelly Drugs?

Linus What are the right answers here?

Kelly *shrugs.*

Silence.

Linus Kelly, wasn't it?

Kelly Kelly.

Linus Surname?

Kelly Why do you ...?

Linus No harm in a surname.

Kelly You could Google me … Facebook me … cyber-stalk me.

Linus Not going to do that.

Kelly How do I know?

Linus Not going to do it.

Kelly *nothing.*

Linus Fine. (*Pause.*) I'm not into mystical things … spiritualism … cosmic-ordering … angels …

Kelly I'm not an angel.

Linus And you're not a ghost.

Kelly No.

Linus And this is a small town.

Kelly It is.

Linus So I'm going to take a punt and say you were related to Melissa.

Kelly *no response.*

Linus Because it's uncanny.

Kelly My face?

Linus Your face.

Kelly I must have one of those faces.

Linus No. Melissa … her surname was Lowe. You're Kelly Lowe.

Kelly I know all of Melissa's friends – Melissa's friends are my friends.

Linus I'm not a friend.

Kelly That's a sinister fucking thing to say.

Linus I didn't mean it like that.

Kelly How did you mean it?

Linus   Well … you know.

Kelly   Say what you are.

Linus   Grateful. (*Beat.*) She did a very special thing.

Linus' *mobile rings once more, he ignores it and drinks his water.*

6.

A bandstand in the centre of a park.

Simon *has been waiting for a while.*

Marnie *in new clothes, has only just turned up, camera in hand.*

Simon   I was going to leave.

Marnie   I'm sorry I'm late.

Simon   I've been here nearly twenty-five minutes.

Marnie   Sorry.

Simon   It's fine … it's just …

Marnie   Thank you for waiting.

Simon   It's been threatening to rain.

Marnie   I couldn't find my brother.

Simon   He didn't want to come?

Marnie   Yeah … no … I don't know.

Simon   Are you going to cry?

Marnie   No … I just …

Simon   Are you alright?

Marnie   Give me a moment.

Simon   Okay.

Marnie (*deep breaths*)   Your name is Simon?

Simon Yes.

Marnie I'm Marnie.

Simon Right. (*Beat.*) Like the film.

Marnie No.

Silence.

Simon So ... er ... what do you want to know?

Marnie I've come up with some questions.

Simon Shoot.

Silence.

Marnie I'm sorry ... I ... I'm a little weirded out.

Simon Right.

Marnie How are you?

Simon How am I?

Marnie Are you finding this weird?

Simon Is that one of your questions?

Marnie Er ... no ... yeah ... well ... it *is* a question obviously, but ... you say that like there's a limit. Is there a limit?

Simon A limit?

Marnie Yeah ... like three wishes ... twenty questions ... because if there is a limit then I don't want to waste one on something as mundane as –

Simon 'How are you?'

Marnie Yes.

Simon There are worse things you could ask.

Marnie Is there a limit?

Simon If I don't want to answer something, then I won't answer it.

Marnie   Fair enough. (*Beat.*) How are you?

Simon   I'm fine, thank you.

Marnie   Good.

Simon   I'm an estate agent … you know that, right?

Marnie   Yeah.

Simon   Yeah, they're not making any more land, so …

Marnie   Who aren't?

Simon   No one. 'They're not making any more land'. It's just a thing that estate agents say. (*Pause.*) Are you going to take my photograph?

Marnie   No.

Simon   Oh.

Marnie   Do you want me to?

Simon   No … not especially … but you brought a camera, so …

Marnie   Yeah, I always carry …

Simon   Right.

Marnie   I don't like staged photos … I don't do portraits … all forced smiles and straight backs.

Simon   Okay.

Marnie   It's fake. I like to take shots of people unawares. There's more truth in it that way.

Simon   Not even for birthdays … Christmas …?

Marnie   This is not 'treasured memories' – I have a brain for that sort of thing. This is pictures for the sake of pictures.

Simon   It's an expensive looking camera.

Marnie   It was a gift – 'get well soon'.

Simon Of course. (*Beat.*) I'm sorry for what you've been through.

Marnie Not your fault.

Simon But still …

Marnie Such is life.

Simon How old are you?

Marnie Twenty-one.

Simon And your brother?

Marnie Twenty-five.

Simon He's all you have?

Marnie *shrugs*.

Simon Ask me something else.

Marnie Where do you live?

Simon Lincoln Street.

Marnie I don't know this town.

Simon It's about half a mile from here.

Marnie Is it a nice house?

Simon It's got a loft conversion.

Marnie Terrace? Detached? Semi-detached?

Simon Semi.

Marnie Large garden?

Simon Not especially … little patio area …

Marnie Have you lived there long?

Simon Five years.

Marnie Alone?

Simon Yes.

Scene 6   29

Marnie   You didn't raise your family there?

Simon   No.

Marnie   Not the family home?

Simon   No.

Marnie   Where's that?

Simon   It's … er … it's at the bottom of the sea.

Marnie   What?

Simon   We lived on the coast. The coast is being eroded. It fell into the sea.

Marnie   Really?

Simon   The winds and the water … it's a punishing stretch of … most of the village has gone.

Marnie   So you moved here.

Simon   So I moved here.

Marnie   Were there swings? And climbing frames?

Simon   There was a climbing frame.

Marnie   And how many kids did you have?

Simon   Just the two.

Marnie   You, the two kids and your wife?

Simon   Yes.

Marnie   Your wife is …?

Simon   My wife is …

Marnie   … no longer around?

Simon   No.

Marnie   Why did that happen?

Simon   She got very sick.

Marnie I'm sorry. (*Beat.*) I would've liked to have met her.

Simon Yeah ... well ...

Marnie Where is she buried?

Simon Why?

Marnie I might visit ... I might ...

Simon Cremated.

Marnie Where was she scattered?

Simon In the sea.

Marnie How old were the kids?

Simon Twelve. (*Beat.*) Last thing she said ... last coherent words ... before she stopped making sense ... drugs and delirium ... she said 'look after them'.

Marnie And you did.

Simon Well ... evidently I did not.

Marnie You, two kids and a wife ... in a house by the sea. (*Offers her wrist.*) Do you want to feel my pulse?

Simon I ...

Marnie Go on.

Simon *takes her wrist.*

Marnie Can you find it?

Simon No ... I ...

Marnie Under where the thumb meets the wrist ... about an inch down.

Simon *finds it.*

Marnie Got it?

Simon (*moved*) Yeah. It's strong.

Marnie It is.

Simon (*close to tears*) It's strong.

7.

Kelly's *flat.*

Kelly I'm drinking – are you drinking?

Linus I ... er ...

Kelly Come into the room. Are you drinking?

Linus Water's fine.

Kelly I don't think so. (*Pours two drinks.*)

Linus I'm not very clean.

Kelly Is that so?

Linus There's no shower ... where we're staying ... or, at least, not a working one.

Kelly But you haven't been doing anything strenuous?

Linus No, I suppose not. Still ... two days without a shower.

Kelly Uncivilised.

Linus Prehistoric.

Kelly Can't have that.

Silence.

Linus So ... your sister.

Kelly My sister.

Silence.

Linus You teach. That's ... that's ... laudable.

Kelly *shrugs.*

Linus No?

Kelly Crowd control. I feel like I'm drowning.

Silence.

Linus An accident.

Kelly Yes.

Linus A car accident.

Kelly Yes.

Silence.

Linus If you don't want to …

Kelly No … it's not …

Linus … if you can't talk … bring yourself to talk …

Kelly … it's fine … it's just …

Linus … I totally understand if you …

Kelly … it's not that I …

Linus … can't or won't … it's …

Kelly … more that I haven't … ever. I should be able to … no reason why I shouldn't … but who would listen? Who would ask? We were twins. People pre-empt … stop themselves from … because they think that I think that they won't understand.

Linus I'm asking.

Kelly Good. Thank you. (*Beat.*) I was going to show you … some stuff … her stuff … albums … her and me together … I was going to … but I've put it all in a box and that box is … I don't know where that box is.

Linus It doesn't matter.

Kelly It does matter, because, even though it's away it should also be to hand. I should have ready access to … to …

Linus I don't have to see.

Kelly Why've I put it all away? Why did I think I wanted to do that? (*Beat.*) Sorry.

Linus It's okay. (*Beat.*) A car accident ...

Kelly She was on the passenger side ... in a car that collided with another car.

Linus Were you ...?

Kelly I wasn't. My dad was. (*Beat.*) And your sister?

Linus She's left me a message.

Kelly Why did she need ...?

Linus She had a heart problem ... all her life. Never worked as it should. And progressive. A stiffness in the muscle wall ... couldn't ... couldn't pump well enough. It would never fully relax in the time between the heartbeats. Could never fill ... with blood ... not properly. It needed to come out and for something better to take its place.

Kelly She's good now?

Linus Yeah. There or thereabouts.

Kelly Well ... that's ... um ... that's ... um ...

Linus Yeah.

Kelly This is ... this is 'thank you'?

Linus I guess. To an extent. But also 'goodbye'.

Kelly She's with my father?

Linus Yeah.

Kelly I hope he's not being a dick. (*Pause.*) She didn't want to see me?

Linus She doesn't know about you.

Kelly Oh.

Linus Only the next-of-kin was mentioned ... your dad.

Kelly Right ... yeah ... no ... okay.

Linus I didn't know you existed until I ...

Kelly ... recognised.

Linus Yeah.

Kelly So she doesn't know you're ...?

Linus She doesn't know where I am.

Kelly She's been calling you. (*Beat.*) I wanted to show you her graduation portrait. I don't know why that's important. (*Beat.*) Did she have to wait long? For a ... for a suitable ...

Linus Matches can be difficult.

Kelly I thought there were protocols ... systems in place ... to keep the donor's family ... recipients ... separate? Didn't we sign something? I thought we signed something.

Linus You want a thing done – you get a thing done. (*Beat.*) She's a good person. She has a lot of warmth. Witty. She has wit. She's very funny ... I find her funny ... and talented ... and nice. She's good. She's one of the good guys. The world is a better place for having her in it.

Kelly Hooray.

Linus Hooray.

Kelly You're the eldest?

Linus Yeah.

Kelly I'm the eldest. Only by ten minutes, but still ...

Long silence.

Linus What time is it?

Kelly Nearly half past three.

Linus I left her at one. That's two and a half hours. Two and a half. Wow. (*Laugh.*) It's like I'm my own person.

Kelly You're not being cruel?

Linus She needs to stand on her own two feet. This I have decided. This I have decided today.

Kelly And you need the break?

Linus That doesn't make me bad ... wanting a rest. Not a bad person – just a knackered one. I'm heavy the entire time. Everything is effort. Just stumbling ... one thing to the next. I'm strong ... being strong ... have to be strong. You carry someone for a while ... it's the thing to do and I don't begrudge it. You start with a straight back and light in your eyes ... but no matter how you pace yourself ... their arms around the back of your neck ... you start to get pulled down. Pulled down and beset by dogs.

Silence.

Kelly Do you want to use the shower?

Linus I would love to use the shower.

Kelly And I'll find you some clean clothes.

Linus These were fresh on this morning.

Kelly But you weren't.

Linus No.

Kelly You've done good things ... and I know she appreciates it.

Linus I'm not saying she doesn't.

Kelly *kisses him lightly on the lips.*

Linus That was nice.

Kelly Yes.

Linus Why?

Kelly I wanted to.

Linus Okay.

Kelly Go. Jump in the shower.

Linus Thank you.

8.

A service station.

Simon *and* **Marnie** *are sat drinking tea at a plastic table.* **Marnie**'s *camera is on the table.*

Marnie *on her mobile phone.*

Simon No answer?

Marnie Nothing.

Simon Is it the signal? That will only get worse. (*Offers his phone.*) Try mine.

Marnie It's ringing, he's just not picking up.

Simon Leave a message.

Marnie Hi … it's me … can you give me a call? I'm with Simon … he's taking me to the coast … I won't have any signal. Where are you? I'll try again later. (*Hangs up.*)

Simon You and your brother … you're close?

Marnie Usually. (*Beat.*) It doesn't bother you … doesn't seem to bother you.

Simon What doesn't?

Marnie Driving.

Simon The car?

Marnie You seem alright … behind the wheel.

Simon What do you mean?

Marnie I'm not saying you have skills … I'm not saying you're rally-cross … but you seem competent.

Simon Shouldn't I be?

Marnie I'd never get in a car again.

Simon Do you drive?

Marnie No.

Simon Public transport is piss-poor and when necessity dictates ...

Marnie Still ... it can't be much fun.

Simon I do what I do.

Marnie I admire that.

Simon Um ... thanks. (*Pause.*) Nice to have a brother.

Marnie Yes. (*Playing with a pack of sugar.*)

Simon You'll make a mess. It'll burst and it'll make a mess.

Marnie Won't.

Simon She used to do that ... play with the sugar packets.

Marnie It's not uncommon.

Simon I suppose not. Still ... you'll make a mess.

Marnie I don't believe in that.

Simon What?

Marnie What you're talking about.

Simon What am I talking about?

Marnie Cellular memory.

Simon I don't know what that is.

Marnie When people inherit traits ... traits from ...

Simon I see.

Marnie Did she have languages?

Simon French and Spanish.

Marnie I can't speak either. Did she play a musical instrument?

Simon The flute ... for a while ... at school.

Marnie I can't play the flute.

Simon Have you tried?

Marnie I have no musical skills whatsoever.

Simon You never know until you try.

Marnie Would you want that? If it were true ... if I turned up ... speaking French and Spanish ... playing the flute ... playing with the sugar packets the way she used to ... would you actually want that?

Simon No.

Marnie So don't ask about it. (*Beat.*) Before the surgery ... I read up on ... because the heart is pretty symbolic ... symbolic of who you are as a person ... the core ... and to have that removed ... to have that replaced ...

Simon Sure.

Marnie Yeah ... so ... cellular memory ... it's bullshit ... like ghosts and angels and spiritualism. It's all anecdotal. I am not my heart.

Simon Can I ask ...?

Marnie You can ask.

Simon Can I ask ... what was it ... what you had?

Marnie Restrictive cardiomiopathy.

Simon I see. (*Beat.*) I don't know what that is.

Marnie The walls of the heart ... the muscle ... it starts to stiffen ... the walls of the heart get denser and blood becomes harder to pump.

Simon That sounds ...

Marnie Rigidity of the muscle wall.

Simon ... painful. And there was no cure?

Marnie Yeah, there was. I am cured. Took it out ... gave me a new one.

Simon And it won't happen again ... to the ... to the ... transplanted ...

Marnie The problem was with *my* heart ... couldn't beat properly ... just a hard little lump ... muscle walls like jerky. My heart has gone ... so has the problem.

Simon I'm sorry.

Marnie Don't see how it's your fault. (*Pause, starts taking a few photos – though not of* **Simon**.)

Simon Can you not ...?

Marnie (*puts the camera down*) Okay. (*Pause.*) All these places look the same.

Simon You feel like you've been here before?

Marnie That's not what I said. (*Pause.*) How far to go?

Simon About half an hour.

Marnie I want to see the sea.

Simon You will.

9.

Kelly's *flat.*

Linus, *wet from the shower, towel around his waist.*

Kelly *with fresh clothes in her hands.*

Kelly Better?

Linus So much so.

Kelly A semi-naked man in my flat. (*Hands him the clothes.*)

Linus *takes them.*

Kelly *looks away, covering her eyes.*

Linus (*gets dressed*)   All done.

Kelly   Hello.

Linus   Hi. (*Leans in and kisses her.*)

Kelly *doesn't fully respond.*

Linus   Is this not alright?

Kelly   It's fine.

Linus *kisses her again.*

Kelly *still not a full response.*

Linus   I'm sorry ... I ... perhaps I'm out of practice. Reading signals was never my ...

Kelly   The signals are all there.

Linus   Yeah ... I thought they were.

Kelly   Try it again.

Linus *kisses her.*

Kelly *kisses him back.*

Linus   Yeah ... okay ... yeah ... nice.

Kelly   Nice?

Linus   Very nice.

Kelly   Good.

They stand there ... holding each other.

Kelly   A human person in my flat.

Silence.

Linus   I can feel your heart beating.

Kelly   Is that so strange?

Linus   Not strange.

Kelly   Is 'Linus' your real name?

Linus   How do you mean?

Kelly   Is it your actual name?

Linus   It's the realest one I've got.

Kelly   It's a Snoopy name.

Linus   What do you want me to say?

Kelly   What music do you listen to?

Linus   I don't really … haven't had the time …

Kelly   Who's your favourite author?

Linus   I don't have one.

Kelly   You must do.

Linus   I not much of a reader.

Kelly   Charles M. Schulz.

Linus   I don't know who that is.

Kelly   Who's mine?

Linus   I don't know.

Kelly   Stab in the dark.

Linus   Is this a game?

Kelly   Games are fun to play.

Linus   I can't think of any authors.

Kelly   Not one?

Linus   I don't really read.

Kelly   It's almost adorable.

Linus   You're making me feel stupid.

Kelly We're playing a game.

Linus The purpose of which is to make me feel stupid.

Silence.

Kelly I'm sorry.

Linus Thank you. (*Pause.*) I can read. I have read. Someone left … in a waiting room … a book. Just on a chair. I've spent a lot of time in waiting rooms. I read a good four or five chapters before … (*Beat.*) I can't for the life of me remember it now. (*Pause.*) Were you identical? Do you mind if I ask?

Kelly No. (*Beat.*) No – I don't mind. Yes – we were identical.

Linus You looked the same?

Kelly We were … genetically … the same.

Linus That would freak me out.

Kelly I never knew anything else.

Linus Even when …

Kelly Even when … what?

Linus No.

Kelly What?

Linus It doesn't matter.

Kelly Go on.

Linus It was crass … it was a crass comment … question.

Kelly I speak crass.

Linus I don't want to.

Kelly I have a tough hide.

Linus Still …

Kelly Ask your dumb question.

Linus Alright, but I'm sorry for it.

Kelly   Apology accepted.

Linus   Did you see her?

Kelly   When?

Linus   After the accident ... the hospital ... the funeral ... open casket? See – crass.

Kelly   It was not like looking at my dead self. It was like looking at my dead sister.

Linus   I apologise.

Kelly   I'm used to it – honestly. Questions ... people ... all my life. People are so used to individuality ... snowflakes ... fingerprints ... it's similarity that fires people's imagination. Do you know what we were asked the most? The one question people felt they just had to ask? Did we swap boyfriends? That or ... did we go to each others classes? Did we try to fool our parents by answering to each other's name?

Linus   Right ... I'm sorry.

Kelly   Don't be sorry. Don't apologise. What are you apologising for?

Linus   Curiosity, I guess.

Kelly   You can't apologise on behalf of every person that's ever asked a dumb question.

Linus   No.

Kelly   I kind of miss it actually ... walking down the street ... the doubletakes ... I kind of miss that. Where we grew up ... we grew up by the sea and we'd walk along the cliffs ... people would doubletake ... and have to catch themselves before they reached the edge.

Linus   Did you swap boyfriends?

Kelly   No. (*Beat.*) She itches everyday ... like a lost limb. I know she's not there ... I know she's not there because I don't buy into that ... but she itches everyday.

Linus   And a twin, as well ... I suppose that must be –

Kelly   Why must it? Why must it be worse?

Linus   I don't know ... I just assume that ... is it not?

Kelly   I lost my mum when I was twelve ... and I can't say which was worse ... I can't quantify that ... I can't. (*Beat.*) Argh! Downbeat. We seem to have run out of booze.

Linus   I'm fine ... I don't really need ...

Kelly   It's dishonest ... sobriety ... it's deceitful ... it's scaffolding. Inhibitions are scaffolding – let them fall. Because if it's the scaffolding that keeps the house together, then it's no kind of house. Let it crumble. (*Beat.*) I need to get out of here.

Linus   Right ... okay ...

Kelly   There's a human person in my flat and it's freaking me out a bit. Just a smidge. (*Pulls* **Linus** *in close and snogs his face off.*) I think we should go and get absolutely shit-faced.

10.

The coast.

A cliff-edge.

Marnie *and* **Simon** *looking out to sea.*

Marnie *taking photographs.*

Simon   As close as we can get.

Marnie   Sorry?

Simon   To where it used to be.

Marnie   It's cold.

Simon   Time of year.

Marnie   It goes on forever.

Simon Have you not seen the sea before?

Marnie I have.

Silence.

Simon When we first moved here ... god ... near on thirty years ago ... there were four other houses between us and the sea. (*Beat.*) How did you find us?

Marnie Linus made friends with a hospital porter.

Simon A porter?

Marnie A night porter with movable ethics and an open wallet. (*Beat.*) My heart's already been here ... isn't that strange? Beat most of it's beats here. (*Beat.*) You know when a song gets stuck in your head? Round and round ... over and over ...

Simon An earworm.

Marnie I've got that now ... only it's not a piece of music ... it's not a tune ... it's a phrase: 'home is where the heart is ... home is where the heart is.' An earworm? Is that what it's called?

Simon It's a German word, I think. Ohrwurm.

Marnie Didn't know it had a name.

Simon Everything has a name.

Marnie How often do you come here?

Simon Not ...

Marnie No?

Simon Not often.

Marnie Too painful?

Simon No ... no ... places don't ... don't hold much for me. I barely recognise this patch of ... whatever. It's not even this patch, is it? My patch is over there somewhere ... that void of space ... six foot from the cliff-edge ... however many feet from sea-level. Where's my landing? Where's my spare room? Where's my greenhouse? I guess the bricks are down there somewhere, but I doubt they're even recognisable as bricks anymore. The tides would've worn them round ... broken them apart ... scattered them across a thousand miles ... dissolved them in the guts of fish. There are no rooms here, and no one walking those rooms. I mean ... *they're* not here, are they? Caroline, my wife ... and Melissa. They're not here.

Marnie Was this where you scattered Melissa too?

Simon Yes. Her sister said ... her sister's idea ... I mean ... she grew up ... and she always loved the ... loved the ... to her this was home ... and she didn't leave any wishes ... why would she – she was young ... and she used to visit ... I knew she used to visit ... when she was down ... when she was blue ... to talk to her mum ... she would come back ... to the sea ... so ... (*Beat.*) Where are your parents?

Marnie Not in the picture.

Simon A child should be with their parents.

Marnie I'm not a child.

Silence.

Simon Why did you seek me out?

Marnie Why wouldn't I?

Simon You say that like it's obvious.

Marnie (*shrugs*) It was a car crash, yeah? Sudden.

Simon I suppose.

Marnie It wasn't cancer ... it wasn't months of ... treatment ... appointments ... chemo and coming to terms with ...

Simon No.

Marnie That's what I thought. And I wanted to give her that ... the farewell tour.

Simon That's what this is?

Marnie Yeah. (*Beat.*) When they took my heart ... my faulty heart ... I don't know where they took it. I don't know what happened to it. I assume it was incinerated ... I assume it was incinerated as medical waste. I'm already part-cremated ... already part-buried. And I don't have a place to mourn. I know that sounds self-centred ... I know that sounds self-obsessed ... but it was *my heart* ... you know? When they sent me home ... first time I was alone ... I made myself sick. Fingers down my throat. Head down the toilet. Retching and heaving and ... and ... because it felt *wrong* ... it felt ... and they said there was no problem with my body rejecting it ... that it was being accepted ... but part of me ... a part of me was like ... 'no ... no, I don't accept this ... something foreign where my heart used to be'. The heart I loved my grandma with ... the heart that fluttered when I kissed Darren Michaels ... that was gone ... and this something else was there instead. So ... fingers down my throat ... bring it up ... trying to vomit this invader out ... purge ... even though I knew I couldn't ... even though in my brain I knew I couldn't physically ... and that even if I did, it wouldn't help ... because you need a heart ... you need your blood to pump. I would imagine ... I would fantasise ... as I dry-retched and my ribcage convulsed ... I would fantasise that the stitching would come undone ... that the muscle would tear ... that the sack around the heart would burst and pull itself away from the chest-cavity wall. I was on the floor ... my head on the toilet seat ... Linus at the bathroom door ... 'Are you alright? Can I get you a glass of water?' And I knew I couldn't go on as I was ... with a stranger's heart in my chest. So I set about ... we set about ... making the heart not a stranger. (*Pause.*) It must be odd to see the sea where your house once was.

Simon (*shrugs*) It's the past. It's the bottom of the ocean. (*Pause.*) Look at that sky ... it'll open up in a minute.

Silence.

Marnie Would you like to see the scar?

Simon Yes. I would.

Marnie *unbuttons her top and shows him a neat, dark scar – vertical between her breasts.*

Simon (*holds her shirt open and looks directly at the scar*)   There you are.

11.

An off-licence.

Linus   I don't recognise this brand of vodka.

Kelly   Does it matter?

Linus   It's on offer. I've got ten quid. I don't want to spend all of it. Does this place look reputable?

Kelly   What do you mean?

Linus   Does it look … does it look … like the sort of place that would stock … because this could be … fake.

Kelly   It's vodka.

Linus   You hear it on the news … bootleg spirits … bootleg vodka that's mostly paint thinner or anti-freeze. You could wake up blind. You could strip your insides.

Kelly   Your phone hasn't rung in a while.

Linus   Don't …

Kelly   What?

Linus   Can we not …?

Kelly   I didn't mean to …

Linus   I am a person in my own right.

Kelly   Sure. Okay. (*Beat.*) You should try being a twin. (*Pause.*) It's Danish. Is vodka a Danish thing? Is it something they are renowned for?

Linus   I don't know.

Kelly Polish and Swedish, certainly … but Danish?

Linus You know what … I'm alright.

Kelly You're alright?

Linus I've drunk enough. The nice stuff is expensive.

Pause.

Kelly Is he watching?

Linus Who?

Kelly The guy … the behind-the-counter guy. Can he see us?

Linus He's on the phone.

Kelly Lift your jumper.

Linus What?

Kelly Your jumper is baggy – lift it up.

Linus Stop it … no!

Kelly One up your jumper … one down your trouser leg …

Linus Get off … what if …? I'm not going to …

Kelly Walk with confidence … that's all it is. Walk with confidence.

Linus Cameras …

Kelly No one watches that.

Linus Morals …

Kelly No one cares.

Linus Stop.

Kelly Have you got a car?

Linus No.

Kelly Would you know how to get one?

Linus Would I know how to get a car? A loan … I guess … and monthly repayments.

Kelly A screwdriver … a wire coat-hanger? Let's knock this place over. I'll be Bonnie … you be Clyde.

Linus I'm not playing sidekicks.

Kelly Not a sidekick – a partner. Lift up your jumper.

Linus *doesn't.*

Kelly (*defeated*) I'm being a dickhead, aren't I? I'm not … not usually … like this. (*Beat.*) Pick out something you want … whatever you like. I'll pay.

12.

Simon*'s car.*

The car is stationary.

Simon *behind the wheel.*

Marnie *on the passenger side.*

It is raining. We can hear the droplets lightly on the roof of the car.

Marnie *is fiddling with the radio – snatches of the shipping forecast. She becomes bored and turns it off.*

Marnie Can we go back now?

Simon It'll pass. It's just a shower.

Marnie Then we'll head back?

Simon Yes.

Marnie *takes a picture of him.*

Simon Hey …!

Marnie Sorry.

Simon I wasn't smiling.

Marnie That's the point.

Simon Can I see?

Marnie *passes him the camera.*

Simon (*cycles through the photos*) These are … these are really quite good.

Marnie Thank you.

Simon They're all really well done.

Marnie Thanks.

Simon Seriously.

Marnie I believe you.

Simon Do you exhibit?

Marnie (*laughs*) What?

Simon Is that a stupid question? These should be hung on a wall somewhere.

Marnie No.

Simon These would look great in someone's hallway … above a fireplace …

Marnie I don't sell them.

Simon Do you put them on the internet? Is it … Instagram? Do you have an online … portfolio?

Marnie They don't even leave the memory card.

Simon Have you got any printed off … blown up?

Marnie No.

Simon No?

Marnie No.

Simon In an album or …?

Marnie I don't do that.

Simon Put photos in albums?

Marnie It's not what I'm interested in.

Simon I've got a colour printer. Inkjet. Any use? You can get that photo-paper ... professional quality ...

Marnie I don't see the point.

Simon What are you going to do with them?

Marnie Nothing ... I don't know ... nothing.

Simon What would you ideally ... what is the best thing that could happen to you and your photos?

Marnie I don't know.

Simon You should get them published somewhere.

Marnie Where?

Simon Magazines ... coffee table books ... upload them to those stock-image sites – get them used in advertising.

Marnie I don't know anything about that.

Simon I could help.

Marnie How?

Simon I could ... I could ... well ... I could be supportive ... or help you ... in some way ... with whatever it is you want to do with them. Invest.

Marnie They stay on the card. Why should I want to do anything?

Simon Then why do it at all?

Marnie Just to be better, I suppose.

Simon To be better?

Marnie Yeah ... I take a picture ... see what I did wrong ... see what I can improve on ... I take another ... I get better. Understanding the conditions ... understanding the camera ...

Simon Right. (*Beat.*) And that's enough?

Marnie I like it.

Simon Still ... you should get them ... processed.

Marnie I don't see why.

Simon That little LCD screen ... that's no good. It can't do justice to your ... they should be allowed a larger canvas ... a greater reach. You just keep them on the memory cards?

Marnie Card – singular. I've only got the one. Came in the box. It's not that big. It can only store about four hundred images.

Simon And when it fills up?

Marnie I delete.

Simon I don't see how you can do that.

Marnie *shrugs.*

Simon *takes out his wallet.*

Marnie I don't want your money.

Simon (*finds the photo, hands it to her*) Take a look. Go on.

Marnie Is this ...?

Simon Yes.

Marnie I like her hair.

The rain is getting harder.

Marnie Can we ...?

Simon It'll pass. Soon. It always does. (*Beat.*) Did you see in the papers this week ... the chap with the face transplant?

Marnie No.

Simon Yeah ... it was ... it was in all the papers.

Marnie I don't read the ...

Simon No, okay. (*Beat.*) It didn't look right ... but then I've no idea what he looked like before. You assume it's an improvement. He just looked strange ... like a child's drawing of a face. It's the brain, you see ... the brain ... the way it constructs images ... it has a whole separate system for recognising faces. If you bypass that ... if you mess with that template ... well ... it feels uneasy ... odd. It's why masks are so potent in tribal cultures ... it's why barbarians would paint their face with woad ... it all interrupts the brain's natural process for seeing faces. It doesn't look natural ... some object where there ought to be a human being. It can be frightening.

Marnie It's why I hate clowns.

Simon Exactly. Exactly that. Because we want to see faces ... want to see other people in the world ... when you look at clouds ... when you see patterns in the lino of the bathroom floor ... Jesus in the burnt toast. My subconscious wants to trick me ... wants to show me her face where I know her face isn't. It's important to have photos ... important to have evidence ... of actuality not remembrance ... because you cannot trust your brain ... because your brain wants her not to be dead ... wants her to be in the world. It's a cheat ... it's a lie ... to show me her face where I know her face isn't. (*Beat.*) Does it hurt ever? Does it itch or ...?

Marnie I try not to think about it.

Simon You should.

Marnie I'd rather not.

Simon I think it would be important to remember.

Marnie No.

Simon I think you should.

Long silence.

The rain on the roof of the car.

Marnie Can you take me back now? (*Pause.*) It's not going to pass.

Simon *a moment, a pause ... he turns the key in the ignition and the engine fires up.*

13.

The bandstand.

Kelly *dancing in the rain, swigging from a bottle.*

Linus *taking shelter.*

Linus   Come in out of it.

Kelly   I'm dancing. Don't you like to dance?

Linus   You'll catch cold.

Kelly   Are you looking out for me?

Linus   You'll get soaked through.

The rain eases off.

Kelly   It's stopping. Don't stop rain ... don't stop ...

The rain has stopped.

Linus   The rain doesn't listen to you.

Kelly   I shouldn't find that such a surprise. (*Sits next to* **Linus**.) Okay. You're looking out for me. It's sweet. (*Kisses him, cuddles him, offers him the bottle.*)

Linus *shakes his head.*

Kelly   Take a drink. (*Beat.*) We could put it in a paper-bag if you're feeling self-conscious.

Linus   I don't want a drink. (*Pause.*) You grew up by the sea?

Kelly   Yes.

Linus   You mentioned ... back at your flat ...

Kelly   Right.

Linus Do you miss it? Do you miss your home?

Kelly No.

Linus Oh.

Kelly Should I?

Linus I always thought people who grew up by the sea … with a seaside upbringing … always hankered for …?

Kelly 'Hankered'?

Linus … yeah … always wanted to return.

Kelly It wasn't sandcastles … candyfloss … arcades …

Linus No?

Kelly I can't skim stones. I can't swim.

Linus You can't …?

Kelly I could probably keep afloat … just about … but I'm not a strong swimmer.

Linus Right.

Kelly Mel would go back … but I don't miss it. There's nothing left there anyhow.

Linus Nothing?

Kelly Erosion … coastlines get battered … they're exposed … they're the open nerve-endings of the country. The ground beneath your feet taken away from you in slices. It's death-by-a-thousand-cuts. I was so happy when we moved inland. I know Dad felt the same. Safe. Away from the edge. But Mel would go back … kept going back … after every big storm … after every heavy night of rain … she'd drive out there to see how much more the sea had taken. There was this one time … there had been gales … and snow, I think … and she went out to survey the damage. She said the dining room had fallen into the sea. Yeah … she said … half of it … during the night … had pulled itself away … bricks and dust and wooden floorboards. Carpet and wallpaper … the wallpaper

... the rubble at the bottom of the cliff ... the newer, topmost layers had been ripped away and shreds of this old wallpaper were exposed ... some green with birds that had since been many times decorated over ... and I knew the one she meant ... I knew the one she meant ... not from ... you know ... childhood ... not from actually remembering ... but from Christmas family portraits ... tissue paper crowns ... woollen Rudolph jumpers ... and this green wallpaper ... green with birds ... in the back of every photograph. Family. Happy. A life taken away in layers ... why would you ... why would you go back? Why would you want to see bits ... bits ... snapped off ... broken off ... in a heap at the bottom of a cliff? Say goodbye ... say goodbye and be done. Not bit by bit. Not increment by increment.

Linus *kisses her.*

Kelly That was the nicest one yet. (*Beat.*) Tell me your name.

Linus I told you ...

Kelly No, no ...

Linus I don't know why you're ...

Kelly What's your real name ...?

Linus ... so obsessed with ...

Kelly ... the one you were born with?

Linus You're not born with a name.

Kelly Some people are. I was.

Linus No you weren't.

Kelly I was.

Linus How could they know which one was coming out first?

Kelly You're being slippery.

Linus Am not.

Kelly Tell me your birth certificate name.

Linus *silence.*

Kelly Why won't you tell me?

Linus I'll give you a multiple-choice.

Kelly What?

Linus I'll give you a multiple-choice.

Kelly Why?

Linus It's fun.

Kelly Okay ... I'll guess. Don't make it too hard.

Linus Stephen – Martin – Dennis. Make a choice.

Kelly Say them again.

Linus Stephen – Martin – Dennis.

Kelly You don't look like a Dennis.

Linus Maybe my mother was blind.

Kelly Martin. I'm going with Martin.

Linus Sure?

Kelly Martin. Am I right?

Linus Not a Stephen? Not a Dennis?

Kelly Martin. Tell me I'm right.

Linus If you want to be right, be right. I'd rather be Linus.

Silence.

Kelly I might be a little drunk.

Silence.

Linus I should be getting back.

Kelly No ... stay ... wait ...

Linus What for?

Kelly I could come with … meet your sister.

Linus I'm not … maybe you shouldn't … fuck … I don't …

Kelly You think I shouldn't?

Linus I don't … I don't know what's the right thing to do. I don't always know the right thing to do.

Kelly I think you've done pretty well.

Linus All I was doing … for so long … day after day … was treading water. I gave her assurances … certainties. I had to be certain that all would be well … for her. The truth is I didn't know … didn't know how bad … or for how long. I became a parrot … 'not long now … a little longer … a little further … it's only pain and pain passes' … a prince of white lies. And Marnie was … when she was at her worst … and we would've done anything to speed through the waiting … for it to be over and complete … she was believing me … because what else was there for her? She was … every day … another fraction … less. Until … one bad night in the rain …

Kelly Melissa.

Linus Yep. And after that … every day … a fraction better.

Kelly Hooray.

Linus Hooray.

Kelly And now you can relax.

Linus Some time for myself?

Kelly Yes.

Linus And how should I fill this Linus-shaped time? Read a book? Watch a movie? Travel the world?

Kelly You've earned it.

Linus You think?

Kelly Haven't you?

Linus It's not a question of earning ... of balance ... 'I do this ... I deserve that' ... no. Years of 'if we just wait long enough ... hold out for a heart ... then everything will click ... everything will fix.' These things are not so neat. Woken in the middle of the night ... her retching and crying behind a locked bathroom door. You don't know what you get. It could've been the heart of a bad man ... the heart of a cheat ... a racist ... a molester ... a dickhead ... or a ... or a ... it could've been anyone in that accident ... it could've been ...

Kelly But it wasn't ... it was ... it was ...

Linus We didn't know what we got, and that's what Marnie couldn't cope with – a stranger in her chest. It came with a history ... of course it did. A thousand heartbreaks maybe. Who knows?

Kelly That can change now.

Linus What can?

Kelly I have not had a good time recently. It has been difficult ... lonely. I seem to be surrounded by mirrors. And you ... I think you have done incredible things. What you have done for your sister ... that support ... that love ... that is family. Whereas mine ... my father ... he is a weak man. (*Beat.*) There's an overlap now ... between our two ... a Venn diagram of ... and perhaps we can help each other ... perhaps we can find coherence ... of some sort ... maybe.

Linus No.

Kelly No?

Linus I'm not going to hold your hand. I'm not going to give you comfort. I'm not going to take you in my arms and tell you you're all sparkly and magic. I was having fun ... this was fun ... a distraction. I enjoyed your company ... but now ... what? Sorry. I'm not in the market for burdens. I'm not going to hold your hand through the tough times. We came here to say goodbye.

Silence. Distance between **Linus** *and* **Kelly**. **Kelly** *drinks.*

14.

The B&B.

Marnie (*the photo is still in her hand*)   You can go.

Simon   I want to be here when he gets back.

Silence.

Marnie   It's alright …

Simon   It's not alright.

Silence.

Marnie   Thank you for staying.

Simon   There's a damp patch on the ceiling. (*Beat.*) Get your stuff together. I think it would be better if –

A door slams.

Marnie   What's that?

Simon   I don't –

Marnie   Listen.

Linus *is suddenly through the door, supporting an unconscious* **Kelly**.

Linus   Don't just … don't just … give me a hand!

Simon *helps* **Linus** *move the unconscious* **Kelly** *into the room.*

Simon   What's going on? What have you been …?

Linus   She's had a little too much to drink.

Simon   I don't know how you …

Linus   She passed out coming up the stairs.

Simon   I don't know how the two of you would be … why would you be …?

Linus I recognised her face ... we got to talking ... we got to drinking ... (*To* **Marnie**.) Have you had a good day?

Marnie, *confused and close to tears, is staring at* **Kelly**'*s face.*

Simon (*taking* **Marnie**'*s face in his hands, reassuring*) It's okay ... it's okay ...

Marnie I ... I ... she ...

Simon They were twins. Okay? They were twins. This is Kelly.

Linus Marnie ...?

Marnie Twins.

Simon Yes.

Marnie Okay ... okay ...

Simon Okay?

Kelly *coughs up a little sick*

Linus Oh god ... (*Cleans the muck from* **Kelly**'*s face.*)

Simon What's she done to herself?

Marnie Where have you been?

Linus Round the corner ... on the pavement ... for the last half hour. She was being sick in the gutter.

Simon You bring her here ... why are you bringing her here?

Linus I'm supposed to leave her in the park ... face down in a puddle of rainwater and vomit?

Simon No ... no ...

Linus (*offers his hand*) It's good to see you again, by the way. I hope she hasn't been too much of a pain?

Simon No ... no ... not at all.

Linus Have you had a good day? Have you bonded?

Simon She's been trying to call you.

Linus This town is a communications blackspot.

Marnie Is that all I'm going to get?

Linus *shrugs*

Marnie Ask me if everything's alright.

Linus Is everything alright?

Marnie Yes. Ask me where we went.

Linus Where did you go?

Marnie To the seaside.

Linus You took her to the seaside?

Simon She wanted to go … so we went.

Linus Did you paddle?

Marnie It wasn't that kind of seaside.

Linus Did you buy her an ice cream? (*Beat.*) You went to see the crumbling house?

Marnie Crumbled – past tense.

Linus She told me about … um … dining rooms at the foot of cliffs. (*Beat.*) I'm sorry to have scared you. I'm sure you were fine.

Simon She was very concerned.

Linus I know how to look after myself.

Marnie You could've told me.

Linus It wasn't planned.

Marnie You abandoned me.

Linus I didn't answer my phone for a few hours – that's all.

Marnie I didn't know where you were.

Linus Good for you.

Marnie Good for me?

Linus Maybe you learnt something about self-reliance.

Simon There are ways to –

Linus Don't.

Marnie You were teaching me a lesson?

Linus That makes it sound vindictive and all I wanted was …

Marnie It's a shitty lesson … a shitty … useless … smug lesson. Idiot-hole.

Linus … some time to myself.

Marnie He could've been anyone … he could've been …

Linus But he wasn't.

Kelly *coughs*.

Linus (*squats down next to her*) Hey.

Kelly I'm sorry.

Linus Are you alright?

Simon I'll get her a glass of water.

Marnie Those taps don't work.

Kelly Oh no.

Simon Kelly.

Kelly For fuck's sake … don't say anything … please.

Simon I wasn't going to.

Kelly I'm a mess … I know. Fuck off.

Simon Nice.

Linus Are you going to … do you need a bowl or …?

Kelly Are we …? Where are we …?

Simon I think I'm going to go.

Linus Can you take her home?

Simon I ...

Kelly You remember where I live, don't you?

Simon Why would you let her get into this kind of state?

Linus She's not my responsibility.

Simon But still ... Jesus ...

Linus Not my responsibility.

Marnie *staring at* **Kelly**.

Kelly Have I got something ... have I got something on my face ...?

Marnie No.

Kelly You're ... um ... you're ... um ...

Marnie Marnie.

Kelly That's right.

Marnie Hello.

Linus Can you take her in your car?

Simon No.

Marnie I saw your house ... or, at least, where your house once was.

Kelly Yeah?

Marnie It's gone now.

Kelly I imagine it would be. (*Takes the photo out of* **Marnie**'s *hand.*) Where did you get this?

Marnie It's his.

Kelly I took this.

Marnie Yeah? It's a good shot.

Kelly I think I'm going to vomit.

Linus Put your head between you knees.

Simon (*takes the photo from* **Kelly**, *goes to put it back into his wallet, changes his mind. To* **Marnie** ...)   You can hang onto this, if you want.

Marnie No, I ...

Simon I think you should.

Marnie I don't want it.

Simon I'm not saying you have to carry it with you at all times ... just take it ... put it in a drawer ... every now and again throughout your life ... once a month ... once every six months ... take it out, look at it ... remember why you're alive.

Marnie No.

Simon I think you should.

Marnie No.

Linus She doesn't want it.

Simon Important to remember ... important to ...

Kelly Dad ...

Simon You get to grow old ... you get to do all those things ... so live for her ... live for ... live your life, by all means ... but don't ever forget ... don't ever ...

Linus We came here to say goodbye.

Marnie (*takes the photo, takes* **Simon***'s wallet, places the photo inside the wallet, and places the wallet back into* **Simon***'s inside jacket pocket*)   First person to have a hand transplant. His right hand. It was a success. He had feeling. He had fine detail in his movement. But the hand came from a slightly larger man ... with a slightly different skin-tone ... with slightly coarser hairs. And when seen alongside the remaining left hand ... well ... the disparity was disconcerting. And there was a lip ... a ridge ... a step ... where donor met recipient ... no neat Frankensteinian scar ... but a rim around the wrist. It looked like one man was wearing the other's hand as a glove. This is the hand that he touched his wife with ... the hand that smoothed down his children's hair. He had it amputated. Couldn't live with it. It so obviously didn't belong to him. At least I don't have to look at mine. At least mine has been tidied away. Yes, there's a scar ... from my throat to my navel ... but it's a closed door. Out of sight. Though I'm still left with this creeping sense of unease ... everything's fine and I'm going about my day-to-day ... happy-happy ... smiley-smiley ... but something ... at the centre of it all ... is ever so slightly off. So ... thank you ... thank you very much ... but I'm going to say no. You keep that. I'm not likely to forget.

Simon You get to grow old.

Marnie The longest a transplanted heart has ever lasted is twenty years.

Linus *crosses to* **Marnie**, *takes her in his arms.*

Linus *and* **Marnie** *stand holding each other for a time.*

Marnie (*pushing him gently away, wiping a tear*) I'm alright ... I'm alright.

Kelly (*standing up*) I'm sorry ... could you point me in the direction of the bathroom?

Linus I'll show you.

Kelly Just ... point me in the direction.

Linus Down the corridor ... second door on the left.

Kelly Thank you. (*Doesn't quite make it to the door.*)

Marnie I'll go with her.

Linus Yeah?

Marnie Yeah.

Kelly *and* **Marnie** *exit.*

Silence.

Simon *picks up his coat, nods a goodbye to* **Linus** *and exits.*

Linus *alone.*

With a creaking of metal and a juddering of pipes, water begins gushing from the taps. The pressure goes up and up, water spilling out over the edge of the bowl. **Linus** *tries to stop the flow, tries to turn the taps off, but the water keeps coming – a flood, a baptism. Water arcs out across the room, showering* **Linus***, as he tries to stem the flow. He's laughing. He's laughing so very hard.*

15.

Railway station.

Marnie *and* **Linus** *with their bags.*

Marnie When are you back at work?

Linus I'll give them a call this afternoon.

Marnie Which train are we ...?

Linus Six twenty-five.

Marnie We're on the correct platform?

Linus We're on the correct platform.

Marnie I still haven't had a shower. (*Beat.*) He didn't say goodbye.

Linus No. (*Beat.*) Does it matter?

Marnie I suppose not.

Linus It's just a word.

Silence.

Marnie I held back her hair ... as she ... in the bathroom. I held back her hair. Nothing really came up ... a bit of spit ... dry-retching. Her face went bright red ... she was coughing really hard. Then the strength went out of her arms ... her legs ... and she kind of just fell into me ... one hand on the toilet seat ... her head in my chest.

Linus She'll be fine.

Marnie What if she's sick in her sleep?

Linus I left her on her side. And ... as you say ... nothing was coming up.

Marnie Did you think she was pretty? I mean ... ignoring the vomit.

Linus *shrugs.*

Marnie Did you sleep with her?

Linus No.

Marnie It's totally fine if you did.

Linus I know.

Marnie Did you kiss her?

Linus *no answer.*

Marnie Did she kiss you?

Linus I don't recall.

Marnie She kissed you ... not the other way around. She kissed you.

Linus Is it better that way?

Marnie I don't know.

Linus I have kissed girls before. I intend to again.

Marnie She has my heart.

Linus No.

Marnie Or rather ... I have her heart.

Linus No.

Marnie Genetically identical. I have her identical heart.

Linus No. (*Beat.*) I think you should get a job.

Marnie   What?

Linus   A job.

Marnie   What would I do?

Linus   What does everybody else do? I'm not talking vocation.

Marnie   Oh.

Linus   I'm talking work.

Marnie   Right.

Linus   Retail …? Administrative …? Data-entry …? Money-work.

Marnie   I don't … I don't think I …

Linus   Don't give me 'not strong enough' … don't give me that.

Marnie   I could come work with you.

Linus   If you're capable of a day-trip to the seaside, you're capable of folding some t-shirts.

Marnie   My CV will look a bit …

Linus   I can help you with that.

Marnie   Thank you.

Linus   It's nothing. (*Beat.*) Train's coming. Get your stuff.

Marnie *picks up her camera and takes a picture of him.*

Linus *manages to turn and pull a massive cheesy grin as she takes the shot.*

Marnie   Hey!

Linus   Did I get a smile in?

Marnie   You got a smile in.

Linus   Good.

16.

Kelly's *flat.*

Simon *in the doorway.* **Kelly** *not letting him in.*

Kelly There are a billion possible variations on the human face. A billion. It's a number … a real number … finite and countable. So with over seven billion people on the planet, there are six people out there who look exactly like you. And the amount of land we have to share is shrinking … the world is getting smaller … it's being washed away … coastal erosion and rising sea levels. Someone once told me that they're not making any more land. The odds on meeting a doppelganger – of yourself or of someone you know – are improving. There are fewer and fewer places to hide. And that is how I can square this circle … how I can explain your presence. Because I cannot believe that you are my father. Because my father never comes to my door … never asks to see me … never says a word. So … therefore … it is perfectly feasible … in my mind … to accept that you are some … salesman … or Jehovah's Witness … who just so happens to hold an uncanny resemblance to –

Simon Stop it.

Kelly I'm sorry, but I do not need any dishcloths or scouring pads today … and neither do I wish to consider the teachings of Our Lord and Saviour, Jesus Christ. Thank you. Please leave.

Simon Stop. (*Beat.*) Can I come in?

Kelly *lets him in.*

Silence.

Simon Is that true … about a billion faces?

Kelly *shrugs.*

Simon How are you feeling?

Kelly A little rough.

Simon I can imagine.

Kelly They put me to bed ... put me to bed and I woke up ... they had gone. The bill had been paid.

Simon That was nice of them.

Kelly Yeah.

Simon Are you drinking?

Kelly Right now?

Simon Hair of the dog.

Kelly I ...

Simon I've been drinking.

Kelly And you wish to continue in that vein?

Simon I would.

Kelly *finds some booze, pours two glasses.*

Simon I don't know how I'm supposed to ... um ...

Kelly Are we going to talk?

Simon Yes. (*Long pause.*) I was incredibly jealous of you ... of both of you ... for a long time ... after your mum died. 'At least they have each other' is what everyone said. People say such funny things about twins ... ask such funny questions ... talk about telepathy and special bonds. I don't ... I don't understand any of that I suppose ... I was an only child so I never got any kind of sibling ... anything. But you very much ... the two of you ... had your own little world ... during those last months and those months after the fact. You retreated into it. You imagined pirates ... and swashbuckling ... treasure maps and cutlasses. The two of you shared adventures ... shared a universe ... and I was left in this one ... this one without your mother. I wanted to be aboard your galleon ... even if it was just to walk the plank. (*Beat.*) You didn't like me very much back then.

Kelly Dad ...

Simon Neither of you did. You were on the verge of becoming teenagers ... you had adult eyes in a child's face. Every attempt at discipline ... every foot down ... you wished me dead ... you wished me exchanged for your mother ... the both of you.

Kelly We were kids.

Simon I know. (*Beat.*) I've given up. I don't care for anything anymore. When your mum died it was all I could do to keep afloat ... but after Mel ... well ... I'm not even panicked ... I'm not even scared ... I'm not even drowning ... I'm just suspended in the water ... I'm not fighting for breath because my lungs are already full ... and my eyes are open ... and it's cold and it's dark and there's not even a tide to drag me further out. I'm just a bloated corpse ... too far down to find the surface.

Kelly I'm still here.

Simon No you're not. You're too much like your father ... you've let it defeat you ... like a part of you has died.

Kelly I know.

Simon I see your mother in your face ... I saw your mother in you both ... and now ... in you ... I see all three and ... (*Beat.*) Do you blame me?

Kelly Does it matter?

Simon I don't know. Tell me if you blame me and I'll tell you whether it matters.

Kelly You were driving.

Simon Is that a yes?

Kelly I don't know.

Simon The oncoming driver had fallen asleep at the wheel.

Kelly So technically not your fault.

Simon Technically, no. Within the eyes of the law, no.

Kelly I don't blame you.

Simon There was all this metal ... and glass ... twisted metal ... shattered glass ... and she was looking at me ... and the rain was coming in ... and her blood ... the rain was diluting her blood ... washing away ... and I was all 'no ... she needs that ... she needs that.' (*Beat.*) That little girl ... that little girl with Melissa's heart ... I liked her. I'm glad she's alive.

Kelly So am I.

Simon But I would exchange her for my daughter in a heartbeat.

Kelly So would I. But that wasn't an option, was it?

Simon No. (*Breaks down.*) I don't want to live in a world where everyone I love is dead.

Kelly (*Hugging him.*) You don't.

Simon I'm sorry ... I'm sorry ... I'm sorry ...

Kelly It's okay ... it's okay ... it's okay ...

Simon You came as a unit ... a two-for-one deal ... and there are moments when I'm thinking I would've preferred it if you had both died ... I think that would've been easier to cope with. And then I pull myself out of that thought pattern and I'm a little bit sick with myself because I was just that moment wishing you dead ... and I don't ... I don't wish you dead ... not at all.

Kelly (*a little laugh*) Thank you.

Simon I've been a bit of a shit.

Kelly Yeah.

Simon I'm sorry. (*Beat.*) Will you come round for dinner?

Kelly Er ... okay.

Simon Are you free next Wednesday?

Kelly I ... er ... I don't know ...

Simon There's this ... woman I've been seeing ... Elizabeth ... she has her own kids and ... and ... I've met them ... a couple of times ... I don't know where it's going, but ... but I want to keep with it ... I think I could be happy ... happier ... and ... I'm not suggesting we plan Christmas together or anything ... but ... dinner ...

Kelly That would be nice.

Simon I think it would.

Kelly Yeah. I'm free.

They drink.

17.

A shopping centre.

Marnie *has set up a portable studio – a backcloth, a few lights, lots of example portraits of toddlers, babies, happy families. She stands amongst it, her camera in hand.*

Kelly *stands to one side, a pram in front of her.*

Kelly Hello.

Marnie Hello.

Kelly Hello, Marnie.

Marnie Hello, Kelly.

Kelly I wasn't sure if ... whether you would ...

Marnie Of course I ...

Kelly ... recognise. After however many ...

Marnie How could I not? It's ... come ... let me ... (*Hug.*)

Kelly Oh ... okay.

Marnie How have you been?

Kelly Well. Really well.

Marnie You've got a little one.

Kelly Yes. A boy.

Marnie What's his name?

Kelly Noah.

Marnie That's adorable. Can I see?

Kelly Yes. He's sleeping.

Marnie I won't wake him?

Kelly No.

Marnie (*looks inside the pram*) Oh, he's beautiful.

Kelly Yes. I don't know where he gets that hair from.

Marnie I love it. How old?

Kelly Four months.

Marnie You look good on it.

Kelly Thanks. I look awful.

Marnie No.

Kelly You're too kind. (*Beat.*) I was hoping for twins.

Marnie What brings you to …?

Kelly My husband is from round here … visiting his family.

Marnie Small world.

Kelly Yes.

Marnie You got married. Congratulations.

Kelly Met him online.

Marnie Nevermind.

Kelly I'm very happy.

Marnie Good.

Kelly And you …? You seem … your own business?

Marnie I work for myself but as part of a franchise. I set up in shopping centres ... supermarkets ... libraries sometimes. It's good ... fun ... I do what I do.

Kelly They're good.

Marnie People hold onto them, you know? They're the sort of thing you keep in a frame ... or printed on a canvas ... hung on a wall. Even when the kids grow up and move away. It's nice. These photos get kept. I'm writing myself into their lives a little ... invisibly though ... I like that.

Kelly How's your brother?

Marnie He's alright.

Kelly I'll tell my Dad I saw you. He'll be interested to know that you're doing well.

Marnie Good ... thanks ... he's ...?

Kelly He's fine.

Marnie Good.

Kelly And you're alright? Healthy?

Marnie Yes. Absolutely. Yes.

Kelly No complications?

Marnie No. Nothing.

Kelly She was always a hard worker. Are you ... are you breaking for lunch at any point? I'd love to ...

Marnie I'm meeting my ...

Kelly I see.

Marnie ... my boyfriend, he's ...

Kelly Okay ... that's ... that's fine.

Marnie It would've been nice ... and thank you ... but ...

Kelly Sure.

Marnie It's only been two months ... I'm still at the stage where I get palpitations when I see him ... I'm not used to ...

Kelly It's a nice stage to be at.

Marnie Yes. We had the scar conversation last week ... so ... well ... I guess that makes it a bit serious.

Kelly How did he take it?

Marnie Good. He didn't freak out ... he didn't run away ... didn't treat me like I was made of glass.

Kelly I'm glad things are working out for you.

Marnie So am I.

Kelly Say 'hi' to Linus for me.

Marnie I will. Say 'hi' to your Dad.

Kelly I will. It was really good to see you.

Marnie If you want ... I'm not busy ... I could take a portrait ... no charge.

Kelly That's kind, but he's sleeping ... he'll just be grumpy if I wake him ...

Marnie No one wants a picture of a grumpy baby.

Kelly Thank you though.

Marnie What about you?

Kelly Me?

Marnie I could take your portrait.

Kelly I ...

Marnie I'm getting really good.

Kelly I can see.

Marnie Come on. On me.

Kelly Oh … alright then.

Marnie Excellent. (*Positions* **Kelly** *on a stool in front of the backcloth, adjusts the lights and gets behind the camera, takes a couple of shots, the lights flash.*) Okay … okay … smile.

Kelly *smiles a genuine smile.*

Oppenheimer

Tom Morton-Smith

Oppenheimer

'Just because some of us can read and write and do a little math, that doesn't mean we deserve to conquer the Universe.' *Kurt Vonnegut*

For Jen.

With thanks to Angus Jackson, Professor David Wark, Gregory Doran, Erica Whyman, Michael Boyd, Jeanie O'Hare, Réjane Collard-Walker and all at the RSC. Thanks also to Laura K Diehl for her help with the German translation.

Special thanks to Pippa Hill for championing my work over the past few years and for urging me on.

Oppenheimer was first performed by the Royal Shakespeare Company at the Swan Theatre, Stratford-upon-Avon, on 15 January 2015.

Edward Teller	Ben Allen
Haakon Chevalier/Richard Feynman	Ross Armstrong
Little Boy	Fred Barry/Christopher Kingdom/Barney Fitzpatrick
Joe Weinberg/Paul Tibbets	Daniel Boyd
Kenneth Nichols	Vincent Carmichael
Ruth Tolman	Laura Cubitt
Jackie Oppenheimer	Hedydd Dylan
Charlotte Serber	Sandy Foster
Genereal Leslie Groves	William Gaminara
Frank Oppenheimer	Michael Grady-Hall
J. Robert Oppenheimer	John Heffernan
Robert Wilson	Jack Holden
Giovanni Rossi Lomanitz	Oliver Johnstone
Peer de Silva	Andrew Langtree
Klaus Fuchs/Richard Harrison	Joel MacCormack
Hans Bethe	Tom McCall
Luis Alvarez/Doctor	Josh O'Connor
Kitty Puening Harrison	Thomasin Rand

Jean Tatlock Catherine Steadman
Bob Serber/Albert Einstein Jamie Wilkes

All other parts played by members of the Company.

Director	Angus Jackson
Designer	Robert Innes Hopkins
Lighting Designer	Paul Anderson
Music	Grant Olding
Sound Designer	Christopher Shutt
Choreographer	Scott Ambler
Video Designer	Karl Dixon
Dramaturg	Pippa Hill
Casting	Hannah Miller, Annelie Powell

Characters

J. Robert Oppenheimer
Frank Oppenheimer
Giovanni Rossi Lomanitz
Bob Serber
Jackie Oppenheimer
Jean Tatlock
Joe Weinberg
Robert Wilson
Haakon Chevalier
Charlotte Serber
Kitty Puening Harrison
Hans Bethe
Edward Teller
Leslie Groves
Kenneth Nichols
Peer de Silva
Richard Feynman
Luis Alvarez
Klaus Fuchs
Richard Harrison

Albert Einstein
Ruth Tolman
Little Boy
and others

Act One

1 – LECTURE SERIES: INTRODUCTION

A lecture theatre.

*J. Robert Oppenheimer (**Oppie**) addresses a gathering of students. He reads from a slim, red book: Atomic Theory and the Description of Nature – Niels Bohr, 1934.*

Oppie 'The task of science is both to extend the range of our experience and to reduce it to order.' So says Niels Bohr. It is only by experience that we can discern the laws that govern our universe. So as we learn ... as we grow ... we must be prepared to alter our methods for ordering our experience ... because we come to surpass those techniques ... those patterns ... that once instructed us. Life is nothing if not a constant re-evaluation of what we believe to be correct, and a constant reassessment of the ways we gauge that correctness. What was true yesterday can be less true today, because we have learnt ... and will learn ... better. My name is J Robert Oppenheimer. You will come to know me as Oppie. I expect you to be attentive. I expect you to be present. And if some aspect of the lecture doesn't make sense, then perhaps we are getting somewhere. There is no negotiation ... no debate ... with the complexity of the universe. If the work eludes you ... if you simply lack the ability ... then take your leave. I can make it clearer, but I cannot make it simpler. Let us begin.

2 – A FUNDRAISER FOR THE RELIEF EFFORT IN SPAIN

The Oppenheimer residence – Berkeley, California.

A party is in full swing. Music plays. The room bustles with people – people who are drinking, dancing, laughing and generally having an excellent time.

People present include: **Oppie**, **Frank** *Oppenheimer, Giovanni Rossi* **Lomanitz**, *Bob* **Serber**, **Jackie** *Oppenheimer,* **Jean** *Tatlock, Joe* **Weinberg**, *Robert* **Wilson**, *Haakon* **Chevalier** *and* **Charlotte** *Serber.*

Frank Roosevelt!

Lomanitz Ha! Roosevelt!

Frank Franklin Delano Roosevelt!

Serber My god, Frank, you've got to give it a rest.

Frank Roosevelt's greatest achievement has been to get people thinking … about employment … about economics … once the working man actually considers employment, economics, race-relations … that's the start … that's the route to socialism … communism.

Serber Frank … you're kicking at an open door!

Lomanitz A specter is haunting Frank Oppenheimer.

Frank What the New Deal has done … the legacy of the New Deal … it has opened people's eyes … the Great Depression … the Wall Street Crash … that way no longer works. Robert … brother of mine … big brother … big Robert … back me up …

Oppie If booze is present in your glass then your argument cannot maintain its structure. It will inevitably collapse.

Frank My glass is empty.

Jackie Frank, will you lay off the sermons?

Frank Hey baby … hey sweet-cheeks … how's about I spin you round the floor?

Lomanitz Please, Jackie … take him dancing.

Serber Burn off some of that liquor.

Jackie Show me your moves, mister.

Oppie Frank's not wrong … the people's eyes are open.

Lomanitz To be fair to the guy … if you're going to air your leftist politics … where better than a Communist Party fundraiser?

Serber I thought we were raising money for the relief effort in Spain?

Oppie It's getting dispersed ... distributed ... through the Party.

Lomanitz What difference does it make? Sign me up to the union. For ... with ... through ... I'm there.

Jean (*standing on a table, banging on a collection bucket*) Workers of the world – unite!

The music and dancing stops and everybody turns their attention to **Jean**.

Jean For too long the White House has ignored the rise of fascism in Europe. Our government sits impotently by while Franco marches on Barcelona. Civilians fleeing the violence are interned in camps across the French border. I ask you – do you believe, even if there are thousands of miles between you, that your brother is any less your brother? We are not asking for money to fight a war ... we are asking for money to feed children ... to pay for medicines ... to return some dignity to those who fascism has stripped bare. Compare their sacrifice with the dollar bill in your wallet and please give generously. Thank you.

Cheering and applause. Some voices in the crowd start singing 'L'Internationale[1]*'. More and more people join in until eventually everyone is singing.*

3 – THE DEPARTMENT OF THEORETICAL PHYSICS

The theoretical physics department – University of California, Berkeley.

Lomanitz Joe ... Joe ... how are you finding it?

Weinberg Rossi, hey. Bob.

Serber How are you settling in?

Weinberg The work here is ... well, it's a great deal more intense to what I'm used to.

---

[1] L'Internationale – Eugène Pottier (lyrics – 1871), Pierre De Geyter (music – 1888). An anthem of international socialism and the de facto national anthem for the Soviet Union (1922–44).

Serber Where were you studying before?

Weinberg Wisconsin.

Lomanitz That would … yeah … Berkeley's a little more … than Wisconsin … a little more …

Serber European. In terms of thinking.

Weinberg It used to come so easy to me.

Serber You'll have to work for it here.

Weinberg My professor told me I belonged at Berkeley … that I belonged with Oppenheimer. I wasn't sure.

Lomanitz No?

Weinberg Oppenheimer … his articles … in the Physical Review … they're the only ones I don't get.

Lomanitz And that is why.

Weinberg And that is why.

Lomanitz Well, on behalf of the University of California's theoretical physics department … welcome.

Serber You are among your own kind now.

4 – A FUNDRAISER FOR THE RELIEF EFFORT IN SPAIN [cntd.]

Jean *approaches with a collection bucket in hand.*

Lomanitz Here she comes … prepare yourself for a fleecing.

Jean So, gentlemen … dust off your wallets. (*To* **Serber**.) Are you a socialist?

Serber Yes, ma'am.

Jean Then put your money in the pot. (*To* **Lomanitz**.) Are you a socialist?

Lomanitz Through and through.

Jean In it goes. And you?

Weinberg I'm a fully paid-up member of the Communist Party USA.

Jean Lyubimaya! Babushka!

Lomanitz Comrade!

Jean Robert! Robert, your boys … you must be a proud Papa Bear.

Oppie Give the nice lady your donation.

Jean I want to see paper money. This nickel and dime crap is weighing me down.

Weinberg I just wanted to take this chance to introduce myself properly …

Jean Oh yes?

Weinberg You have such a lovely home … and I'm a great admirer of your husband …

Jean Is that so?

Weinberg It's a pleasure to make your acquaintance, Mrs Oppenheimer.

Oppie Joe, Jean and I aren't married.

Weinberg Oh, I … god … I'm sorry … I just assumed …

Oppie It's quite alright.

Weinberg Oh god.

Lomanitz This way, Joe … there are some folks over here you've yet to embarrass yourself in front of.

Jean Not very smart, your new disciple.

Oppie He's a bright kid. They're all bright kids.

Jean (*to* **Serber**) How old are you?

Serber Thirty.

Jean 'Kids'.

Oppie Serber doesn't count. Rossi, how old are you?

Lomanitz Eighteen.

Jean That proves nothing. (*Takes* **Lomanitz**'s *drink.*) And you … you should not be drinking.

Lomanitz And how old are you?

Jean I don't think I like this one.

5 – THE DEPARTMENT OF THEORETICAL PHYSICS [cntd.]

Wilson (*waving a magazine*) Have you read this?

Serber Hey … ease up, Wilson … you're going to take out someone's eye.

Wilson Sorry.

Lomanitz What is it?

Wilson This month's *Nature*. Have you read it?

Serber He's talking about Hahn and Strassman.

Lomanitz I haven't read it.

Wilson (*reads*) 'Hahn and Strassman were forced to conclude that isotopes of barium are formed as a consequence of bombardment of uranium with neutrons[2].' Can you believe that?

Weinberg I don't … I don't …

Serber Weinberg's new … his brain's still playing catch up.

Wilson An atom of uranium … they broke it down … they broke it up … into all these little pieces … these little pieces of other elements. It's alchemy.

---

[2] 'Disintegration of Uranium by Neutrons: a New Type of Nuclear Reaction', Lise Meitner and O. R. Frisch, *Nature* (1939).

Serber By bombarding the uranium nucleus with neutrons … it disintegrates … it falls apart … the atom splits into all these lesser … lighter elements.

Lomanitz Has Oppie read this?

Serber It was published this morning, it's … what … two o'clock now. I'd be surprised if he wasn't already the world's foremost authority on the subject.

6 – A FUNDRAISER FOR THE RELIEF EFFORT IN SPAIN [cntd.]

Oppie Haakon – thank you so much for coming.

Haakon For the cause and for you – how could I not?

Oppie How was France?

Haakon Excellent, excellent. Tout est possible!

Oppie And how is the novel coming?

Haakon Slow.

Oppie Send me what you have.

Haakon I have a chapter … a chapter and a half …

Oppie Let me read it.

Haakon Thank you. If it's not too much trouble?

Oppie My friend, you bring me poetry. It's no trouble at all.

Lomanitz Oppie … I wanted to return that book you lent me …?

Oppie On the bookcase is fine.

Lomanitz I wanted to say … I haven't quite … I'm still taking notes from it … wondering if I could …?

Haakon What's the book?

Lomanitz Henri de Saint-Simon.

Oppie It's fine. Rossi. Hang on to it.

Lomanitz Thank you.

Haakon You have your students reading socialist philosophy?

Oppie I have them learning about the world.

Charlotte *enters. She has lifted the front of her skirt in front of her so that she can carry a large amount of change.*

Serber There she is … the love of my life. Where have you been hiding yourself?

Charlotte There were some pockets unpicked in the kitchen.

Jean In the bucket it goes!

Jackie Have any of you seen Frank?

Serber He was headed to the bathroom.

Jackie Oh god.

Jean Lost your dancing partner? Here, let me … (*Pulls* **Jackie** *to the middle of the floor.*)

Jackie Oh, I … I couldn't …

Jean Don't worry your pretty little face … I'll lead!

Jean *proceeds to dance* **Jackie** *around the floor.*

7 – THE DEPARTMENT OF THEORETICAL PHYSICS [cntd.]

Wilson You can make sense of this?

Oppie Hahn and Strassman? Absolutely.

Serber These two Germans … are we certain they've actually done this?

Oppie I had one of the boys in the radiation laboratory recreate the experiment. We broke apart an atom this morning. I've seen the results.

Act One 93

Lomanitz Two chemists in a tiny laboratory in Berlin! For all our machines ... these huge great cyclotrons ... the entire rad-lab ... all this resource ... and *still* the Germans make us look like schoolboys.

Oppie There are still so many questions to be answered. Does the uranium come apart in only certain ways or randomly? Is barium always produced?

Wilson So ... inside the uranium atom ... you crack it open and all these other elements tumble out?

Serber Atoms within atoms ... like a Russian doll?

Oppie Not quite. Hahn and Strassman thought that by bombarding uranium-238 with neutrons ... they thought that they would stick ... that they might add to the nucleus ... creating a heavier form of uranium.

Weinberg But that didn't happen.

Oppie No.

Wilson They didn't add to the nucleus ... they split it.

Oppie The energy that holds the nuclei together – you'd expect that to be released.

Lomanitz And the neutrons ...

Oppie Precisely.

Serber My god.

Weinberg What am I missing here?

8 – FUNDRAISER FOR THE RELIEF EFFORT IN SPAIN [cntd.]

Charlotte Gabble gabble gabble ... blah blah blah.

Serber Charlotte ...

Charlotte You haven't danced with me once tonight.

Jackie (*nursing a drunk* **Frank**) I think it's time we left.

Charlotte You're leaving?

Jackie I'm going to drive him home.

Charlotte It's been so lovely seeing you both.

Jackie Give my apologies to Robert.

Frank I've cleaned up the bathroom as best I can.

Charlotte Goodbye, Jackie.

Jean Do svidaniya, comrade!

Jackie Goodbye, Jean.

Wilson Hey, Jean … how much did you make?

Jean Enough to topple all the fascist regimes of Europe!

Wilson That much, huh?

Weinberg My brain hurts.

Wilson You need a glass of milk … a glass of milk with a raw egg cracked into it.

Weinberg Why would you say that?

Serber I don't want you vomiting in the back of my car.

Lomanitz Any chance of a ride?

Serber Grab your stuff.

Charlotte Goodnight, Jean. Goodnight, Oppie.

Serber Wilson, you coming?

Lomanitz *pulls* **Wilson**, **Serber** *and* **Weinberg** *together and leads them in song. They reprise the chorus of L'Internationale.* **Jean**, **Oppie** *and* **Haakon** *applaud as* **Serber**, **Weinberg**, **Wilson**, **Lomanitz** *and* **Charlotte** *exit.*

Haakon And then there were three.

Oppie It's late, Haakon.

Haakon It is. (*To* **Jean**.) Can I offer you a lift?

Jean No.

Haakon Goodnight, then.

Oppie *ushers* **Haakon** *to the door.*

Haakon Laissons les jolies femmes aux homes sans imagination.

Oppie Good night.

Haakon *exits.* **Jean** *and* **Oppie** *are alone.*

Jean That was a night.

Oppie It was.

Jean What did you make of my speech?

Oppie Your clarion-call to the global proletariat?

Jean Yes. Did it stir you? Were you stirred?

Oppie I was worried your shoes might scuff my tabletop.

Jean *sings the first lines of the British translation of 'L'Internationale' and starts to strip.*

Arise ye workers from your slumber,
Arise ye prisoners of want …

Oppie Jean … stop it.

Jean Not a chance.

Oppie It has been two months.

Jean Has it?

Oppie Two months and no word … no telephone call …

Jean You sound like my mother.

Oppie What do you expect? Open arms? Where have you been?

Jean You are not my only man.

Oppie I am abundantly aware.

Jean You need to relax. You have nothing to lose but your chains.

Oppie You let yourself in as though you've been to the corner store. You take on the role of hostess. You fling my brother's wife around the floor like ... like ... I don't know what.

Jean Jackie was having a great time.

Oppie Jackie doesn't know you like I do. Jackie's a waitress.

Jean Phooey.

Oppie Put your clothes back on. You're embarrassing yourself.

Jean I've never been embarrassed in my entire life.

Oppie This was a night of charity.

Jean You think I don't care for the cause? My heart bleeds for the Spanish ... my soul cracks for them ... to think of their suffering ... it kills me.

Oppie I am sure that the starving and the dispossessed greatly appreciate your drunken behaviour.

Jean I may be a lush, but I am a sincere one.

Oppie No doubt.

Jean Look at you ... so aloof, so sanctimonious. I shall think of this moment in forty-five minutes' time ... in that other room ... when you are moaning my name as if it's the only word you have ever known.

Oppie I will throw you out.

Jean You will do no such thing.

Oppie You think I'm not capable of ...?

Jean I'm sure you're well versed in the theory.

Oppie *forcibly grabs* **Jean** *and goes to throw her out.*

Jean Oppie?! Oppie! God damn you, you bastard!

Silence.

The tension dissolves into laughter.

Jean It's cold out there.

Oppie I know.

Jean You want me to catch cold?

Oppie Can't you leave me alone?

Jean I would die without you.

9 – LECTURE SERIES: THE MODEL ATOM

Lomanitz The internal structure of the atom consists of three subatomic particles …

Weinberg … the positively charged proton …

Wilson … the negatively charged electron …

Serber … and the neutron …

Lomanitz … which remains neutral.

Wilson Each chemical element has a differing number of protons at its core.

Weinberg Hydrogen …

Serber … the simplest element …

Wilson … the lightest element …

Weinberg … has only a single proton at its heart.

Lomanitz Helium … the next lightest element … has a nucleus with two protons and two neutrons.

Serber This is lithium …

Wilson … third in the periodic table.

Lomanitz Three protons bound to four neutrons and orbited by three electrons.

98 Oppenheimer

Weinberg The electrons are desperate to be part of the nucleus ...

Serber ... they're negatively charged ... the protons positively charged ... there's an attraction.

Wilson But electrons are fidgety ... they can't keep still.

Serber They've got all this energy but they're tied to the nucleus.

Weinberg It's like having a firework on a piece of string.

Wilson They want to be up in the sky but the center won't let them go.

Lomanitz So they pull in all directions at the same time ... a cloud of tethered energy.

Wilson But that is nothing compared to the energy held within the nucleus.

Serber Let's look at something at the other end of the periodic table ... a much heavier nucleus ...

Wilson ... let's look at uranium.

Serber Uranium is still made of protons, electrons and neutrons ...

Weinberg ... but in far greater quantities.

Lomanitz There are 92 protons in the nucleus of a uranium atom ...

Wilson ... orbited by 92 electrons ...

Serber ... and it can bind between 141 and 146 neutrons.

Weinberg That's a whole big heap of sub-atomic particles.

Serber Half of a perfect atom is an imperfect one.

Lomanitz So if you were to use a neutron to split a uranium nucleus ... it wouldn't divide neatly into two equally sized stable elements.

Wilson It's a watermelon shot by a rifle … it will be blown into chunks.

Lomanitz As we said, uranium can hold a lot of neutrons at its core. Lighter elements cannot contain nearly as many.

Serber So if you start splitting uranium into lighter elements … that's a lot of neutrons left with no place to go.

Weinberg You split one atom and you'd have neutrons firing off in all directions …

Wilson … bombarding any surrounding atoms …

Serber … any surrounding *uranium* atoms …

Lomanitz … and what you'd have …

Wilson … would be a …

Serber … in all likelihood, would be …

Weinberg … a chain reaction.

Lomanitz The nuclear force that bonds particles together is incredibly strong.

Wilson You start tearing into atoms … start pulling them apart … that's an awful big mess of energy you're releasing.

Serber An awful big mess.

10 – FRANK AND JACKIE JOIN THE PARTY

Jackie There was a membership coupon in *People's World* …

Frank … the local communist newspaper in Pasadena …

Jackie … Frank was reading it at the time …

Frank … at the kitchen table …

Jackie … there was an article about the working conditions of Negro farm workers …

Frank … horrendous state of affairs … inhuman treatment …

Jackie   ... I was reading over his shoulder and I saw the coupon ...

Frank   ... and without a word exchanged between us ...

Jackie   ... I fetched some scissors from the drawer ...

Frank   ... and I took an envelope from my desk ...

Jackie   ... we posted it that afternoon.

Frank   It was some time before they contacted us ...

Jackie   ... they sent us these little green Party cards ... like library cards ...

Frank   ... they assigned us to a 'street unit' ...

Jackie   ... all people from the local community ...

Frank   ... the neighbourhood ...

Jackie   ... some unemployed ...

Frank   ... some Blacks ...

Jackie   ... some Black unemployed.

Frank   We gather every week ...

Jackie   ... it's mostly talk ...

Frank   ... which is frustrating ...

Jackie   ... we hold meetings in our front room ...

Frank   ... my famous avocado dip ...

Jackie   ... we want to get things done ...

Frank   ... we'd like you to attend.

Jackie   The Pasadena municipal swimming pool is segregated. Wednesday afternoons are set aside for Blacks, and then they drain the pool on Thursday mornings. We're trying to get that changed.

Oppie   Have you thought about your career?

Frank I have no problem calling myself a communist. And neither should you.

11 – LECTURE SERIES: A LETTER TO A PRESIDENT

Albert Einstein *reads from a letter.*

Einstein 'Mr Roosevelt ... Mr President ... Sir. I believe that it may soon become possible to set up a nuclear chain reaction in a large mass of the element uranium ... thus generating a vast amount of power. This phenomenon may lead to the construction of a new type of extremely powerful bomb. A single bomb that may very well flatten a city. I understand that, since her expansion into the Sudetenland, Germany has stopped the sale of uranium from the Czechoslovakian mines that she has taken over. Are the Nazis aware of the potential of uranium? Of course. May I suggest that this situation calls for watchfulness and, if necessary, quick action on the part of your administration. Yours truly ...'

12 – THE LINCOLN BATTALION

A garden party in Pasadena.

The sun is shining and music is playing. Partygoers are having an excellent time. **Haakon** *is chatting to a group of people.* **Oppie** *stands to one side.*

A band strikes up and sings a jaunty version of 'Jarama Valley',[3] a soldier's song of the Spanish Civil War. **Kitty** *Harrison approaches* **Oppie** *with a drink.*

Kitty Here.

Oppie What's this?

Kitty A Scotch and soda. You look like a Scotch and soda.

---

[3] 'Jarama Valley' – Alex McDade (lyrics – 1938), to the tune of 'Red River Valley' (folk). This is the Americanized version, as sung by Woody Guthrie.

Oppie Thank you …

Kitty Kitty Harrison.

Oppie Thank you, Kitty.

Kitty That's no problem at all.

Oppie Are you not joining in with the …?

Kitty Discussions … debates? No. My husband dragged me along. This is very much his sort of thing.

Oppie It isn't yours?

Kitty Maybe once. My first husband died pointlessly in Spain. To hear the band sing of the Lincoln Battalion … of the brave Americans … volunteers in the noble battle against Franco …

Oppie I am sorry.

Kitty All of his friends … all of our friends … and that includes my current husband … all believe passionately in the Communist ideal. Europe's either becoming a bootcamp or a graveyard … and these people think they have the answer … but they only ever talk to each other.

Oppie Then why are you here?

Kitty There's a free bar.

Haakon *waves for* **Oppie** *to come over.*

Oppie *declines.*

Kitty A friend of yours? He wants you to go meet some people.

Oppie He wants to wheel me around. I expect he's losing an argument he'd like to win.

Kitty You're his secret weapon?

Oppie Hardly.

Kitty Please. I cannot bear false modesty – my husband is British. (*Beat.*) What is it you do?

Oppie I'm a professor of physics.

Kitty You're a smart one then … you're a thinker.

Oppie It has been known.

Kitty If we left together now … where would we go? If we said 'screw it'. If we flipped the bird to all the Party Men … the card carriers … the ideologues. If we threw off the bullshit of the world … where would you, professor of physics, take me?

Oppie If we were to leave right now?

Kitty Right now.

Oppie I have a ranch … up in the mountains of New Mexico. A simple, wooden ranch. A forest glade … horse riding … the stars in the sky. A wood burning stove.

Kitty It sounds perfect.

Oppie It's a bit of a drive.

Kitty If we could swing by a drugstore, I could pick up a toothbrush.

Oppie You don't want to stay for the lecture?

Kitty Spontaneism and the dialectics of revolutionary yadda yadda yadda … I would rather eat glass.

Richard *Harrison approaches.*

Richard Darling … the talk is about to begin …

Kitty Richard, do you know …?

Oppie Robert Oppenheimer.

Kitty Robert, my husband Richard.

Richard We should take our seat.

Kitty Will you not join us?

Oppie Please. I know what will be said.

Kitty Yes.

Richard Darling … we really must …

Kitty It was a pleasure to meet you, Robert.

Oppie And you.

Kitty I hope that our paths cross again.

Oppie We should make certain of it.

Kitty Yes. We should.

13 – PEAS IN A POD

Haakon I want your advice … suggestions … rewrites if necessary. Will you cast your eye over …?

Oppie I'm flattered that you would ask, but you're the novelist, not I.

Haakon This isn't the novel, this is … this is a pamphlet on behalf of the League of American Writers. This is for the College Faculties Committee of the Communist Party of California. This is a letter to be sent to *Soviet Russia Today* … to be published in their September issue.

Oppie And what do these pamphlets say?

Haakon They are petitioning against war. Now, more than ever, we have to be vocal. Hitler is getting bold. Europe is on a precipice and political discourse in this country is lurching to the right. The politicians are stoking our hate … stoking our fear … priming us for violence.

Oppie You would have me throw my weight behind the Communist Party?

Haakon The Party's beliefs are your beliefs.

Oppie My beliefs would not allow for treaties with fascists.

Haakon That is not … that is …

Oppie The soviets have signed a treaty of Non-Aggression with the Nazis. Is Eastern Europe a carvery now? The carcass of a roasted bird ... stripped for soup ... stripped for stock. People are tearing up their Party cards ... cursing Engels ... cursing Marx ... because the German military machine has no counter ... no balance ... no equal and opposite ... if the Soviet Union does nothing. And this treaty of theirs is formalized nothing.

Haakon   I cannot claim to understand diplomacy ...

Oppie   And the word ... from Russia ... the purges and the show-trials we hear of ... the forced labour camps ... the famine ...

Haakon   We all know the rumours.

Oppie   And so far we have dismissed them ...

Haakon   ... as Trotskyite lies and disinformation.

Oppie   But in light of the Non-Aggression Pact?

Haakon   It's bullshit! The capitalists will say anything to discredit ... to harm ... to have us fighting amongst ourselves.

Oppie   So it's the Trotskyites and the capitalists ...?

Haakon   Yes!

Oppie   ... and we are to lap this up ... hold our nose ... and believe that water is milk?

Haakon   You say the Soviets are the only answer to the black-boots. I believe that. I believe you.

Jean *enters.*

Haakon   I didn't realize ...

Jean   So good to see you, Haakon ... but Oppie's a little busy right now ... so perhaps some other time?

Haakon   Sure ... I'll ...

Oppie   Leave me your pamphlets.

Haakon   You'll look at them?

Oppie   I will.

Haakon Comrades?

Oppie Comrades.

Haakon *exits.*

Jean He lives up your ass.

Oppie He respects my opinion.

Jean Come back to bed.

Oppie No.

Jean Fine. I am taking you out to dinner. I am treating you to oysters across the bay. I have booked us a suite at the Majestic. I have charted a boat to sail us down the coast. I have booked us on a flight to New York. I have organized tickets to the hottest show in town. I have bought you a new gold watch and a platinum plated cigarette case, inscribed inside in beautiful flowing script: 'Jean and Oppie – two peas in a pod!' (*Beat.*) Come and hold my hand. Come and kiss my face. (*Beat.*) I heard you and Haakon talking about purges … show-trials … famine.

Oppie It's an ugly habit to listen at doors.

Jean These stories … these rumors … tell me they are lies and I'll believe you.

Oppie They are unsubstantiated.

Jean I have to believe that everything is better in Russia … that it is better somewhere … but that belief is being taken from me in strips. I want to take the world … shake it … and scream in its face: 'This is how we live! United! And with love! And with fair pay and the means of production in the hands of the people!'

Oppie When was the last time you spoke to …?

Jean I don't need to speak to anyone. I've read those books … I've studied them … I can do it myself. And I have you – the smartest man I know. Why would I speak to some dullard? I am not special – everyone is suffering. I feel as though I want to sneeze. I want to look at the sun but it is covered by clouds …

smoke from destroyed Polish towns ... and it blots out the light, but not with a darkness ... not just with a darkness ... it drains the color ... Poland is a newsreel and German tanks gray the landscape. If we cannot rely on Russia ... fascism will swarm over us like ants on a dead bird.

Oppie I'm going to drive you home.

Jean Let me stay.

Oppie That's not going to happen. That isn't how this works anymore.

Jean Then tell me how it works.

Oppie You are not my only woman.

14 – THE HOT DOG

Perro Caliente – the Oppenheimer brothers' isolated ranch in New Mexico.

Jackie, **Charlotte** *and* **Kitty** *enter.*

Jackie Let me take your ... let me take your bags ...

Kitty That's very kind. Thank you.

Jackie Not at all.

Charlotte Those roads are getting worse.

Jackie Ain't that the truth?

Charlotte I swear the trip gets longer every time.

Kitty Is Robert here?

Jackie Somewhere. With Frank, I think.

Charlotte The car was shaking apart. I thought we might lose the back axle.

Jackie You got here in one piece though.

Kitty It's some beautiful countryside.

Charlotte It sure is.

Jackie Have you been to New Mexico before?

Serber (*enters*) Am I the only one unpacking the car?

Charlotte Don't do that now. Get settled … show Kitty around.

Kitty I'm dying of thirst.

Jackie I'll get you something … what do you want? We've got beer. Do you drink beer?

Kitty I drink beer.

Frank (*enters*) I thought I heard voices. How the hell are you all?

Serber Stiff as a board.

Frank Those roads are hell, aren't they?

Charlotte I was just saying.

Frank Charlotte … give me a kiss. And you must be Kitty?

Kitty I must be.

Jackie How do you guys all know each other?

Kitty Oh … I don't really … I only know Robert.

Serber We're purely providing a taxi-service today.

Kitty Oh, I didn't mean …

Serber No … I was joking.

Charlotte Over five hours in the back of that jalopy … I'd say we were fast friends by now!

Kitty Sure.

Serber You've got a sweat on, Frank.

Frank I've been chopping wood like the natural-born woodsman I am.

Jackie Ha!

Act One   109

Charlotte   I fall in love with the place every time.

Jackie   Yes.

Charlotte   I fall in love …

Serber   … with New Mexico … with this country.

Frank   Sometimes you need to just get away …

Jackie   … away from the bustle and the orders and the burgers, the chili, coffee and shakes … the poor tips and the 'Miss? Miss? I asked for fries and you brought me wedges … I asked for root beer, you brought me sarsaparilla.' Away from that … away from people.

Kitty   Is Robert …?

Frank   He's smoking his pipe.

Charlotte   Bob …

Serber   Are we unpacking the car?

Charlotte   We're unpacking the car.

Serber *and* **Charlotte** *exit.*

Jackie   So Kitty … what is it … what is it you …?

Kitty   I'm a botanist.

Jackie   Oh perfect!

Frank   Then you'll love it up here.

Jackie   The woodland is … is just full of …

Kitty   Yes.

Jackie   … trees.

Silence.

Oppie *enters.*

Frank   Here he is.

Oppie   Hello.

Kitty Hello.

Jackie Frank ... let me help with that firewood ...

Frank It's all done ... it's all ...

Jackie Frank?

Frank Oh.

Frank *and* **Jackie** *exit.*

Kitty This is your ranch?

Oppie This is my ranch.

Kitty It's beautiful here.

Oppie It's a shame Richard was unable to make it.

Kitty Don't.

Oppie Don't ... what? (*Kisses her firmly and passionately.*)

15 – A PHONECALL TO RICHARD HARRISON

Oppie Doctor Harrison?

Richard This is Richard Harrison.

Oppie We met some months ago in Pasadena.

Richard Oh yes?

Oppie At a garden party in Pasadena.

Richard Oh right.

Oppie My name is Robert Oppenheimer.

Pause.

Richard Oh yes.

Oppie I wish to talk to you about Katherine.

Richard Katherine?

Oppie Kitty.

Richard Yes, I know who Katherine is.

Oppie Of course. (*Beat.*) She's pregnant.

Richard I see.

Oppie Yes.

Richard I suppose you'll need me to get divorce proceedings underway.

Oppie I would appreciate that.

Richard Of course. Congratulations.

Oppie Thank you.

16 – LECTURE SERIES: CHAIN REACTION

Oppie There was a Maharaja who had a great passion for chess. Travelers … as they passed through his court … were invited to his throne room and challenged to a game. One day a visiting sage appeared at the palace gates. He was welcomed and brought before the king. 'Do you know chess?' 'I do.' 'Then let us play.' The sage smiled and politely inquired as to what his prize would be if he were to win. The Maharaja laughed and offered any reward that the old man could name. The sage modestly asked for a few grains of rice. 'How many grains?' enquired the king. 'Place one grain of rice on the first square of the chessboard … two on the next … four the next … then eight … sixteen … and keep doubling the number of grains on every following square.' 'Very well.' And so they played. It was a hard fought game, but it did not go the way of the king. Having lost … and being a man of his word … the Maharaja ordered for a bag of rice to be brought to the chessboard. He placed one grain on the first square … two on the second … then four … eight … sixteen … thirty-two … sixty-four … 128 … 256 … 512 … 1,024 … 2,048 … 4,096 … I could do this all day. By the twentieth square the Maharaja required a million grains of rice … by the final sixty-fourth square he required more rice than had ever existed … enough to cover all of India with a layer one metre thick. Such an amount would require paddy fields covering twice the surface of the world – oceans included. The Maharaja was agog. It was at this point that the Lord Krishna shook off the image of the sage, revealing his true identity to the king. 'Now you are humbled before the power of exponential mathematics.' (*Beat.*) A neutron enters an atom ... splits it ... two further neutrons are released ... and what you have is a chain reaction.

17 – NUMBERS

Serber How's Kitty? Taking to motherhood? And Peter is ...?

Oppie Seven months.

Serber I hadn't realized it had been so ... (*Beat.*) Standing? Crawling? Teething?

Oppie Standing. Teething.

Serber We should definitely ... definitely pay a visit ... Charlotte is aching to ... we have some things ... we bought some things for the baby ... clothes ... for Peter ...

Oppie Thank you.

Serber It's good to see you. Illinois' no Berkeley ... but the department's good ... the work is good.

Oppie Fission ...

Serber Yes.

Oppie ... as the basis for a bomb.

Serber Yeah ... I ... since Pearl Harbor, it's all I can think about. That and signing up. But my eyesight's appalling; I wouldn't make it past the physical. Probably wouldn't make minimum height. And now the Russians have joined the war and I'm ... I'm cheering inside ... like a full-blown warmonger.

Oppie How much uranium do you think we'd need?

Serber The minimum amount ...?

Oppie ... for a chain reaction. Yes. How much?

Serber Well ... I don't know ... we've talked ... in my department ... we've talked ...

Oppie Can you give me numbers?

Serber The amounts people are throwing around range from six hundred grams to a ton.

Oppie A ton of uranium-235?

Serber It would have to be.

Oppie It would take time to separate ... to refine ...

Serber There would have to be a large-scale industrial ...

Oppie It would be easier if I thought it was beyond me. I know it is not. I see it so clearly ... in my mind I can picture a uranium device ... I can picture it's components ... sometimes it has stars and stripes stenciled to its casing ... but more often than not it has a swastika. I see it ... it sails down the Hudson River ... or it hangs in the air above the Upper West Side ... I can see it ... and there I am ... a man of inaction ... knowing that I could have built it first ... perhaps quicker ... even by just a day ... (*Beat.*) So when I ask 'can you give me numbers', what I want to know is: can you give me numbers?

Serber I don't have any for you right now, but I'm certain I can get them.

Oppie Do it.

Serber Sure.

Oppie There needs to be gathering ... of minds ... there needs to be discussion. I'm bringing together people from Cornell and Chicago ... from Princeton ... Harvard. I need you with me in Berkeley.

Serber Sure ... sure ...

Oppie We need to be solid on the theory and we need to consider the practical implications on design. What sort of fissionable material ... what sort of blast radius ... how much energy will be released.

Serber   Of course ... of course ... my god ...

Oppie   Bob ...?

Serber   Yes, Oppie?

Oppie   The uranium bomb is entirely possible, therefore it is entirely inevitable. It's not a question of 'should'; it's a question of 'when' ... of 'where' ... of 'by whom'.

18 – THE FIRST FEASIBILITY DISCUSSIONS

Berkeley campus.

The room is filled with a select group of physicists, including **Oppie**, *Edward* **Teller** *and Hans* **Bethe**. **Serber**, **Wilson** *and* **Weinberg** *and preparing to give a presentation.* **Lomanitz** *enters – he is late.*

Lomanitz   Sorry ... I'm sorry ... I got caught up at meeting about the Rad Lab union.

Serber   There is no Rad Lab union.

Lomanitz   Not yet. Geez ... it's like a Nobel longlist in here.

Wilson   Try not to say anything too stupid.

Weinberg   I haven't pressed my shirt.

Lomanitz   What are we talking about? Halifax?

Serber   Halifax.

The lights darken.

Weinberg *operates a projector.*

Black and white images of the devastated city of Halifax, Nova Scotia.

Weinberg   This is Halifax, Nova Scotia.

Wilson On December 6, 1917, a French cargo-ship, fully stocked with wartime explosives, collided with a Norwegian vessel inside Halifax harbour.

Lomanitz The resulting explosion caused the immediate death of two-thousand people. Nine thousand sustained injury.

Serber All structures within the one-and-a-half-mile blast radius were leveled.

Wilson The subsequent pressure wave bent iron railings ... snapped trees ... dispersed debris ... up to as much as 10 miles.

Weinberg The ship's anchor ... or a portion of it ... weighing in excess of 1,100 pounds ... was carried a distance of 2.3 miles.

Serber One of the gun barrels landed in Dartmouth, a town some 3.4 miles to the east.

Lomanitz The force of the blast is estimated to be somewhere in the region of 2.9 kilotons.

Serber That's the equivalent effect of 2,900 tons of TNT.

Oppie Thank you.

The lights are switched back on.

Oppie This is the level of destruction that we are hopping to achieve. We are familiar with the physicists the Nazis have at their disposal. We have studied with them ... corresponded with them ... worked with them ... lived with them. Heisenberg. If we are capable of building this bomb, then so are they. Tenfold. And we are behind. The British government have been making great strides and, in the spirit of our mutual struggle, they have agreed to share with us what progress they have made. It's not much, but it's as good a starting point as any. I'll be making those documents available to you.

Bethe This British report ... what areas does it concern itself with?

Oppie Hello, Hans. For those of you who don't know, this is Hans Bethe, who is joining us from Cornell.

Bethe Hello.

Oppie As for the report, it mostly deals with the cost estimates and technical specifications for a large uranium enrichment plant ... it also contains some ideas on assembly and some work on efficiency. I would also suggest that you speak with Bob Serber who has been diligently working on critical mass calculations. What I propose we do over these next few weeks is pool our ideas. Collaborate. Bring everything you have ... any epiphanies ... any eureka moment ... however outlandish ... I want to see it. We'll reconvene tomorrow.

The gathered scientists break off into groups. Everyone is chatting. Everyone is excited.

Wilson Professor Bethe?

Bethe Yes?

Wilson I have to say it is an honor to meet you ... and to have the chance to possibly work beside you ... geez ... I mean ...

Bethe That is very kind of you to say.

Wilson Your work on the subject of nuclear reactions ... cross-sections and atomic nuclei ... I mean it's ... wow ... just wow.

Bethe It is always nice to meet a fan.

Wilson I have a copy of *Reviews of Modern Physics* ... with your articles ... would you mind signing ...?

Bethe Of course.

Weinberg Actually, we all have copies ... could you ...?

Bethe Of course ... of course ...

Teller Oppie?

Oppie Edward Teller! I am so pleased you could make it.

Teller Hans and I shared a train carriage from Chicago. I hear it is you I have to thank for the change in my status.

Oppie Ah, yes.

Teller They denied my clearance for classified work simply because I am Hungarian. As though all Hungarians must support that faszszopó of an admiral who conspires with Nazis. This study group of yours ... it is a good start. I am pleased that finally something substantial is being done.

19 – LECTURE SERIES: THE MAN WHO BUILT THE PENTAGON

Groves September 17, 1942. I am called to the office of my superior. I know these corridors ... I built these corridors ... Colonel Leslie R Groves of the Army Corps of Engineers ... the man who built the Pentagon. My blood is in this mortar. These hinges are oiled with my sweat. 'You are familiar with the S-1 Committee?' 'I am, sir.' 'What do you know of the S-1 Committee?' 'The S-1 Committee is in charge of investigating the properties and manufacture of uranium, sir.' 'Do you understand the purpose of the S-1 Committee?' 'Not fully, sir. I can't say that I do, sir.' 'It is weapons development.' 'I see, sir. I was hoping for a combat assignment, sir. Overseas, sir.' 'That is not going to happen.' 'I see, sir.' 'The development of this new uranium bomb is to become a military operation.' 'Yes, sir.' 'It is to be instilled with a sense of urgency.' 'Yes, sir.' 'If you do this job right, it will win us the war.' '...' 'Groves?' 'Yes, sir.' 'I said it will win us the war.' 'We have bombs already, sir.' 'The decision has been made. You will be promoted to the rank of general.' 'Thank you, sir. I was hoping for a combat assignment, sir.' 'Well, you have this instead.' 'Sir, yes, sir.' 'Congratulations, General.' 'Sir, thank you, sir.' I am handed some files. I am appointed a personal aide. If I am ordered to build a wall, I buy bricks. If I am ordered to shoot a man, I count my bullets. If I am ordered to throw myself in front of a train, I consult a timetable. Where to begin ... where to begin ...?

20 – TOBACCO AND GIN

The Oppenheimer household.

Oppie *in one corner.* **Kitty** *on the other, smoking.* **Charlotte** *holds baby* **Peter** *in her arms.* **Serber** *has a ukulele. They sing* **Peter** *a* *lullaby – 'Remember Your Name and Address' from Irving Caesar's* Songs of Safety.[4]

Serber & Remember your name and address

Charlotte And telephone number too
And if someday you lose your way
You know just what to do …

Charlotte Say goodnight to everyone, Peter. Say goodnight to Daddy.

Oppie Goodnight, my darling.

Charlotte Say goodnight to Mummy.

Kitty I have a cigarette.

Charlotte I'll put him to bed. Bob …?

Serber Sure.

Serber *and* **Charlotte** *exit.*

Kitty I smell of sick. I smell of sick, off-milk and baby-shit.

Oppie You smell of tobacco and gin.

Kitty It masks the odor of baby-shit. (*Beat.*) He has sharp little fingernails and he claws at me … he's constantly sucking … sucking and biting and scratching and …

Oppie Kitty …

Kitty I'm chapped. I'm cracked. I'm broken and sore. He doesn't sleep.

Oppie He's sleeping right now.

Kitty He doesn't sleep for me. I am falling apart!

---

[4] 'Remember Your Name and Address' – Irving Caesar and Gerald Marks (1937).

Act One   119

Oppie   You have Charlotte. You have Bob. And what am I paying the nanny for? Four days a week she comes.

Kitty   I cannot cope.

Charlotte *enters.*

Charlotte   A teething baby is trying to sleep.

21 – THE GENERAL AND THE PINKO

The offices at Berkeley.

Groves *and* **Nichols** *stand before* **Oppie** *and* **Serber**.

Groves   The eagle on this man's collar ... do you know what it signifies? It signifies that this man has risen to the rank of colonel. Quite the achievement. A colonel in the United States army can command up to two thousand men. (*Removes his jacket.*) My uniform, as you can see, is adorned with these silver stars. (*Hands jacket to* **Nichols**.) See that this is dry-cleaned.

Nichols   Sir. Yes, sir. (*Exits.*)

Groves   Four silver stars, Professor. I am a commander of men. The rank of general puts the fear of a righteous god into the heart of the average serviceman. But I understand that rank alone is not enough to impress you ... not enough to earn your respect. So let me tell you this ... I am an engineer. I have a degree from the University of Washington in Seattle and a second degree from the Massachusetts Institute of Technology. I graduated fourth in my class at West Point. I am an educated man. I may not be your equal, but I am damn close. And I have these stars.

Oppie   Bob, would you fetch the General and I some coffee?

Serber   Sure thing. (*Exits.*)

Oppie   I am also a commander of men.

Groves   Washington has decided to bring all of the governmental committees ... all of the civilian contracted projects ... all of the work on this new form of bomb ... under one banner. A military banner. My banner.

Oppie I see.

Groves Are you a Communist? It is a yes or no question.

Oppie It really isn't. 'Are you a card-carrying member of the Communist Party?' is a yes or no question.

Groves Are you?

Oppie No.

Groves Have you ever been?

Oppie No.

Groves Would you consider yourself a Marxist?

Oppie That is a ridiculous question.

Groves How so?

Oppie I understand gravity. I understand the laws of motion. I understand optics. Do I go around calling myself a Newtonian?

Groves This symposium of yours ... this gathering of minds ... it shows initiative. It is proving ... fruitful?

Oppie I would say so, yes.

Groves It smacks of ambition. I do not disapprove. May I offer you a word of advice, Professor Oppenheimer?

Oppie Please.

Groves You are, it seems to me, a uniquely useful individual. Your ambition is great and your capability is great. That one does not outstrip the other is something of a marvel. So listen to me as I say: your affiliations and your associations with the Communist Party ... with members of the Communist Party ... (*Shakes head.*) If you wish to progress, then there must be distance. Do you wish to progress?

Oppie Yes.

Groves The US military is now the proud owner of 1,200 tons of as yet unrefined uranium ore. I placed that order on my first day. On the second day I purchased a refinement facility in Oak Ridge, Tennessee. That this had not already been done tells me that no one involved in this project is thinking practically. So think practically. If you had resource … if you were 'the guy' … what would be our next move?

22 – THE OPPENHEIMER BROTHERS

Frank *and* **Jackie***'s house.*

Oppie Is he here?

Jackie (*calls off*) Frank? (*Beat.*) He won't be long.

Silence.

Jackie Hello, Jackie. Good to see you, Jackie. How have you been? Well, I trust. You're looking well. How's work, Jackie? Have you done something new to your hair?

Oppie When did you last meet with your street unit?

Jackie Excuse me?

Frank (*enters*) Hello, Robert. It's good to see you.

Oppie When did you last meet with your street unit?

Frank Oh god … I can't remember … when was it? Weeks ago …

Oppie When was the last time you held a meeting here?

Frank Month before last. Why?

Oppie You're not to do it again. You're not to host meetings … you're not to attend. Do you still have your Party card?

Frank I guess.

Oppie Let me see it. Let me see you tear it up.

Frank Now just one second …

Oppue Where is it?

Jackie In the desk.

Oppie Fetch it.

Frank What is all this ...?

Oppie Fetch it.

Jackie No.

Oppie You're to destroy your Party cards ... you're to sever all Party contact ... you're to avoid any and all known Party members ...

Jackie They're our friends.

Oppie ... you're to resign from the teacher's union.

Frank Okay ... no.

Oppie You need to put away your childish idealism.

Frank The Communists are the only answer to fascism ... in Europe ... here ... in Spain ...

Oppie To hell with Spain! To hell with the Spanish Cause! I am sick of it! How many martinis ... how many buckets filled with nickels ... how many ineffective, chattering parties ... how many pamphlets ... how many lectures ... and still the fascists take Spain!

Frank The labor movement ... workers rights ... segregation ... tell me which other party – ?

Oppie This is not the time for those things.

Frank Not the time? Well ... either way ... whatever your thoughts ... whatever your protests ...

Oppie Your career ...

Frank Let us not kid ourselves that this is in any way about *my* career.

Oppie You're a child.

Frank No. I am not. And these are my decisions to make.

Oppie You have a tendency to make very poor decisions.

Frank I'm sorry?

Jackie I think it's time you left.

Frank I'm sorry ... because I married a waitress?

Oppie You have to ... you have to ... distance yourself from ...

Frank What I should've done ... what I should've done was to find myself a nice, wholesome girl ... someone of a comparable status perhaps ... someone of breeding ... and fuck her behind her husband's back until she falls pregnant.

23 – THE COORDINATOR OF RAPID RUPTURE

The Oppenheimer residence.

Oppie, Kitty, Serber, Charlotte, Bethe, Haakon *and* **Teller** *are in little groups talking and drinking.*

Kitty *opens a bottle of champagne.*

Serber We were drinking in this dive-bar ... on the quayside ... by the ferry terminal ...

Charlotte This was before the Bay Bridge had opened.

Serber ... we're drinking tequila ... we're drinking gin ... and this beautiful Mexican waitress brings round a ceramic dish of red peppers ...

Charlotte ... a little ceramic dish ...

Serber ... and so I grab a handful ...

Charlotte ... a couple ...

Serber ... a few. And I knock them back like they were peanuts. Every nerve-ending in my mouth bursts into flame. My eyes are streaming ...

Charlotte   ... his tongue's lolling out like a dog ...

Serber   ... and I grab for this vase ...

Charlotte   ... this carafe ...

Serber   ... this jug ... of water. Only it's not water ... I down it in one and I get to the bottom and it's not water – it's gin. Neat gin.

Charlotte   He fell off his chair and landed on his ass!

Serber   I'm insensible.

Charlotte   I'm laughing ... Oppie's laughing ... the waitress is laughing. Bob vomits in a plant-pot.

Serber   A little dignity?

Charlotte   Not a stitch.

Serber   So I get bundled into Oppie's car ... it's one of those Packard Roadsters with a rumble seat in the back. I put my head in my hands and Charlotte says something like: 'See ... what do I tell you ... alcohol is not the solution.' To which Oppie says ... 'No, for it to be a solution you'd have to add tonic.'

Charlotte   The car ... it had a cute name ... what did he use to call it?

Serber   Garuda.

Charlotte   That's right.

Bethe   Garuda? What is that? Is that ...?

Serber   It's Sanskrit. Garuda is the mount of Lord Vishnu.

Bethe   Which would ... in this story ... make Oppie Vishnu, correct?

Kitty *goes to pour* **Bethe** *some champagne.*

Bethe   Thank you, no.

Kitty   You don't like champagne, Hans?

Bethe I was raised on the French-German border. I like champagne just fine. This – not so much.

Haakon You're a professor?

Teller Indeed.

Haakon As am I.

Teller I've not heard of you.

Haakon Of the Romance Languages.

Teller Ah.

Haakon Do I detect a German accent? I own an 1867 edition of *Das Kapital*.

Teller I am Hungarian. And I have not read Marx.

Haakon Oh?

Teller People might mistake me for a Democrat.

Serber What are we celebrating?

Kitty Can we tell them about it?

Serber Tell us about what?

Kitty They'll know soon enough.

Oppie I'm not supposed to talk about it.

Kitty Robert had a visit from the military.

Teller Is this about the bomb?

Oppie It's all very hush-hush.

Bethe We are all inside the circle here.

Serber Well, with the exception of Haakon perhaps.

Haakon Do you want me to leave?

Oppie No … I …

Haakon I'm not in your department ... I'm not even the spouse of someone in your department ... it's fine. I need a trip to the little linguist's room anyway, so ... (*Exits.*)

Bethe Oppie?

Oppie You must understand, the details are not yet finalized ...

Charlotte Tell us!

Oppie A laboratory is going to be built. A laboratory dedicated to the building of this bomb ... probably somewhere quite remote. It will be a continuation of our discussions and work at Berkeley, but now ... well ... as a legitimate and sanctioned part of the war effort.

Teller A central laboratory?

Kitty A national laboratory.

Oppie And I will be its director.

24 – LECTURE SERIES: EDWARD TELLS A JOKE

Teller A joke. President Roosevelt is being informed that Hungary has entered the war. 'Hungary? What is Hungary?' 'It is a kingdom,' says his aide. 'Then tell me about their king.' 'They have no king, they are ruled by an admiral.' 'Then tell me about their navy.' 'They have no Navy, they lost their coastline after 1918. They have an army.' 'Where is their army?' 'Fighting in Russia.' 'Because they want land from the Russians?' 'No, they want land from the Romanians.' 'Then why do they not fight the Romanians?' 'Because the Romanians are their allies!' (*Beat.*) Perhaps you have to be Hungarian.

25 – THE CHEVALIER AFFAIR

Haakon Oppie, may I have a word? (*Pause.*) I will never suffer nor ever comprehend the suffering felt by those at the heart of this war ... but don't deny my empathy. The Russians ... Stalingrad ... they're fighting with their teeth and their hands ... with pitchforks and kitchen knives. (*Beat.*) It is clear to everyone on campus that the physics department is involved in ... that you are working on ... something very important. I have a proposition for you ... I think that you will want to hear it. I saw a friend of mine recently ... a man ... you are known to him ... he shares our sympathies. He has a means of getting technical information to the Soviets.

Oppie *silence.*

Haakon Do you not believe that the Russians have a right to know? Or, indeed, that they may be able to help? I am no physicist ... I have no useful skills here ... but I can do this. So let me do this.

26 – THE BOY WITH A BEAR ON A LEASH

The Los Alamos Ranch School for Boys.

High in the New Mexico mountains. A haze of light snowfall.

Oppie *and* **Groves** *inspect the grounds.*

Groves It's remote, I'll give you that. What are we at here? Seven thousand feet?

Oppie Seven two.

Groves Why New Mexico?

Oppie Out here there is space to think. Out here the ideas will find you. I have a cabin not far ... forty-miles due east ... across the plateau.

Groves You don't strike me as your typical Old West frontiersman. (*Consulting a map.*) 'The Los Alamos Ranch School for Boys'.

Oppie I read the reports coming out of Chicago ... humanity has its first nuclear reactor. It's little more than a stack of uranium and graphite bricks, but ...

Groves ... it's the first step towards your bomb?

Oppie Yes. It's on its way. They built it beneath a football stadium … in the center of Chicago.

Groves Population density is not going to be an issue here.

Oppie No. The grounds comprise eight-hundred acres … there's the main school building … a dormitory … a pond behind the lodge that the boys use for ice-skating in the winter … canoeing and swimming the rest of the year.

Groves We're not building a summer-camp, Oppenheimer.

Oppie We're building something a little more terrible than a summer-camp.

Groves You need this?

Oppie We do. We need the blank page.

Groves Very well. (*Exits.*)

Oppie *is alone. He raises his face to the sky and catches some snow on his tongue.*

A ball rolls toward **Oppie**. *A* **Little Boy** *of about eleven or twelve steps in the clearing to collect it. He is dressed in a gym slip.*

The **Little Boy** *and* **Oppie** *stare at each other. The* **Little Boy** *runs away.*

27 – IGNITION

Teller We were discussing Hans' work on the cycle of nuclear fusion in stars …

Bethe … stars generate power by fusing elements together …

Teller … in the case of our sun it fuses the lightest element to make the second lightest …

Bethe … hydrogen plus hydrogen equals helium …

Teller … it is with the sun's own gravity … the weight of itself … the incredible pressure at its core that gives rise to fusion …

Bethe ... those particles have no place to go and yet are travelling at astonishing speed ... slamming into each other like blind and angry dodgem cars ...

Teller ... and it occurred to me that ... in the split second of a uranium device's detonation ... an equivalent heat or pressure may exist ... equal to that found at the core of our sun ... and if you were to surround that fission device with enough fuel ... deuterium – heavy hydrogen ... then maybe ... maybe it would cause a fusion reaction.

Bethe We could make a star on the surface of the earth.

Teller Why stop at splitting the atom ... why not forge new ones?

Oppie Not just a nuclear device ... but *thermo*nuclear. The energy released would be ...

Bethe ... colossal.

Teller A super bomb.

Bethe A much higher yield.

Teller Much higher. Thousands of times more powerful ... than a mere fission device ... a mere uranium bomb.

Oppie A hydrogen bomb.

Teller A blast radius of not just one or two miles ... but ... what? Thirty-five? Forty? Fifty?

Bethe A star on the surface of the world.

Oppie A fundamental element of your hydrogen device is a uranium device.

Teller Yes.

Oppie So we build that first.

Bethe With a uranium device ... even with just a uranium device ... the temperatures and the pressures we are talking about ... what if we were to set fire to the earth's atmosphere?

28 – PEEL THAT POTATO

A bar in San Francisco.

Weinberg *is drinking heavily and smoking.*

Wilson *and* **Lomanitz** *enter.*

Lomanitz   Joe?

Waitress   Is he a friend of yours? You should get him home … get some coffee into him.

Weinberg   Shut your yap.

Waitress   He's a charmer, that's for sure.

Weinberg   Screw you.

Lomanitz   What the hell's this about?

Weinberg *hands a crumpled letter to* **Lomanitz**.

Waitress   Hey, I'm not unsympathetic … my brother got the draft just last week.

Weinberg   Fuck your brother.

Waitress   Get him out of here.

Wilson   I'm sorry about this, ma'am. We'll take him home.

Waitress   See that you do.

Lomanitz   You've been drafted?

Weinberg   Off to fight the good fight … to the killing fields of Alaska … got to peel potatoes for justice, liberty and the American way.

Lomanitz   Tell them you're needed here … tell them you're already working on a project for the military.

Weinberg   My guess is that they already know.

Wilson   If they knew they wouldn't be sending you to Alaska.

Weinberg Because I'm so important to the project I can beat the draft? I've been … I've been running my mouth … keeping people informed … keeping them in the loop.

Lomanitz What people?

Weinberg I'm a card-carrying member.

Lomanitz How would they know?

Weinberg Walls have ears, don't they? Phonelines have ears. The project is military now … you think they're not going take an interest in who our friends are … who we talk to … our beliefs? I'm no genius … I'm a perfectly competent but replaceable schmo … so … off I go. To fight the good fight. To peel that potato. I wish I could have been of more use.

29 – 128 POUNDS OF PROUD AMERICAN SOLDIER

An army hospital in San Francisco.

Oppie *is being given a physical exam by* **Doctors**.

He is made to stand on scales, X-rays of his chest are held up to the light. Blood pressure is taken. A stethoscope is placed against his chest.

Groves *stands nearby.*

Groves So, doc … does he pass?

Doctor He's underweight. Eleven pounds short of the minimum required for active duty … twenty-seven pounds under what would be ideal for a man of his age and height. He's had a chronic cough for some years …

Groves 'Some years'?

Oppie Since 1927.

Doctor … and x-rays of his lungs confirm a mild case of tuberculosis. The patient also suffers from lumbosacral strain … lower back spasms … and experiences moderate shooting pains down his left leg every two weeks or so. My considered opinion is that this man is not army material and that the physical defects I have mentioned render him permanently incapacitated for active service.

Groves You understand all that?

Oppie I do.

Groves (*passes* **Oppie** *some forms*) Sign here to acknowledge these pre-existing medical conditions and to request extended active duty.

Oppie (*signs*) Can I ask … what rank will I receive?

Groves You will be commissioned at the rank of Lieutenant Colonel. Stand up, soldier. Welcome to the United States Military.

30 – THE UNITED STATES ARMY UNIFORM

Oppie's *office at Berkeley.*

Alone with a neatly folded pile of clothes – his US Army uniform.

Oppie *gets dressed.*

Kitty *enters.*

Kitty Hello, soldier.

Oppie Ma'am.

Kitty Hello, officer.

They kiss.

Kitty Everything is packed. Peter is staying behind with Charlotte until they move to Los Alamos next week. I like your uniform.

Oppie Thank you.

Kitty Can you order a man to kill?

Serber *enters, also in US Army uniform, that of the rank of sergeant.*

Serber Lieutenant Colonel Oppenheimer, sir ... Sergeant Robert Serber, reporting for duty, sir!

Kitty Look at you, Bob!

Serber Very natty, don't you think? Very authoritative.

Oppie Atten-SHUN! Chin up, chest out, shoulders back, stomach in. Eyes front, soldier!

Serber Hey now, that's pretty good.

Oppie Drop to the floor and give me twenty. That's an order soldier!

Serber Sir! Yes, sir! (*Starts doing press-ups.*)

Kitty Frank called the house.

Oppie When was this?

Kitty This morning. I told him not to call again.

Oppie Was there a click on the line? Did you hear the click?

Kitty I don't know.

Oppie How is he?

Kitty I told him not to call again and I hung up.

Oppie That was the right thing for you to do.

Serber No more ... no more ... I have a body designed for mathematics ... no more ...

Kitty I'll leave you boys to play dress-up. Look at you two ... glasses like milk bottle bottoms ... limbs like bamboo ... all dressed up to go to war. (*Exits.*)

Serber You heard about Joe Weinberg?

Oppie What about Joe Weinberg?

Serber He's been drafted.

Oppie Yes, I had heard that.

Serber Well?

Oppie We're all in the military now.

Serber He should be at Los Alamos with the rest of us.

Oppie What would you have me do?

Serber Gee, I don't know, Oppie … get him reassigned. You have the stripes now – bark some orders.

Oppie And why would I do that?

Bethe *enters.*

Serber You're out of uniform soldier.

Bethe It's not possible … under these conditions … to do as you ask. We will never find the manpower … the grad students … the PhDs. How am I to recruit them to a project I am not authorized to discuss?

Oppie Any scientist worth our time would surely have guessed what it is we are asking of them …

Bethe It is unpalatable to me to coerce men onto this bomb project without the full facts …

Serber We are not to call it the bomb project.

Bethe Excuse me?

Serber It is the Manhattan Engineer District … for reasons of security.

Bethe This world of codewords and obfuscation … it is not my world.

Oppie I'm sorry, but it is.

Bethe I am already within the circle?

Oppie You are.

Bethe These are academics and free-thinkers … they are perhaps not so eager to be press-ganged into the military.

Oppie Then appeal to their patriotism.

Bethe Take to the seas when the men start wearing flags … flags and thick-soled boots. I will build the bomb if I must. But I will do it as me … as Hans Bethe … not as … not as a buzz-cut … as a broken and rebuilt man. I would feel more comfortable if you were to build it as J Robert Oppenheimer … as a professor, not as a colonel.

Oppie Fascism is tearing Europe apart and you want to argue about the symbolism of our shirts and our pants?

Bethe I know of fascism! As a German … as a man with family still in Germany … perhaps my understanding is just that little touch sharper. It must be built here … I cannot fathom the other. But I will not wear a uniform. I suspect I will not be alone.

Serber You are a US citizen, Hans.

Bethe You think I would wear a German one? The Cult of the Soldier is not for us all … not even in wartime.

Oppie I will talk to the General.

Bethe Thank you. And my recruitment drive?

Oppie There is no room for movement on matters of security.

Bethe Fine. (*Beat.*) I am sorry to hear of your Joe Weinberg.

Oppie It is what it is.

Bethe To lose good men when we are trying to recruit …

Oppie Is that all?

Bethe No uniforms?

Oppie No uniforms.

Bethe Thank you. Oh, and … (*Hands* **Oppie** *a folded piece of paper.*)

Oppie What is this?

Bethe The proof that we are in no danger of igniting the atmosphere. A near zero possibility. Perhaps it slipped your mind between salutes. (*Exits.*)

Silence.

Oppie Get out of that uniform – you look ridiculous.

Serber At least I'll have something to wear for Halloween.

Oppie I need you on a train to Santa Fe in the morning. I need you in Los Alamos as soon as possible.

Serber Charlotte and I … the plan was to move next week … we were to look after Peter …

Oppie Then Charlotte stays behind. It's not an inobvious solution.

Serber I can't ask that of her … you can't ask … of us.

Oppie You need to take your share of responsibility for what we are doing.

Serber Yes, Oppie. (*Exits.*)

Lomanitz *enters.*

Lomanitz Everyone is packing for Los Alamos. Apart from me. I am supposed to remain at Berkeley.

Oppie Yes.

Lomanitz Could you explain to me the reasoning behind …?

Oppie Rossi … I have a great many things to …

Lomanitz You want me to join the Rad Lab … under Professor Lawrence?

Oppie Yes.

Lomanitz The man is a Republican nightmare … the merest hint that the boys in the lab might form a union and he –

Oppie Giovanni Rossi Lomanitz – that you would even take the idea of a union to Earnest Lawrence … it boggles the mind.

Lomanitz The radiation laboratory is a workplace ... the boys who work there are workers. The fillings in their teeth have become radioactive. Hold a Geiger counter to their mouths ... the damn thing sings like fat in a pan. You expect me to work in that kind of environment without representation from a union?

Oppie I expect you to acknowledge that there are sacrifices to be made during wartime.

Lomanitz I should not have to throw myself on a fucking spear to prove that I am willing to die for my country.

Oppie You need to be less vocal ... in your politics ... in your dealings with people ...

Lomanitz Are you punishing me? Are you ... for what? Because of the books I have read ... the convictions that I hold? The books you lent me ... the convictions that you instilled. Your lectures ... those first few weeks of lectures ... those discussions ... drinking in the small hours ... science and art ... Niels Bohr and FDR ... social reform ... Engels ... Hindu scripture ... and I find myself in my spare time trying on porkpie hats ... training myself to enjoy pipe tobacco ... reading Marcel Proust. I'm from Oklahoma!

Oppie The Berkeley work will be good work ... essential work ... isotopes ... electromagnetic separation. Professor Lawrence is a good man. You will learn a great deal.

Lomanitz I guess I should be grateful I'm not being shipped off to Alaska!

Oppie Do you think I had a hand in that?

Lomanitz No – I think you were, in fact, a little too hands off. I think you ought to have stood up and said ... 'hey ... he's one of my boys ... he stays with me.' But I guess that leash of theirs is a little shorter than you were expecting, huh?

31 – THE HARVARD CYCLOTRON

The muddy streets of Los Alamos.

The brand new town is awash with **Soldiers**. *Brand new timber-frame buildings are being erected. It is chaos. Men straddle beams ... nailing roof tiles into place ... there is an urgency to the building. Blueprints are held down on jeep bonnets with rocks. Lengths of wood are being sawed in two. The men sing a comedy song as they work.*

Wilson, *the only civilian to be seen, is at somewhat of a loss in amongst all these army men.*

Soldiers When der fuehrer says we is de master race
We heil heil right in der fuehrer's face
Not to love der fuehrer is a great disgrace
So we heil heil right in der fuehrer's face

When Herr Goebbels says we own the world and space
We heil heil right in Herr Goebbels' face
When Herr Goring says they'll never bomb dis place
We heil heil right in Herr Goring's face

Are we not the supermen
Aryan pure supermen
Ja we are the supermen
Super duper supermen

When der fuehrer says we is de master race
We heil heil right in der fuehrer's face
Not to love der fuehrer is a great disgrace
So we heil heil right in der fuehrer's face

Wilson Excuse me ... excuse me ...

Soldier 1 What's up, buddy?

Wilson You don't happen to know which of these buildings is meant to house the cyclotron?

Soldier 1 The what?

Wilson The cyclotron.

Soldier 1 What's that?

Wilson A particle accelerator ... an atom-smasher.

Soldier 1 Geez. What the hell are we building here?

Wilson Please. I'm to inspect the building that's to house the cyclotron ... it's being shipped here from Harvard in a couple of days. Professor Oppenheimer sent me here to ...

Soldier 1 I don't know who that is, buddy.

Wilson Well ... what building are you working on? If you could point it out on a plan ... on a layout ... maybe I could figure ...

Soldier 1 It's a dormitory or a barracks or ... I don't know. Hey! Bill! What this building we're working on?

Soldier 2 Mess hall.

Soldier 1 Mess hall? Then what's with all the bunkbeds?

Soldier 2 Bunkbeds?

Soldier 1 I got Eddie putting together a hundred and fifty bunkbeds.

Soldier 2 I don't know what to tell you, Dan.

Soldier 1 I don't know what to tell you.

Wilson Who does know? Does anyone know?

Soldier 1 *points* **Wilson** *in the direction of* **De Silva**.

Wilson Excuse me ... excuse me ...?

De Silva Captain de Silva.

Wilson Captain de Silva, hello. I'm Robert Wilson ... from the Rad Lab in Berkeley.

De Silva What can I do for you, Mr Wilson?

Wilson I've been sent here to inspect the building that's to house the cyclotron ... but ... I can't seem to work out which one that is. None of these buildings seem anywhere near finished enough.

De Silva Now wait just one goddamn minute ...

Wilson That wasn't a criticism … it's just … well, we're taking delivery of the cyclotron in a couple of days and …

De Silva Look, I don't know anything about that.

Wilson Well, he said … your man there said … that you were …

De Silva I'm not in charge of anything other than my men.

Wilson Well, who is in charge?

De Silva Hang on. I've got it written down here somewhere. (*Takes out a pocket notebook.*) Here you are. Here's the guy.

Wilson Great. I really appreciate …

De Silva You want to talk to a … (*Reads.*) Professor J. Robert Oppenheimer. Glad to be of help.

Wilson But … but … but …

32 – A TOWN OF TIMBER FRAMES

Los Alamos.

Richard **Feynman**, *Luis W.* **Alvarez** *and Klaus* **Fuchs**.

Bethe *enters, his shoes are caked in mud, he carries a clipboard.*

Bethe Zum Teufel noch mal … dieser verdammte Schlamm … (*Beat.*) Welcome, gentlemen, to Los Alamos. The site is encompassed on all sides by a nine-and-a-half-foot fence, which you will find patrolled by military policemen. The roads are not roads … they are strips of mud between the shantytown houses – houses which are not houses … corrugated iron roofs and plywood walls. We live in a town of timber-frames … a thousand people in a town of timber-frames. As part of my theoretical division you will be working in the Technical Area … the 'T'. The 'T' is a white badge zone. These are your white badges. These must be displayed at all times, or you will not be admitted entrance into the 'T'. As part of my division you will also be required to wear a second badge … a badge with your name.

Feynman Is this a security requirement?

Bethe   No, this is a Hans Bethe requirement. What is your name and what university are you joining us from?

Feynman   Dick Feynman … from Princeton.

Bethe (*writes*)   Feynman … Princeton. (*Pins badge to* **Feynman**'s *shirt.*) And you?

Alvarez   Luis Alvarez … from Berkeley.

Bethe   From Berkeley? Are you one of Oppenheimer's boys or Lawrence's?

Alvarez   I studied under Professor Lawrence.

Bethe   Well, you are one of Oppenheimer's boys now. And you?

Fuchs   Klaus Fuchs … I am coming here with the British contingent … from the University of Birmingham, England.

Bethe   Wo kommst du her?

Fuchs   Leipzig.

Bethe   Hat Leipzig im Krieg gelitten?

Fuchs   Bisher noch nicht.

Bethe   Hast du noch Familie dort?

Fuchs   Alle aus meiner Familie sind tot.

Bethe   Wir leben in einer schrecklichen Zeit. (*Beat.*) Now are there any questions before I assign you to your bunks?

Fuchs *raises hand.*

Bethe   Yes?

Fuchs   What are we building here?

33 – LECTURE SERIES: TAMPER MATERIALS

Serber   How to Build an Atom Bomb 101.

Wilson Get yourself two lumps of uranium ... smack 'em together. Boom.

Serber Here endeth the lesson. Any questions?

Wilson 'Then why is it so difficult?' I hear you ask.

Serber Ah, well now you're moving out of the theoretical world ... now you want to be practical.

Wilson Raw uranium ore won't cut it ... it needs to be enriched ... and the infrastructure you'd need to do that would have to be massive.

Serber I mean, there's a handful of countries with the right level of industry and infrastructure.

Wilson And uranium is rare ... and the refined stuff you'd need from it ... the isotope uranium-235 ... makes up maybe 0.72 per cent of the naturally occurring stuff.

Serber There's also plutonium ... but that's a bit too new.

Wilson We just don't know that much about it yet.

Serber Well, shoot ... you want to do this quickly, right?

Wilson You're in kind of a rush?

Serber Then you're going to need several processing plants ...

Wilson ... you're going to need about 10 per cent of the national grid of the US to run these plants ...

Serber ... and still you'll be lucky if you get a couple of hundred pounds of uranium in a year.

Wilson 'Well, how much do you need?'

Serber We don't know ...

Wilson ... and this stuff is far too precious for Trial and Error testing.

Serber Getting it together and keeping it together – that's the trick.

Wilson You bring it together too slowly ... you bring not enough of it together ...

Serber ... and hey, you'll kill everyone in the room ... well done.

Wilson But it won't be a bomb.

Serber A billion dollar suicide and the Reich won't give a damn.

Wilson So we've got to make the most of every last ounce.

Serber Which brings us to ... tamper materials.

Wilson You know on a flashlight how you've got a reflective surface behind the bulb? It's the same deal, only we're putting two flashlights together – face on. No escape.

Serber This diagram represents a mass of uranium that is currently undergoing fission ... but it's wasteful. We are losing quite a lot of neutrons through the surface of the mass.

Wilson But surround it with a tamper material ... a material that will reflect those neutrons back into the uranium ...

Serber ... a jacket of something reflective and non-reactive ... tungsten, say ...

Wilson ... and those neutrons attempting to escape can't get out.

Serber They're corralled. They're a pack of wolves in a broom cupboard and they'll tear themselves apart.

34 – THE COMPLAINTS OF CAPTAIN DE SILVA

De Silva I have complaints.

Oppie Captain, I'm sorry, but we're in the middle of ...

De Silva I will not have it. I will not. This is a military base and ...

Oppie Captain de Silva ... whatever your complaints, I am certain General Groves ...

De Silva This is not a matter for the General. This concerns the behaviour of your men.

Oppie I'm sorry, Bob.

Serber No problem.

Oppie What seems to be your concern?

De Silva Part of my role as Chief Resident Security Officer is to serve as liaison between you scientists and the army ... and my office ... my office is not some ... rumpus-room. I had a man ... a white badge scientist ... come into my office to talk to me and ... and he sat on my desk!

Oppie He ...?

De Silva On the edge of my desk! Like some damn paperweight! (*Beat.*) I did not appreciate it, sir, I can tell you. No, sir – not one bit.

Oppie In this laboratory, Captain, anybody can sit on anybody's desk.

De Silva It is symptomatic of a greater indiscipline, sir.

Oppie I see.

De Silva There are other examples.

Oppie Go on.

De Silva Your man Serber there ... he and his wife are entirely saturated with Communist beliefs.

Serber Charlotte may have mentioned that she believes that fascism is the inevitable result of a capitalist society in decay, and that the proletariat ...

De Silva 'Proletariat'! Geez!

Oppie I am aware that Bob was formerly active in Communist activities. He assures me that is no longer the case.

De Silva If I may say, sir, I do believe you to be incredibly naïve. It is my recommendation that he is dismissed immediately, sir.

Oppie Then send me with him!

De Silva If it were up to me, sir, I would.

35 – FANTASIES OF A HYDROGEN BOMB

A military **Policeman** *enters.*

Policeman Excuse me, Professor Oppenheimer …?

Oppie Yes?

Policeman Professor Teller is here to see you.

Oppie Of course.

Policeman Professor Teller isn't wearing his white badge.

Oppie Let him in, for god's sake.

Policeman Yes, sir. (*Exits.*)

Teller There you have it! Right there! Unbelievable. One cannot visit the bathroom without the correct certificate … the appropriate permission slip. (*Raises his voice to the* **Policeman** *outside.*)
I might piss microfilm, eh? Szánalmas idióta! I said 'I might piss microfilm'!

Oppie Hello, Edward.

Teller I am tired. I sleep in a dormitory with ten other men. I shower in a communal shower. When my wife and son join me we will be given a house. It will not be such as yours … but as long as there is space for my piano … (*Beat.*) My mail is being censored. My wife complains in her letters that my correspondence is mostly thick black lines. Any names – redacted. Any mention of the building situation – redacted. Any complaint about my lack of privacy – redacted.

Oppie You think they would allow them to pass unchecked?

Teller Two more weeks and they will come. Until then there is the work. I am not tired when I work. I am not tired when the work is interesting.

Oppie No, Edward.

Teller No?

Oppie No, you cannot work on the super.

Teller But a hydrogen bomb! The processes of the stars themselves! This is what is fascinating to me … not lumps of rock … not lumps of degrading rock …

Oppie There is not the resource to follow up on the super … not at the moment …

Teller The numbers you have me working on … the calculations … any member of Hans' theoretical division …

Oppie But they would not do it as fast or with as few mistakes as you. You will do the work that you are assigned.

Teller No, I will not.

Oppie No?

Teller It is beneath me.

Oppie Beneath you?

Teller It is a nonsense to have someone of my ability scratching out sums that would barely challenge a college freshman.

Oppie Take your offence and your boredom and your ego – I have no use for them.

Teller There is opportunity here. The things we are learning about atomic structure – a decade's worth of peacetime research in a handful of years! We have funding … we have resource … and you would have me hold back?

Oppie Our enemies are upon us! We have within our reach a blunt instrument and we will grab it and we will use it and we will win.

Teller There is no beauty or elegance in these equations.

Oppie Thousands of people – at Los Alamos, Oak Ridge, Berkeley, Chicago and across the entire country – are working toward a single purpose ... and, contrary to what you may believe, that purpose is to end this war ... not to enable fantasies of a hydrogen bomb.

Teller   I have not fantasized this science ... it is reality.

Oppie   It is not! It is not a reality unless I say it is. It cannot exist unless I say it exists. And I say that there is no resource for a hydrogen bomb ... not here ... not now. Oh ... oh ... but excuse me ... I have forgotten myself ... you are the great Edward Teller ... how remiss of me. Of course you may work on your pet project, Edward. The world will simply all have to tolerate a little more war ... a little more slaughter. How shortsighted of me. You may have an hour.

Teller   I'm sorry?

Oppie   I will give you one hour ... every week ... to come and discuss with me your ideas on the super. That is what you want, isn't it?

Teller   An hour is no ...

Oppie   Edward ... it is all that I will give.

Teller   And I am supposed to be grateful?

Oppie   It is an hour or it is nothing.

36 – THE MAYOR OF BOOMTOWN

Kitty *and* **Oppie***'s Los Alamos home.*

Nighttime. A party in the distance.

Kitty *and* **Oppie**. **Kitty** *is visibly pregnant.*

Military **Policeman** *enters from the bedroom.*

Policeman   Peter's tucked up snug as a bug in there, Mrs Oppenheimer.

Kitty   Thank you.

Policeman   Just yell out the window if you need anything, sir.

The military **Policeman** *exits.*

Oppie Our security detail double as babysitters now?

Kitty I may as well make use of them.

Oppie Groves is unhappy that all the women are pregnant ... and that my wife is leading by example.

Kitty You build a new town in the mountains ... kids running in the street ... tricycles ... jumpropes ... you provide free government funded healthcare for the men and their families ... and you're surprised by the birthrate? It's a boomtown, Robert. You've built a boomtown.

Oppie You reek of booze.

Kitty It's the chemists' punch. They mix in the alcohol from the lab. Two hundred per cent proof. I can still feel it in my throat ... feel it in my blood. Do you begrudge me a social life?

Oppie No.

Kitty What else is there for me to do?

Oppie No ... go ahead ... besides, we may need some new friends.

Kitty What does that mean?

Oppie Don't expect a dinner invitation from Edward and Mici Teller.

Kitty I can live without the Tellers. I can live without his godawful records ... his godawful Beethoven.

Oppie He smarts because I made Hans a division leader and not him.

Kitty He smarts because Groves gave you Los Alamos ... but he could not build this bomb. He could not rally the men and guide the work. Can you imagine Edward Teller as the Mayor of Boomtown? He has the arrogance ... and there is an arrogance required to build this weapon of yours ... to even consider the idea. What is rare is when arrogance is partnered with sacrifice.

Oppie And what have I sacrificed?

Kitty Oh Robert ... Robert ... where is your brother?

Oppie There has to be distance.

Kitty Yes.

Oppie There has to be distance. (*Beat.*) Haakon ... before we moved up here ... before work truly began ... Haakon said ... he came to me and said that he had been approached by someone who was in contact with the Soviet consulate in San Francisco. He was asking if I wanted to feed information about the bomb to our Soviet allies.

Kitty What did you tell him?

Oppie I told him nothing. I may have used the word 'treason'.

Kitty You need to tell Groves.

Oppie Yes.

Kitty You see that, don't you?

Oppie I do. But Haakon ...

Kitty ... should never have come to you.

Oppie He's my friend.

Kitty Not if he were to ask that. Cast him off. The bomb will not be built by some spineless, milquetoast man.

Oppie No.

Kitty The man who builds this bomb will be hailed a hero.

Oppie I have never asked for that.

Kitty But you have wanted it. Everyone will know your name. Everyone will want to bask in your light.

Oppie My 'light' … if I were to show it … would strike the world blind.

Kitty You cannot be scared of your own potential.

Oppie I have it within me to murder every last soul on the planet – should I not be scared?

Act Two

1 – THE SERBERS TRY THEIR HAND AT ESPIONAGE

A bar in Santa Fe.

The bar is full of locals, a band is setting up in the corner, beer is being drunk, burgers are being served.

Serber *sits alone at a table. He is reading a newspaper and wearing sunglasses (even though he is indoors).*

Charlotte *enters, she is also wearing sunglasses. She sits down at* **Serber***'s table, but they are pretending not to know each other. They share a little laugh, but quickly stifle it because what they are doing is meant to be serious.*

Charlotte   What have you volunteered us for?

Serber   Well, I thought it couldn't hurt … bolster our reputation among the top brass. Assuage some of their doubt. We are, after all, patriotic Americans. Are you ready to disseminate some disinformation on behalf of the United States government, Mrs Serber?

Charlotte   Oh absolutely, Mr Serber.

Serber   Alright then. You start.

Charlotte (*clears throat, with a raised voice*)   I haven't seen you around here before, mister.

Serber (*with a raised voice*)   No, that's right. I am new to the area.

Charlotte   What brings you to Santa Fe?

Serber   I am on my way to the former Los Alamos Boys School.

Charlotte   Oh, is that the top secret military base?

They look around the room to see if anyone is listening. No one is.

Serber   Yes, that is correct. The top secret military base.

Still no one is listening.

Charlotte Oh, how fascinating. Please, do tell me more.

Serber How do I know if you are trustworthy?

Charlotte You can share all of your highly classified information with me. I won't tell a soul.

Serber Well, okay, as long as you promise not to tell. This information would be extremely valuable to the krauts.

Charlotte Or the Japanese?

Serber Even maybe the Russians.

Charlotte Yes.

Serber Do you promise not to share this highly classified ...

Charlotte ... and valuable ...

Serber ... and valuable information?

Charlotte Oh, I swear. Cross my heart.

Serber Well then, I will tell you. We are building ... electric rockets!

They look around to see if anyone is listening. No one is.

Charlotte Did you say 'electric rockets'?

Serber I did say 'electric rockets'.

Charlotte My, how fascinating.

Serber (*normal speaking voice*) No one's listening.

Charlotte Let's try a more direct approach.

They start approaching the locals individually, all of whom could not be less interested.

Serber I sure am thirsty after a long day working at the Los Alamos ranch school ...

Charlotte Hey there, do you know anything about the top secret military base? Would you like to?

Serber … yes sir, hot and thirsty work at the Los Alamos ranch school …

Charlotte Do you wonder what they could be building up there? Are you curious? Well let me tell you …

Serber … hot thirsty work building *electric rockets.*

Charlotte They're building *electric rockets.*

Serber We're building electric rockets! Electric rockets!

The locals 'shush' them and the band begins to play Lil Hardin Armstrong and her Swing Orchestra's 'My Secret Flame'.[5]

Band … one day and it ain't far away
I'll call a spade a spade
And let you know I love you so
You are my secret flame

2 – A VISIT TO JEAN

Jean*'s apartment in San Francisco.*

Jean Don't stand in the doorway … don't stand in the hall … come in … come in. There is wine … I know there is wine … there is gin and there is scotch. There is vodka! We shall have music and there will be dancing … though the needle has broken … it doesn't matter … we can sing! Sing me a little song and dance with me a little dance … if I stop moving I'll die … so spin … spin me around the floor.

Oppie You have tired me out.

Jean (*sings*) One day and it ain't far away
I'll call a spade a spade
And let you know I love you so …

Oppie *holds her still.*

---

[5] 'My Secret Flame' – Armstrong, Avon (1938).

Silence.

Jean You smell of pipe tobacco.

Oppie We should open some windows.

Jean No ... no ... fresh air brings with it fresh problems.

Oppie It's stale ... breathed in, breathed out, a thousand times.

Jean You smell of pipe tobacco. You smell like my father. She has you dressing better.

Oppie You think so?

Jean Oh yes. Very smart.

Oppie She is ... she's ...

Jean You can talk about her. I don't mind.

Oppie I don't have to. So I won't.

Jean Do you only do things when you have to?

Oppie Mostly.

Jean And you don't *have* to reply to my letters?

Oppie Jean ...

Jean Was that unsubtle? Was that a brickbat?

Oppie They open them. They read them. They copy them out and file them.

Jean I don't care.

Oppie There are all these sounds on my telephone ... clicks where I've never known there to be clicks before. That car across the street ... across the street from your apartment ... that black sedan ... do you see it?

Jean I see it.

Oppie FBI.

Jean How can you tell?

Oppie That car follows me. This … this will be getting them excited … a married man visiting his former lover … his former lover who has been so very vocally communist. The pencils in their notebooks … you can hear them if you listen. So I wave at them … smile at them … make it clear that I know that they are there. It tells them that you are nothing to hide.

Jean I can't picture you. I could picture you on the Berkeley campus … with your students … with your blackboards … but now … (*Beat.*) I send my letters to a post office box … it's a number … it's not a location … it's not where you are.

Oppie No.

Jean Where are you?

Oppie You can't ask that. I can't answer.

Jean I need to know.

Oppie Stop.

Jean Please …

Oppie If you ask again I shall get suspicious and I shall leave.

Jean No … no … I'm sorry … I'm sorry …

Oppie Have you gone back to therapy? Look at me.

Jean I am a doctor now … do you know that? I have a job at a hospital.

Oppie But not today?

Jean Patients don't like their doctors to be sick.

Oppie When was the last time you went into work?

Jean 'The work of the proletarians has lost all individual character, and, consequently, all charm for the workman. He becomes an appendage of the machine, and it is only the most simple, most monotonous, and most easily acquired knack, that is required of him.'[6]

Oppie *touches her face.*

Jean What do you see?

Oppie A fire I can't put out.

Jean Kiss me if you want to.

Oppie Is that what you want?

Jean I want it to make me happy.

Oppie We know it won't.

Jean The world is ugly. It is full of ugly things. And ugly people. Doing ugly jobs. Under ugly light. For ugly money. To buy ugly food. To feed their ugly children. So that their ugly children can kill someone else's ugly child in an ugly way. I find myself embarrassed … for my youth. Is there anything more pathetic … more arrogant … more self-centered … than 'I want to change the world'? (*Beat.*) Are you going to stay? If it's the last time – stay.

3 – IN GENERAL GROVES' OFFICE

Groves This Tatlock woman … she is …?

Nichols … a known Party member.

Groves Very well.

Nichols A wiretap will be placed on her phone.

De Silva Despite his reassurances, sir, Oppenheimer has failed to fully distance himself from his many dubious associations. Sir.

Nichols The question must arise … is this one man's contribution worth risking the security of the entire project, sir?

---

[6] *The Communist Manifesto* – Karl Marx, Fredrich Engels (1848).

Groves His clearance will not be revoked. His inclination is to protect his own future and reputation. Trust in his vanity. He has asked to come talk with me. I would like you to be present.

Nichols Of course.

Groves He says he has been approached.

Nichols Approached?

De Silva Permission to speak freely, sir. This project is awash with pinkos and fellow travellers. You have given these scientists too much. The informality of the Technical Area ... the discussion and debate between divisions ... the men wear slacks and jeans and open collared shirts ...

Groves The work required of these men comes not from any structure or discipline that I recognise. I personally would prefer to pin each man jack of them down, cut their hair, scrub the chalkdust from their pores and polish the living hell out of their damn sueded leather shoes. However ... their country has called on them to perform an incredible feat ... it is completely right that they are allowed to tackle that feat in the way that they see as best fit.

De Silva With the greatest respect, sir, this is not how wars are won ... and if ... if this war can be won ... by these men with their woolly and undisciplined ways ... and this violent, horrific bomb I hear them talk of ... damn it, sir ... I don't see how you could call that a true win, sir.

Groves You would rather we lost?

De Silva We would at least lose as soldiers, sir ... with a gun in our hand and a flag on our arm ... not ... not as some ... I don't know ... as something *else* ... with marks on a blackboard and olives in our martinis ... sir.

Groves There was a time ... in Medieval Europe ... just after their invention ... that crossbows were banned during warfare. The church deemed them a 'deadly art, hated by God'. These were dishonourable weapons ... not worthy of a true soldier. You think

Richard the Lionheart gave a hot damn? Or do you think he fired a million metal bolts into a million Saracen hearts?

De Silva Sir. Yes, sir.

Groves Do not mistake me, I would much prefer to have my blade hilt deep in the belly of some slit-eyed sonofabitch on the atolls and islands of the South Pacific.

De Silva Yes, sir.

Groves Yes, sir. But my job is with these men ... these men of intellect ... and my concern is with the transference of valuable information from within these laboratories.

A military **Policeman** *enters.*

Groves Yes?

Policeman Sir, Professor Oppenheimer is here to see you, sir.

Groves Send him in.

Policeman Sir. Yes, sir.

The military **Policeman** *exits,* **Oppenheimer** *enters. He is wearing his trademark porkpie hat.*

Groves Professor.

Oppie General. Captain.

Groves This is Colonel Kenneth Nichols – Chief of Counter-Intelligence on the West Coast.

Nichols We have, in fact, met once before.

Oppie Forgive me if I don't recall.

Groves That will be all, Captain.

De Silva Sir. Yes, sir. (*Exits.*)

Groves You said you had a matter of great urgency to discuss.

Oppie Well ... a couple of things ... minor things ... I was hoping that you and I could ...

Groves   Pay no mind to the colonel. Everything that you may say to me, I will end up telling him anyway.

Oppie   Chief of Counter-Intelligence?

Nichols   You have your work and I have mine.

Oppie   I have heard that Rossi Lomanitz has been promoted to group leader of the Berkeley Rad Lab. I thought the promotion was apt and justified.

Groves   Have you spoken to him?

Oppie   Yes. He said that three days after his promotion he received a letter from the draft board. I cabled the Pentagon to say that they were making a mistake. I'm waiting for a reply.

Groves   I can tell you the reply.

Oppie   Please.

Groves   Lomanitz will be inducted into the army ... and most likely sent to the Pacific.

Oppie   He promised me, if he were to come aboard the bomb project that he would abstain from political work. I am willing to talk with the boy ...

Groves   You want to throw yourself on this grenade? You want to take a bullet for him? How many do you think you can take? I am being pressured to dismiss Bob Serber.

Oppie   Bob was never very active ... he and his wife are dedicated to the project ... dedicated and invaluable ...

Nichols   As is Rossi Lomanitz?

Oppie   Yes.

Groves   You chose to keep him at Berkeley. You chose to put that distance between you. You must have known he was still active.

Nichols   Your brother is a member of the Communist Party. And his wife.

Oppie   They have been. At one time or another.

Nichols No longer?

Oppie You would have to ask them.

Nichols I am asking you.

Oppie I haven't spoken to my brother in months.

Groves That's wise.

Nichols Your wife is a member of the Communist Party.

Oppie No she is not. She was in love. Her party membership expired on the battlefields of Spain.

Nichols Jean Tatlock – listed here as an 'illicit association'. Is that a fair description?

Oppie *silence*.

Groves No one condemns you for being unable to foresee this war. Had you known, you may have been a touch choosier when it came to the friends that you made.

Nichols I am not interested in a man's political beliefs. I am interested in security. The general tells me that you have been approached. Approached by … what is the correct term … what is the apposite term? Emissaries. Of the Soviet consulate. Is this correct?

Oppie Yes.

Nichols And you can see how this is of serious concern?

Oppie Yes.

Groves Take off your hat.

Oppie Excuse me?

Groves Your hat. Take it off. I find it incredible that the head of a top-secret military operation should remain so goddamn identifiable.

Oppie A man needs a hat.

Nichols You say you were approached.

Oppie Yes.

Nichol Go on.

Oppie By an individual ... someone who was known to me. A friend of his was in a position to transmit ... to our Russian allies ... any information that I deemed appropriate.

Nichols Here is a list of names. Are any of the men who have approached you listed?

Oppie (*reads*) Yes.

Nichols Could your circle ... could you underline ...?

Oppie Here.

Nichols George Eltenton?

Oppie Yes.

Groves I don't know that name.

Nichols We are aware of him. This is the man that approached you?

Oppie No. This is the man that approached the man that approached me.

Nichols I see. This ... intermediary ... his name is not on the list?

Oppie No.

Nichols Would you please write down his name?

Oppie No.

Groves No?

Oppie It is unnecessary.

Nichols I see.

Oppie He is not a traitor ... he ... like many ... believe that the Russians, who are fighting and dying on our behalf ... with teeth and hands ... pitchforks and kitchen knives ... he believes that they should be informed.

Nichols That is not a decision for a civilian to make.

Oppie I agree. With you. I agree with you.

Nichols You are handing me a broken chain.

Oppie Nevertheless ... you will have to trust me.

Nichols I do not trust you.

Oppie I will not give you the name of a man I believe to be innocent.

Groves Oppenheimer ... Robert ...

Oppie I cannot give it.

Groves Listen to me as I say this. Whether you are wearing the uniform or not, you are a Lieutenant Colonel in the United States army and I am your superior officer. If I were to give an order and if you were to disobey ... (*Beat.*) Let me speak of the concept of court-martial. Let me speak of imprisonment ... of a stripping of rank and responsibility. Let me speak of disgrace. Let me speak to the part of you that will see this job done.

Oppie What does your file say about Haakon Chevalier?

4 – MARKS ONE TWO THREE

Bethe Talk to me of the Mark One design.

Alvarez The uranium gun ...

Feynman ... the Little Boy ...

Fuchs ... a long, cylindrical bomb casing ...

Feynman ... a gun barrel with a bullet of uranium 235 ...

Alvarez ... to be fired using conventional explosive ...

Fuchs ... down and along the barrel ...

Feynman … to hit a target of … again … uranium 235.

Alvarez Apart these two sub-critical pieces are relatively stable …

Fuchs … slam them together and they become super-critical …

Feynman … and we achieve a nuclear detonation.

Bethe Good. This is the simpler design. This is the most achievable. Now talk to me of the Mark Two. Talk to me of the plutonium gun.

Alvarez The Thin Man.

Feynman Similar in principle to the Mark One but …

Fuchs … but …

Alvarez … the first sample of reactor-grade plutonium …

Feynman … received from Oak Ridge this week …

Fuch … it has a higher … much higher … spontaneous fission rate …

Alvarez … higher than we expected …

Feynman … it would require a higher assembly velocity …

Fuchs … and therefore a longer, larger gun barrel …

Feynman … it would require a longer run-up than the U235.

Bethe How much longer? Physically … practically … how much larger would a Thin Man device have to be?

Alvarez A length of around eighteen feet.

Bethe Compared to the Little Boy?

Fuchs Just under ten feet.

Bethe So the Mark Two raises questions of manoeuvrability …

Alvarez … deployability …

Bethe Will it even fit within the hold of a plane? Someone in Ordnance should have the specifications for the bomb-bay doors.

Feynman There is also the chance of premature detonation …

Alvarez … the background fission rate of plutonium is so high it would likely blow itself apart before reaching a critical mass …

Feynman … rendering it no more effective than a stick of dynamite.

Bethe There simply aren't enough stockpiles of uranium for a great number of Mark One devices … not when taking into account criticality tests and prototypes. Plutonium is much more available to us. Which brings us to the Mark Three.

Fuchs The Fat Man.

Alvarez A plutonium implosion …

Fuchs … a more complicated design …

Feynman … questions of timing … questions of engineering …

Alvarez … we are testing jackets of explosives …

Feynman … a core of plutonium …

Fuchs … a sub-critical mass …

Alvarez … a silver ball …

Feynman … the atoms are not close enough in proximity to each other to trigger fission …

Alvarez … but surround this ball with explosives and the pressure …

Fuchs … the pressure will be …

Feynman … will raise the density within the core turning it from a subcritical mass to a supercritical one …

Fuchs … kicking off a chain-reaction …

Alvarez … a neutron handshake …

Fuchs … disintegration …

Feynman … boom!

5 – A TRAM IN MUNICH

The room outside of **Oppie**'s *Los Alamos office.*

Wilson, *with a stack of papers, waits patiently. As he waits he sings a few lines of the Inkspots' 'I Don't Want to Set the World on Fire'.*

Kitty, *heavily pregnant, enters.*

Wilson   Mrs Oppenheimer.

Kitty   Is he in?

Wilson   He's with Professor Teller at the moment.

Kitty   Fine.

Wilson   Do you want to … want to sit down …?

Kitty   I'm not an invalid. She's just kicking like a bitch today.

Wilson   Can I feel?

Kitty   No. (*Takes out a cigarette.*) Give me a light.

Wilson *does so.*

Kitty   When you see him, tell him I'll be drunk.

Bethe (*enters*)   Kitty.

Kitty   Drop dead. (*Exits.*)

Wilson   He's with Professor Teller.

Bethe   Ah.

Wilson   Any news from Strasbourg?

Bethe   Liberated, thank goodness … though still French … that would not please my father.

Wilson   I guess the war will be over soon.

Bethe   At least in Europe.

Wilson   It seems bizarre that these past years' work might come to nothing.

Bethe Why would it come to nothing? (*Beat.*) Did you know he has a false foot?

Wilson Who?

Bethe Edward Teller.

Wilson A prosthesis?

Bethe He fell under a tram when he was seventeen ... in Munich. You can tell ... when he walks ... he favours the right. What've you got there?

Wilson The latest results on the mean inter-particle distance of the tamper materials.

Bethe Are they correct?

Wilson Yes.

Bethe Are they on time?

Wilson Yes.

Bethe Good. After this war all of us will be elevated. You are the youngest of the group leaders ... the cyclotron division ... the world will see what we do with greater respect. You must capitalize ...

Wilson If it works.

Bethe If it works.

Teller *enters from the office.*

Teller Faszkalap ... szar az elet! I cannot simply stop halfway ... I cannot simply say 'well this will do' ... no ... I must know the full extent ... the ramifications ... the ... the ... progression of a thought. A fission bomb is a half finished idea. He talks of war ... he talks of weapons ... but what of discovery? Picsába ... the man is a contractor, delivering to a deadline. There is no science in this.

Oppie (*at his office door*) I am sorry you feel that way.

Teller No you are not.

Oppie No. I am not.

Teller *exits.*

Bethe You goad him as much as you indulge him.

Oppie What are you here for?

Bethe Now that we have our hands on some plutonium, it is clear that the fission rate is too high for a gun-type device. It is a dead end.

Oppie Fine. Transfer all personnel currently engaged on the plutonium gun to the development of the implosion device. I want to start criticality testing within a week.

Bethe Yes, Herr Professor.

Serber *enters.*

Oppie What is it, Bob?

Serber Oppie … Jean …

6 – A PARALYZED SOUL

Jean A car is parked on Montgomery Street …
A black fastback sedan. Clicks and whirrs
On the telephone line. She leaves the house
When she has to. She calls friends who cannot
Come by. She has become a subject of
Wave function collapse. A woman of twenty-nine
Sits down to dinner … to dine
On codeine and pentobarbital. Barbiturates and
Sleeping pills. She runs herself a bath.
She has fought all her life with her tendencies
Which psychiatrists defined as diseased.
A struggled-with homosexuality
That could not be tamped down with the
Breath and sweat of men. A drowned girl …
A chemical sleep … bathwater in her lungs and stomach.

A gull suspended between seabed and surface.
The tapped phone goes unanswered ... knocks
Land on a hollow door. A father climbs through
A window and collapses to the bathroom floor.
A still moment between father and dead daughter.
Wet hair pushed behind an ear.
An ambulance is called. A flurry of rubbernecks ...
Of policemen and coroners and such ... of parents ...
Neighbors ... who block their children's sight.
A stretcher ... a gurney ... a sheet to cover the face ...
To cover the damp hair and open eyes. The
Black fastback sedan pulls from the curb
And rides in the ambulance-wake.

7 – THE WORK OF DASHIELL HAMMETT

The Oppenheimer house on Bathtub Row.

Serber ... at first the assumption is that the victim was a large man ... a fat man ... but it is soon revealed to be the skeleton of this missing eccentric ... who wasn't fat at all ... he was in fact incredibly thin. The murderers had dressed the corpse in this extra large suit to throw the police off the scent ... to give the impression that it was the body of a much bigger man ... and that this thin man had absconded with the stolen cash. It was Dashiell Hammett's last complete novel ... but the run of movies have all gone under the name 'The Thin Man' ... so everyone thinks that the detective is an eponymous hero, whereas, in fact ...

Charlotte Bobby ...

Serber ... the title refers to Wynant, the dead guy ...

Kitty For god's sake ...

Serber ... the fat man is a ... is a ...

Charlotte Please ... stop.

Serber I was just ... I was ...

Charlotte I know.

Serber It's a great book and I ...

Silence.

Charlotte I've not known a suicide before. It's so ...

Serber Hey.

Charlotte ... it's so ...

Kitty ... incredibly self-centered?

Charlotte Well, I wouldn't say ...

Oppie Of course it fucking is.

Serber Someone should contact Frank and Jackie. They were quite close, weren't they? Jackie and Jean?

Oppie I suppose they shared the same infantile politics.

Charlotte All of us did.

Oppie We know better now.

Charlotte I don't.

Serber I'll call Frank ... I'll ... (*To* **Oppie**.) ... or did you want to do that? Where are they these days? Oak Ridge? (*Beat.*) God damn it ... twenty-nine.

Charlotte I'm tired. Let's go.

Serber Should we raise a glass, or ... say a few words ...?

Kitty (*dismissive*) Please ...

Charlotte Let's go.

Serber Yeah ... okay, yeah ... you know where to find me if you need ...

Kitty We'll be fine.

Serber Goodnight then.

Serber *and* **Charlotte** *exit.*

Oppie I'm going to get some air.

Kitty No.

Oppie No?

Kitty You don't get to be alone. Not with this.

Oppie I am falling apart.

Kitty Let her sink … like lead into the sea … let her sink.

Oppie I have given Groves Haakon's name.

Kitty Good.

Oppie He was my friend.

Kitty So? What you're doing here … what you're trying to do … is greater than a mere friendship. These are the last ties to be cut … Haakon … Jean … you are honest now.

Oppie I am broken and rebuilt?

Kitty Yes. (*Pain.*)

Oppie Does she kick?

Kitty I don't claim to understand the detail of what you do … but I pick up some. Heavy elements are unstable … they carry too much at their core … and what radiation is … what radiation is … it's a form of expulsion … am I right?

Oppie Yes.

Kitty All heavy elements are throwing out particles … shedding excess weight … in order to become more stable. What's the bottom of the bell curve? What's the stablest form they can be?

Oppie Iron.

Kitty So be iron.

Oppie I cannot just be … I cannot … she was … she …

Kitty Maybe I'm not capable of helping you with this … but I'm not so proud that I won't let you seek help elsewhere. (*Beat.*) Do you think I don't know … that I don't understand … that I am not abundantly aware that I am not your only woman?

8 – THE STORY OF A FRIENDSHIP

An interview room in San Francisco.

Haakon *sat at a table.*

Haakon   Can I get a glass of water? (*Beat.*) I have told you all I know. (*Beat.*) I said to him … I said to him … I knew of a way … I knew of a man … who could get technical information to the soviets … he said … in no uncertain terms … 'no'. (*Beat.*) Can I have a cigarette? (*Beat.*) I approached no one else … just Oppie … just Oppenheimer. (*Beat.*) I have been here for seven hours. I have told you all I know. (*Beat.*) Can I get a glass of water?

9 – THE ICEHOUSE

The Tolman household, Los Alamos.

Ruth *Tolman sits in a chair.* **Oppie**, *agitated, paces the floor.*

Oppie   How am I supposed to … start? How am I supposed to …?

Ruth   However you like.

Oppie   Shall I lie down or …?

Ruth   However you feel most comfortable.

Oppie   I'll stand.

Ruth   Take all the time you need.

Oppie   Are you going to make notes?

Ruth   I don't have to make notes.

Oppie   I would prefer not.

Ruth   That's fine. (*Beat.*) We have confidentiality here.

Oppie   I understand that.

Ruth   Whatever is concerning you …

Oppie Of course. (*Beat.*) We are two ... maybe three months from a working prototype.

Ruth The war may well be over by then.

Oppie Let's hope not. (*Beat.*) I mean to say ...

Ruth I understand. (*Beat.*) How is Kitty? She must be due any day.

Oppie Yes.

Ruth Why does no one call you Julius?

Oppie That is not my name.

Ruth No?

Oppie That is my father's name.

Ruth Your name is –

Oppie J. Robert Oppenheimer ... with the J standing for nothing.

Ruth It stands for Julius.

Oppie It is not ... the custom ... to name a child for a living relative.

Ruth Whose custom?

Oppie Jewish custom.

Ruth And your father never cared for Jewish tradition ... Jewish ways?

Oppie I have read Freud.

Ruth And what does Freud say?

Oppie Roosevelt is dead. Have you heard? Slumped in his chair ... an aneurysm whilst sitting for a portrait in oils.

Ruth And how does that make you feel?

Oppie As though it has revealed something.

Ruth What has it revealed?

Oppie That I have an incredible capacity for loss. Groves can see it … it's why he picked me … it is what makes me perfect to lead this project … my resolve. I have a core of cold iron … like a planet that has stopped spinning. I have known that since I was fourteen. (*Beat.*) I wrote to him. I was at summer-camp. I wrote to my father. I wrote telling him that I was having a grand old time … that I was learning all kinds of things from the other boys … that they were telling me fascinating things … about women … about the facts of life. I told him I was becoming a man. On receiving my letter he jumped in his car … he drove all night from New York. Strong words were exchanged with the camp leader … who, in turn, came down hard on us. Smutty talk was now banned. Lewd stories and dirty jokes were verboten. And that is when they beat me.

Ruth Who beat you?

Oppie The other boys. They ambushed me … a group of them … dragged me to the icehouse … stripped me naked and trussed me up like a brace of hares. They painted my ass and genitals green. They laughed … said I wasn't a man … said I was 'a poetry reading cutie'. They left me there with my shame. It was hours before I was found.

Ruth And how does that grant you resolve?

Oppie Because I didn't go home. I could've left … I could've crumpled … but no … I stayed … for the rest of the summer … for three weeks … three weeks of laughter and bitching and hate. Yet every day I stared them down. I stared them down from my iron core.

Ruth *crosses to* **Oppie** *and kisses him tenderly.*

Oppie Jean was a psychiatrist.

Ruth I know.

Oppie Thank you … for allowing me to be weak. I may not get the chance again. (*Unfolds a piece of paper and holds it in front of her.*)

Ruth What am I looking at?

Oppie This piece of paper is the sum total of the Nazi atomic bomb project. A simple sketch ... a design ... drawn by the hand of Werner Heisenberg.

Ruth My husband has talked of him.

Oppie Of course.

Ruth He is your counterpart in Germany?

Oppie To call him my counterpart flatters me. His mind is a blade. And yet ... this scrap of paper was smuggled out of Copenhagen in the pocket of his mentor ... Niels Bohr. It is correct ... the science of it is correct ... but ... this is ... well ... it's a workable nuclear reactor. It's not a bomb. Even if they could somehow get it airborne ... (*Shakes head.*) We always believed that they were ahead. (*Pause.*) There's a concept in quantum mechanics ... developed by Bohr ... he calls it 'complementarity'.

> 'It was six men of Indostan
> To learning much inclined.
> Who went to see the Elephant
> (*Though all of them were blind.*)'.[7]

One man thinks he has in his hand a rope ... another that he has his arms around a tree ... a third thinks he is wrestling with a snake. You see we are all blind ... and we are all grasping at elephants. The Nazis had two years on us *and* they had Heisenberg. But this ... this is only the tail. We have the tusks.

10 – A FUTURE GROUND ZERO

The New Mexico desert.

De Silva I'd say we were at the center here of ... what ... an area eighteen by twenty-four miles of nothing. I'd show you on the map, but what's the point? Enough space for you?

---

[7] 'The Blind Men and the Elephant' by John Godfrey Saxe (1872).

Oppie   I should think so. Any residents?

De Silva   A few ranchers ... no one that can't be reimbursed. Hold back there, Professor. (*Pulls his gun, takes aim and shoots a rattlesnake that was winding its way toward them.*)

Oppie   I think we've found our test site.

De Silva   We'll set up camp. (*Exits.*)

Oppie *stands looking at the dead snake.*

He takes a stick and draws a circle around the rattler.

11 – THE IMPACT OF THE GADGET ON CIVILISATION

A meeting room in the Technical Area.

A gathering of civilian workers. They are helping themselves to coffee and cookies.

Wilson *takes the floor.*

Wilson   Hello, everyone. Thank you all for coming. I know how precious our free time is these days so I really do appreciate it. Help yourselves to coffee ... and please save any questions you may have until the end. (*Beat.*) Over the last few weeks it has become apparent that this gadget is going to have a profound impact on humanity at large. This raises serious questions, which I hope to explore with you tonight ...

Oppie *enters.*

Wilson   Um ... I ...

Oppie   Please continue.

Wilson   Right ... I ... er ... with Hitler dead and fascism most likely defeated in Europe ... it is safe to say that the gadget will not be used there. So why haven't we gone home? Why are we working ... harder and faster it seems ...

Oppie   We are still at war.

Wilson Please ... um ... could you hold your questions until the end? If our country deploys this bomb ... and we're talking cities ... we're talking actual human beings obliterated ... could that be justified? And then, of course, politically –

Oppie Okay ... that's fine ... I've heard enough ...

Wilson There has been talk of handing over complete control of nuclear technology to this new international body ... this United Nations ... that no one sovereign state should have access to –

Oppie Wilson ... okay ... thank you ... stop.

Wilson I have immense respect for you. You have taught me so much and you have been my idol, but –

Oppie Stop! (*To the gathered people.*) If you think the security services aren't aware of your presence here, you are mistaken. Finish your coffee, by all means.

Everyone, except for **Oppie** *and* **Wilson**, *leave.*

Wilson I consider myself a principled man.

Oppie No principle is worth having a file in J. Edgar Hoover's cabinet.

Wilson For what I believe? That doesn't matter to me.

Oppie We all knew what we were building.

Wilson I was hoping we might be proved wrong.

Oppie Men are dying ... on the beaches ... in the sand. Iwo Jima ... Okinawa ...

Wilson There was talk of a demonstration ... for the Nazis ... for the Japanese ... the Russians ... we would invite ambassadors to the desert ... detonate the bomb in an uninhabited location ... to show ... to show them that war was pointless now.

Oppie A static demonstration would achieve nothing. Why should they believe it?

Wilson They would believe their eyes.

Oppie What would they see? A big explosion? They'd assume we'd merely stockpiled a large amount of TNT. I don't think that kind of demonstration was ever seriously considered.

Wilson The Trinity test is planned for the week after next … it's not too late … we could invite the Japanese …

Oppie What if the trigger mechanism jams? What if the plutonium degrades? What if it simply doesn't work? We'd send ambassadors home emboldened by our failure.

Wilson Then we slit their throats! Blow out their brains! Shallow graves in the desert! Who gives a fuck?! (*Beat.*) Oh god … (*Beat.*) I could understand that the Germans had the scientists … the capability for a serious atomic program … but the Japanese? I don't think anybody should have this weapon … not the United Nations … not America … nobody.

Oppie That clearly isn't an option.

Wilson You could not give it to them.

Oppie They already have it … it is theirs.

Wilson Tell them the science doesn't work … tell them the yield is no better than dynamite.

Oppie You're a child.

Wilson We are the heirs to Newton, Faraday and Curie – we looked at their beautiful work and we saw *this*?

Oppie The bomb must be used … and used on people … before this war ends. If the world is not aware that these weapons can and do exist … if it was to be kept as a military secret … then the first strike of whatever war comes next would be an atomic one. It would be Edward Teller's super-bomb. The United Nations is scheduled for its inaugural meeting next month … what use would they be in a postwar world if they were ignorant of this weapon. The gadget will end … not just this war … but all war. (*Beat.*) Can you continue in your work, or will I have to reassign you?

Wilson Oppie, I … (*Beat.*) Yes, Oppie.

12 – PARENTS

The Oppenheimer house on Bathtub Row.

Charlotte *is burping baby Katherine, walking her up and down.*

Oppie *has just returned home.*

Charlotte She won't go down. She's just crying. This is the quietist I've got her all day. Oop … oh … a little sick … can you pass me that …?

Oppie *passes* **Charlotte** *a cloth.*

Charlotte (*to the baby*) Are you happy to see your Daddy? Are you? Your Daddy's been working very hard. Yes he has. Yes he has.

Oppie Where's Kitty?

Charlotte Having a lie down.

Oppie Is she …?

Charlotte She's a new mother.

Oppie Yes, of course. (*Beat.*) Did she offer you a drink?

Charlotte I'm fine, thank you.

Oppie No … I meant … when you arrived?

Charlotte She mixed up some martinis.

Oppie Had she been drinking before you arrived?

Charlotte I couldn't possibly say.

Oppie Why is she in bed?

Charlotte She's tired. I told her to lie down. I'm here pretty much every day at the moment … when I'm not at the library … when I'm not doing the work I'm assigned …

Oppie Uh-huh.

Charlotte ... and when I'm not here ... well, there's usually a military policeman ... or one of the other wives ... sitting ... Kitty is not often ... not often about ...

Oppie I appreciate all you are doing for us. I know Kitty does too.

The baby starts to grizzle and cry.

Charlotte Shh ... shh ...

Oppie You seem to have grown to love the little tyke very much. (*Beat.*) You and Bob have never ...?

Charlotte Shh ... shh ... little one ... shh ...

Oppie Would you like to adopt her?

Charlotte (*silence, and then ...*) Of course not.

Oppie I only mean ...

Charlotte She has two perfectly good parents. Why would I want to ... why would you ask such a thing?

Oppie Because I cannot love her.

Charlotte Oppie ... Robert ... it's a common thing ... a very common thing ... for parents ... who perhaps have not spent time as they normally would ... and you have this project ... and you have this bomb ... so that's understandable ... and ideally the two of you would have time to bond with ... but perhaps that hasn't happened here ... and I ... and I sympathise ... but if you were just to hold your daughter ... if you were just to ... take her ... hold her ... the top of her head ... her little fingers and toes ... over time ... and not that much time, I'm sure ... you would become attached ... as a father ... that fatherly attachment ... I'm certain ...

Oppie No. I'm not an 'attached' type of person.

Charlotte Hold her ... smell her ... new baby smell ... she's beautiful.

Oppie I want this child to have a loving home. You can provide that.

Charlotte As can you. (*Close to tears.*) I have to ... I said to Bob I would be home before ... take her ... take her.

Oppie *takes her.*

Charlotte Put her to sleep ... sing to her ... talk to her ... please. (*Exits.*)

Oppie *alone with the baby.*

Oppie (*sings – haltingly, unconfidently*)   Remember your name and address
And telephone number, too
And if, someday, you lose your way
You know just what to do ...

13 – FAT MAN UP A TOWER

Groves I expect you and all of your men to be in uniform during the test.

Oppie Yes ... I ...

Groves I have been accommodating up until now, but the firing of this weapon is a military act ... I expect military discipline and military rigor in all aspects.

Oppie Understood.

Groves Good. I'm combining the staff from the Oak Ridge plant with that of Los Alamos. I figure the extra hands would be appreciated.

Oppie Yes ... that would be ... yes.

Groves Your brother is at Oak Ridge, is he not?

Oppie Yes ... yes, he is.

Groves Well ... that will be nice for you ... working together.

Oppie Yes ... I ... yes. (*Beat.*) Thank you, sir.

14 – BROTHER TO THE GREAT ROBERT

Jackie I baked banana bread.

Oppie How very thoughtful of you.

Jackie It's a little burnt down one side.

Oppie It's just fine, I'm sure.

Jackie Our rooms don't have kitchen facilities ... I had to use the oven at the mess. Those big ovens cook hot.

Frank It's great. Honestly.

Jackie You have to say that.

Oppie I'm sure it'll find a home.

Jackie I'll need that tin back.

Frank Have you made it up to the ranch at all?

Oppie No.

Frank It must be, what ... thirty miles from here?

Oppie Forty.

Frank We managed two weeks last year ... hoped we might run into you ...

Silence.

Jackie I haven't seen the baby.

Oppie She's asleep.

Jackie I won't wake her.

Jackie *exits.*

Frank I was surprised when I heard. A transfer to New Mexico. I thought ... finally, big brother's pulled some strings ... used his considerable influence ... put me where the action is ... the final push ... as it should be. But no ... it was, in fact the whole unit ... the whole kit and caboodle ... the entire Oak Ridge staff ... order from on high. Frank Oppenheimer – the prize watermelon. Frank Oppenheimer – brother to the great Robert. Like that means a damn. (*Beat.*) For what it's worth, I tore up my Party card in '41. As did Jacks.

Oppie Then why didn't … why didn't you …?

Frank It shouldn't've mattered.

Oppie You're here now.

Frank I see there are no Russians.

Oppie No.

Frank Bit of a slap in the face, don't you think?

Oppie It is how it is.

Frank Secrecy is paramount.

Oppie Yes.

Frank This is a secret that cannot be kept.

Oppie There are protocols … there are guards and fences and barbwire and security clearances … white badges … military policemen and the FBI. Everything is contained.

Frank No.

Oppie Any leak … any breach …

Frank But it is discovery … it's not invention. You're a caveman trying to patent fire. (*Beat.*) When will the Russians learn of this weapon? When it's deployed? 'Hey there, Comrade Stalin … thanks for helping us win the war an' all … thanks for all those millions dead … thanks for Stalingrad and whatnot … we've got this great big earth-shattering weapon by the way … scared yet? Fuck you.' You think any postwar relationship with the Soviets should be based on secrecy and lies? Sets an ugly precedent, don't you think?

Oppie These are political decisions.

Frank Yes! Yes, they are! And you have the ear of policy makers. What are you choosing to say? Anything? Nothing? We always talked about what we'd do if we had the power to change the world. The assumption … from me … was that we would change it for the better.

Oppie Every decision I make … every scratch on a blackboard … is life and death. Every second I deliberate over an idea … every moment of consideration or discussion … is a soldier in the Pacific dead. Every ounce of plutonium I purchase is a P-51 Mustang that will never fly. Every order I place for chalk and for pencils is a frontline request for bullets that will never be filled. If that is what you call power and influence –

Frank You're about to scare the living shit out of the entire world – you *don't* call that power? I call that power. I'm sure as all fuck Kitty calls that power. (*Beat.*) If an air of secrecy … of privileged information pervades … if governments start saying this science needs to be protected … this is ours and no one else's … the habit will develop that science will only be discussed by politicians.

Oppie The average man cannot possibly begin to grasp …

Frank Listen to yourself … the 'average man' … as though there's some gaping chasm between the stupid and the smart. Do you honestly believe that intelligence sets a man so far ahead of the rest? The ability to solve differential equations is a minor variant on the marvel that is the alphabet … language … the written word. Being well versed in Joyce or opera or Sanskrit is as nothing next to the child's ability to recognize their mother. Give me a dancer … give me the world's foremost ballerina … all of their skill … it is insignificant next to the miracle that is standing and walking on two legs. Give a man responsibility and he will grow into it. If there is one thing to learn from war, it is that. If you don't trust the human race to stand beside you … if you set yourself apart … set yourself above … why should they trust you … or your words … your facts? If science is coddled in dark shadows and daggers … the sum of human knowledge will begin to recede … old battles will have to be refought … people will question all that is known to be true … antibiotics … vaccinations … evolution … gravity.

Oppie You're wrong.

Frank I've seen you with kneescrapes. I've seen you with tears in your eyes and snot down your face.

Oppie I am glad that you are here. I am glad that you are beside me. But I am your superior in this. Know that and be humble.

Jackie *enters.*

Jackie Frank …?

Frank Let's go.

Jackie What did you say?

Frank (*to* **Oppie**) I will see you in the desert.

Jackie *and* **Frank** *exit.*

Oppie *alone.*

A knock at the door. A military **Policeman** *enters.*

Policeman Professor?

Oppie Is it time?

Policeman It is, sir.

Oppie I'll be five minutes.

Policeman Yes, sir.

Oppie (*hands the* **Policeman** *the banana bread*) Here.

Policeman Thank you, sir.

Oppie It's a bit burnt down one side.

Policeman That's alright, sir. Much appreciated. (*Exits.*)

Oppie *gets changed into his uniform.*

Kitty (*enters*) Hello, soldier. Hello, officer. (*Beat.*) Will I see it?

Oppie The site is 245 miles from here. And I ... I don't know. Perhaps you will. Perhaps you'll feel it. Perhaps you'll hear. Perhaps you'll see the fire in the sky.

15 – WHISKEY AND THE BURNING SKY

The physicists are gathering before heading to the desert.

Teller What will you do if you get bitten by a rattlesnake?

Serber Well, I'll take a bottle of whiskey.

Teller And if we set fire to the atmosphere?

Serber I guess I better take two.

Teller *and the other physicists exit, leaving* **Serber** *alone with* **Charlotte**.

Serber Don't grind your teeth.

Charlotte I'm not grinding my teeth.

Serber I know you.

Charlotte I'm the only department head who won't be present at the Trinity test.

Serber Don't ...

Charlotte I'm not allowed to get pissed off?

Serber We'll be in dug out holes in the desert. There aren't the facilities.

Charlotte What 'facilities' do you think a woman needs? You think I need to be surrounded by potpourri and doilies in order to take a shit?

Serber It is what it is.

Charlotte I'm a goddamn head of division. It may only be the Library Division ... but do you believe ... with the masses of data, paperwork and classified information ... that this project could succeed without an efficient and organized ...?

Serber Hey ... I know ... I know.

Charlotte It pisses me off.

Serber Yeah. Me too.

16 – THIS IS WHERE I AM FOR THE END OF THE WORLD

Fuchs I lie in the dirt ...

Alvarez ... in the dug-out dust of the desert plain ...

Bethe ... in the bunker ...

Feynman ... my eyes to the distance ...

Alvarez ... my eyes to the tower ...

Bethe ... which Wilson is climbing ...

Wilson ... I am the last to see the bomb ...

Fuchs ... he attaches equipment ...

Feynman ... a measuring and monitoring device ...

Teller ... double check ...

Bethe ... and triple check ...

Feynman ... the radio receives weather reports ...

Alvarez ... stormfronts ...

Fuchs ... electrical ...

Bethe ... if lightning were to strike ...

Teller ... to strike a primed plutonium device ...

Feynman ... hoisted high above the desert ...

Alvarez ... the tallest point for a hundred square miles ...

Wilson ... I'd like to not think of that, thanks all the same ...

Teller ... double check ...

Bethe ... triple check ...

Teller ... quadruple ...

Wilson ... from the tower I can see ... through the gaps in the corrugated housing ... from the tower I see ... lightning as it strikes the dust bowl ...

Alvarez ... the stormfront moves on ...

Wilson ... I place my hand on the device ...

Teller ... do you expect it to be warm ...?

Wilson ... no ...

Bethe ... do you expect it to vibrate ...?

Teller ... or radiate ...?

Wilson ... no ...

Feynman ... is it a sleeping bear ...?

Fuchs ... a lizard's egg ...?

Wilson ... it is metal ... but not the sort that sings ... the sort that sits. I am done here ...

Bethe ... he climbs from the tower ...

Serber ... climbs into his jeep ...

Teller ... and drives ...

Fuchs ... the countdown clock begins ...

Bethe ... automated ...

Serber ... I am in the first bunker ...

Teller ... ten miles from zero ...

Wilson ... I find some dirt to lie in ...

Serber ... my welder's mask is heavy on my arm ...

Frank   ... I lie next to my brother ...

Bethe   ... at t-minus two he is heard to mutter ...

Oppie   ... Lord, these affairs are hard on the heart ...

Fuchs   ... I lie in the dirt ...

Teller   ... I lie in the dirt ...

Serber   ... I lie in the dirt ...

Wilson   ... this is where I am ...

Feynman   ... this is where I'll be ...

Serber   ... for the end of the world ...

An incredibly bright light.

The radiance of a thousand suns.

Silence.

Shockwave.

A gale-force wind.

Debris and dust.

A distant rumble followed by the sound of the very matter of the universe pulling itself apart.

17 – ORANGE JUICE!

Feynman *bursts forward with a set of bongos.*

Feynman   Orange juice!

He bangs out a crazy rhythm on his drums and starts singing a nonsense song about orange juice. The space is suddenly alive with a thousand people all in military uniform ... physicists, civilians and army personnel ... all of them dancing ... all of them singing ... all of them celebrating. It is anarchic. It is surreal.

18 – WE'RE ALL SONS OF BITCHES NOW

Serber   It was 2.30 am when the world began … when the light of the universe … the blast of the universe came. My arm was tired from holding the darkened glass to my eyes. Tired … so that when the beginning … the time of the beginning … when it arrived … my grip had slipped and so my sight filled with the entire spectrum of visible light.

Bethe   Light … through my skin … through my flesh … in the spaces between the grains … light through me like sound in a drum … like air in a dry sponge. Light on the inside of my skull … the brainpan lit. The heat of the midday sun. An Old Testament column … a pillar of smoke and fire … thousands of feet in the air … tens of thousands. A tornado of irradiated and molten earth.

Teller   The short seconds pass and the stars and their black return, but now with a purple glow … as though the northern lights … a crisp winter night … an arctic sky … had found its way south in July … in New Mexico.

Charlotte   On the side of Sawyer Hill … the ski slope … outside the fences of Los Alamos … packs on our back and flasks for our coffee … the women left behind. We wait in the dark … we wait for the sun to rise in the south. The light … my god, the light … and then we hear it.

Wilson   Silence or a new deafness … and dust, dirt and sand … carried to us on a pressure wave … and into our open mouths. Human voices cheering. Handclasps and dancing. I hear someone say … hear someone saying: 'We're all sons of bitches now'.

Frank   I look for the man … the hat and the pipe … he holds my arm as he shakes my hand. He is so nearly me. He has skin and eyes and thoughts and teeth. He is carbon and water … the same component parts. We have lived in the same time … with access to the same education and love. But …

Groves   … this man applied his mind to the world as a scalpel. He gathered us in the surgeon's theatre to observe … as he ripped open the veins of God.

19 – HANGOVER

The Oppenheimer house on Bathtub Row.

Feynman *is gently tapping out the 'Orange Juice' rhythm on his bongos.*

Frank *is scrambling some eggs.*

Bethe *is smoking a cigarette.*

Wilson *has a glass of milk.*

Feynman (*quietly*)   Juice juice juice juice …

Bethe *walks over to* **Feynman** *and takes the bongos from him.*

Feynman *dejected, exits.*

Wilson (*cracks an egg into his glass of milk, takes a swig and brings it straight back up*)   That's disgusting.

Frank   I prefer mine scrambled.

Wilson   How do you feel?

Frank   A little worse for wear.

Wilson   But … yes … besides hangover … do you feel any … any change … any difference?

Frank   Has he been …?

Bethe   Has …?

Frank   Robert. Is he asleep?

Frank   I haven't seen him. (*Beat.*) I was sorry to hear about Jean.

Wilson   Yes.

Frank   I wish I had been here. (*Beat.*) My head …! I haven't drunk like that since … well, not since the Spanish Cause. (*Sits on something uncomfortable.*) What the …? (*He pulls out a prosthetic foot that had been hidden on the chair.*) What the hell is this?

Bethe   I believe that to be Edward Teller's foot.

Frank It's dripping … it's …

Bethe That is because … we were drinking out of it … we were using it for margaritas.

Wilson (*getting up*) I'm sorry … I think I need to … sleep or … something … I need to … I need … I don't … (*Stumbles.*)

Bethe Hey …

Frank Can I get you some water?

Wilson No, I … I … (*Beat.*) This project … this is the one thing … we all have that one thing … and all you can hope for is that your one thing is something to take pride in. This … my life's keystone … is carved from one hundred per cent pure ambivalence. And ambivalence is, by its nature … is not an element. Ambivalence is a chemical compound. My particular variation … my particular compound … the molecular structure of my ambivalence … is one part pride bonded to one part horror. I don't know if I will ever be at ease again.

Bethe *supports* **Wilson** *as they exit.*

Frank *looks at his eggs, he cannot bring himself to eat them.*

Oppie *in the doorway.*

Frank Oh … hey. I didn't know you were up. I didn't know you were out. (*Beat.*) I was just saying to Hans … just saying to Wilson … I was sorry to hear about Jean … about … I should've said something before … it should've been the first thing I said. I wish I could've been …

Oppie *falteringly, awkwardly, he finds himself on the ground and begins to shake, begins to rock.*

Frank (*comforts him, holds him*) Hey … hey …

20 – SAYONARA

Serber *is packing.*

Charlotte *hands him a book.*

Serber What is this?

Charlotte It's a book.

Serber So I see.

Charlotte The only book we had on Japan. Left over from the Boy's School ... not one of the ... not one of the titles we brought with us.

Serber Bushidō.

Charlotte It's a chivalric code. Thought it might come in handy ... holding doors for people ... which chopsticks for mains ... which chopsticks for soup.

Serber I don't think it's etiquette. I don't think it's table manners.

Charlotte It's all we had.

Serber I'll treasure it.

Charlotte It's not to keep. I must show no preferential treatment.

Serber Yes, ma'am.

Charlotte I've stamped it out for a month.

Serber I might be longer.

Charlotte Then you'll pay the fine. You have to bring it back.

Serber I'll bring it back.

Charlotte In one piece.

Serber In one piece.

Charlotte Where will you be ... when the first bomb drops?

Serber I don't know ... some airbase somewhere ... a thousand miles away.

Charlotte You can't wear that ... on the plane.

Serber I won't.

Charlotte You should wear your grey slacks ... the ones with the larger waist. You'll need to be comfortable ... such a long flight. You know how you are with flying.

Serber I'll have to be in uniform.

Charlotte The whole time?

Serber The whole time.

Charlotte On the flight?

Serber On the flight. On the ground.

Charlotte You can't.

Serber No?

Charlotte It'll make you a target ... army uniform ... an enemy combatant ... a legitimate target.

Serber By the time I'm actually in Japan they'll be beaten. They won't fight.

Charlotte Ask to be issued with baggier pants.

Serber I'll write you.

Charlotte You must.

Serber Every day.

Charlotte You must.

Serber I'll bring you a dressing gown. Silk. With embroidered cherry blossom.

Charlotte Don't.

Serber No?

Charlotte I won't wear it.

Serber Don't be silly. Kiss me.

Charlotte It's goodbye.

Serber It's sayonara.

Charlotte Stop it. Their walls are made of paper.

Serber Their cities are modern.

Charlotte There will be nothing to learn.

Serber I'm interested. God help me, but I'm interested. We have to know ... the effects ... how bad ... the pressures ... the temperatures ... to compare with our calculations. How else to know if we were right? Sorry ... if we were *correct*. Correct is different to right. I've got to hold this Little Boy's hand ... I've got to see him off. Kiss me.

Charlotte I love you.

21 – ENOLA

The US airbase on Tinian Island, Pacific Ocean.

US military personnel are playing basketball in the sun. As they play, they sing the patriotic song 'Goodbye Mama (I'm off to Yokohama)'.[8]

All Goodbye, Mama!
I'm off to Yokohama,
For the red, white, and blue,
My country, and you!

Goodbye, Mama!
I'm off to Yokohama,
Just to teach all those Japs,
The yanks are no saps!

A million fightin' sons,
Of Uncle Sam, if you please,
Will soon have all those Japs right down,
On their Japan-knees!
So goodbye, Mama!

---

[8] 'Goodbye Mama (I'm Off To Yokohama)' – J. Fred Coots (1941).

> I'm off to Yokohama,
> For my country, my flag, and you!

The game of volleyball makes way for the arrival of the Fat Man device – a large yellow bomb casing, at a length of 3.3 metres and a diameter of 1.5 metres.

Serber *inspects the device.*

Colonel Paul **Tibbets** *approaches.*

Tibbets Doctor Serber?

Serber That's me.

Tibbets Colonel Paul Tibbets, commander of the 509th Bomb Wing. I'll be flying the bird that lays your egg. Is this …?

Serber No, no. This is Fat Man. You'll be dropping Little Boy.

Tibbets I've got some questions … if you don't mind?

Serber Sure.

Tibbets Normal procedure on dropping a payload would be to continue flying in a straight line, but as I understand it …

Serber … you'll be right over the bomb as it detonates. There won't be a trace of you left. You'll have to turn away from the shockwave. (*Takes some chalk and starts doing his calculations on the bomb casing.*) You'll be at a height of …?

Tibbets 30,000 feet.

Serber And travelling at a speed of …?

Tibbets 200 to 250 mph. 400 mph true.

Serber You'll need to turn about 150 degrees.

Tibbets 150 … I can do that … in a B29 I can do that in 30 seconds.

Serber 30 seconds to turn … 43 seconds for the bomb to drop … the shock will reach the plane at a distance of 10.6 miles … an 18 kiloton explosion … pressure in the shock wave will be about 0.16

psi ... that's 41 seconds after detonation ... 84 seconds from the drop ... you'll be fine ... sir.

Tibbets You're sure?

Serber I'm no expert on planes but she looks pretty sturdy, right?

Tibbets Yes.

Serber No one's going to die. I mean ... of course ... people are going to die ... Japanese people ...

Tibbets And that's their tough luck for being there.

22 – HIROSHIMA

Little Boy Twelve hours of flight ... twelve hours of silence
For the little boy in the fuselage. Twelve hours
At a height of 30,000 feet. A city of 350,000 people.
Forty-three seconds from drop to detonation.
Forty-three seconds and 140 pounds of uranium-235.
Twelve hours and forty-three seconds.
And if I speak of numbers now ...
I speak of numbers because
Numbers can describe what lies outside
Our circles of comprehension. I understand
The difference between ten degrees and twenty ...
I understand a tropical heat of thirty-four Celsius ...
I understand a frost of minus four or five ...
But tell me this city burned at three thousand
And I blink ... the singularity reached
And I know not how to think.
I had an uncle who told me ... an uncle who said
'One death is a tragedy ... one million instead
Is a statistic, my boy ... and your audience reacts
Not with horror or revulsion but acceptance of fact.'
So can we talk of a kimono ... of everyday dress ...
It's pattern seared into its wearer's flesh.
And can we talk of the shadows burned into the stone ...

And if I say vaporization ... then yes ... that includes bone.
If I talk of skin that hangs from muscle in strips ...
And if I talk of black rain that runs down broken bricks ...
If I talk of ash ... of corpses in rivers ... of dams made of limbs ...
Of torsos with an absence of skins ...
Then I talk of Hiroshima ...
And of horrors that cannot be spoken ...
That can only be smelt.

23 – THE BATTLE OF THE LABORATORIES

Groves Is he ...?

Kitty Not really ...

Groves Is he ... sick? Is he ill?

Kitty Not up to seeing anyone. At the moment. Anyone. At all.

Groves I see. (*Beat.*) I haven't had a chance to ... as yet ... haven't had a chance to congratulate him. On a job well done. Everything has gone just as it should. Did you hear the radio address? President Truman ...

Kitty I heard parts.

Groves Robert may not have been mentioned by name ... and quite rightly so ... that time will come ... there will be plenty of opportunity for that ... for Time Magazine ... for accolades ... but I did think that President Truman showed great respect ... and gave due recognition ... to the work ... to the achievement ... to what we have done.

Kitty I'm sure.

Groves He referred to 'the battle of the laboratories' – I like that. It was a battle. I was proud to fight alongside your husband. Damn proud.

Kitty Yes. I'm sure he feels the same.

Groves The second bomb ... the Fat Man device ... is due to be dropped later on this evening. I'm sure the president would be interested to talk to your husband.

Kitty I will make sure he knows. (*Beat.*) Why not Earnest Lawrence ... Enrico Fermi ... Albert Einstein ...?

Groves It's true my superiors would've preferred a Nobel laureate ... it's their only barometer for success in his world. But a Nobel marks a career's peak ... I needed a man for whom this project would be his peak. I also needed a man whom I could work with.

Kitty Someone you could control.

Groves Someone I could predict. It is the wisest decision I have ever made.

Kitty I think he may have had his doubts.

Groves I never concurred with them.

Kitty Do you have any numbers yet?

Groves Numbers?

Kitty Figures. Casualties. For Hiroshima.

Groves No. Nothing precise. Not yet.

Kitty He would want the numbers.

Groves I would discourage him from dwelling on any total or figure. These are not lives lost ... these are American soldiers saved.

Kitty Have you ever killed a man?

Groves Thank you for your time and your hospitality, Mrs Oppenheimer. I hope to see your husband at his desk this evening.

Kitty If the Japanese do not surrender ... after tonight's bombing ... after the Fat Man drops ...

Groves They will.

Kitty But if they do not?

Groves They would be fools.

Kitty And if they are fools?

Groves Oak Ridge is still processing uranium.

Kitty He has blood on his hands ... that's what he says ... blood has washed away the chalkdust.

Groves This is why it is important that he wears the uniform. It helps to make that distinction ... the distinction between an act of war and an act of ... (*Beat.*) No one man could bare the weight of those lives ... but the uniform ... the burden is not his alone, and never will be. Good day, Mrs Oppenheimer.

24 – LECTURE SERIES: BOB SERBER IS IN JAPAN

Serber What would you say was the average height of a Japanese? Five six? Five seven? Let's say five six. Those black marks we saw ... those smudges we found at the centre ... are all that remain of those closest to the point of detonation. Shadows burnt into the sidewalk. Fatty stains collecting ash and dust. If we measure those marks ... take the average height of a Japanese ... by the length ... by the direction of the shadow ... we should be able to calculate where they were in relation to the bomb blast. From that we can gauge how high the bomb was when it detonated. Approximately. There will of course be outliers to discount ... those significantly shorter ... children ... but we should be able to take an average ... (*Beat.*) There were these telegraph poles ... scorched with identical markings. One side ... the side that would've been facing the blast ... was totally burnt away. Charcoal. The reverse side ... completely untouched. I followed them for two or so miles. Two miles. I ended up in a field and there's this horse grazing ... only the horse is the same as the telegraph poles ... one side untouched, the other ... the hair ... the skin ... burnt away to nothing. As I stood there ... in this field on the outskirts of Nagasaki ... looking at this horse ... a crow landed on its flank and tugged at the meat like it was slow-pulled pork.

25 – LOMANITZ

Lomanitz You are very poor when it comes to responding to letters ... to messages left ...

Oppie Rossi ...

Lomanitz (*salutes*) Colonel.

Oppie What is it you want?

Lomanitz I thought I would visit the cyclotron ... thought I would visit old haunts. (*Beat.*) After Hiroshima I said to members of my platoon ... members of my unit: 'hey ... I know the guy that built the bomb.' They told me that I had to shake your hand ... because without you they'd all be dead right now ... fighting or dead in Japan. I guess I would be too. (*Beat.*) I can't find a job. No university ... no campus ... no board.

Oppie There are plenty of high schools in need of physics teachers.

Lomanitz You think I haven't tried?! When an interview with me leads to a visit from a handful of FBI goons talking communism ... talking consequences ... how many school principals will take the risk? A car is permanently parked outside my digs. I'm trying to live a civilian life. I only wear this khaki Halloween outfit ... so that at least some patriots might buy me a beer ... but they can't smell the ... smell the ... fucking pacific island sand in my turn-ups. Write me a letter.

Oppie No.

Lomanitz Write me a recommendation.

Oppie No.

Lomanitz You have the ear of the president! You are on the cover of every newspaper, magazine and scientific journal ...!

Oppie No.

Lomanitz I just want to be in a classroom ... with some chalk ... some paper ... a pen ... my brain and a problem to be solved.

Oppie That's not what a physicist is anymore. We all work for the government now.

Lomanitz It wouldn't have to be Berkeley or Princeton or Harvard ... just a small campus ... somewhere I can finish my PhD.

Oppie I am not responsible for what you are.

Lomanitz You lent me books ... you told me of the workers' struggle ... of the Spanish Cause ... of Marx ... of the rights of man ... of any man ... of civil rights ... you taught us to question authority ... to change the world ...

Oppie I was a poor teacher.

Lomanitz You were a radical. And now ... finally now ... you are in a position to act on your ideals.

Oppie Let me tell you how you become a man of power ... of influence: you trade your ideals for self-interest. Oh, what idiots we have all been. This is just as it must be. (*Goes to exit.*)

Lomanitz (*bars his way, sings*) C'est la lutte finale

Groupons-nous, et demain
L'Internationale
Sera le genre humain

26 – THE DESTROYER OF WORLDS

The veranda of Perro Caliente.

Kitty There are no children ... there are no military police ... there are no physicists, chemists, theorists or alchemists ... no FBI ... there are no black sedans ... there are no human beings left on the surface of the world. So you will dance with your wife. It is inevitable.

Oppie There's no music.

Kitty Our bags are packed.

Oppie And where do you suggest we go?

Kitty We should return to Los Alamos.

Oppie Don't say it. It's a cursed word … a new cuss. Hiroshima … Los Alamos … Oppenheimer – shame and bitterness and disgust. There's little point in going back. There is no science left in building bombs. The world knows my name … and it knows what I have done. A skinny … intellectual … elitist … New York Jew with chest problems and sciatica … ended the war. I saved many lives … American lives. Is a soldier comparable to a civilian … of any nationality? A child … a baby … a pregnant mother … a conscientious objector … an old man at the end of his days …? This was so much philosophy … now it is my cold sweat. (*Beat.*) I want to wallow in the adulation … the respect. I want to walk down the street with everyone knowing who I am. I want younger men to stumble as they talk to me. I want university boards to trip over themselves to offer me positions and awards. I want pretty young girls at trendy socialite parties to ask me questions on deep physics and hang to my every word. I want to seem effortless. I want some upstart to question my methodology only so that I may crush them with a withering reply. I accept on my soul … on my back … I accept the weight of those Japanese … if I have brought atomic power to the world … if I have nullified war … then I welcome it all. But … no … instead … instead I feel like I've left a loaded gun in a playground. (*Beat.*) I must remember what those boys said as they painted me green … because they were right about one thing … I am not a man. A man would buckle under this weight. I am something more. I am lead-lined. I am tungsten. There's a passage in the Hindu scripture … the Bhagavad-Gita … it came to my mind at the Trinity test … in order to persuade the prince to do his duty, Vishnu takes on his multi-armed form and says: 'Now I am become Death, the destroyer of worlds.'

The Earthworks

Tom Morton-Smith

The Earthworks

For my grandfather.

With thanks to Erica Whyman, Pippa Hill, and everyone at the RSC for their continued support. Thanks also to Professor David Wark, John Terry, Mel Hillyard, Nicola Samer and Jen Tan.

The Earthworks was first performed by the Royal Shakespeare Company at The Other Place, Stratford-upon-Avon, on 24 May 2017.

Herta	Rebecca Humphries
Clare	Lena Kaur
Frijof	Thomas Magnussen

Director	Erica Whyman
Designer	Rosanna Vize
Lighting Designer	Mark Tolan
Composer	Sarah Llewellyn
Sound Designer	Steven Atkinson
Casting Director	Annelie Powell
Dramaturg	Pippa Hill
Producer	Claire Birch

Characters

Fritjof
Clare
Herta

A hotel in Geneva, Switzerland, on 9 September 2008.

1.

A peculiar light, natural but in the wrong place – like twilight at lunchtime.

The light comes from a rectangle of glass. At a distance this could be confused for a tablet/iPad, but it has no edges.

The light shines from a single side of the glass. The dark side isn't so much black as an absence of light – like an imploded star.

A man turns the glass in his hands. It is precious. It is the world. If he dropped it he would lose everything, but if he wrapped it in bubblewrap and locked it away it would kill the very essence of what it is.

So he holds it – carefully.

This man is called **Fritjof**.

Someone is coming. **Fritjof** *tidies the rectangle of glass away before it is seen.*

2.

Bar.

Clare Can I get you a drink? Can I get you a …?

Fritjof I was going to finish this one and then …

Clare … head back to your room?

Fritjof *draws attention to his wedding ring.*

Clare I'm not seducing you. Oh god … no … I wasn't … I mean … I'm sure you're very attractive, but … I am too. Married.

Fritjof It's fine.

Clare I'm going to order a bottle of wine. I'll get two glasses. God, it does sound like I'm cracking on to you. Red or white?

Would that make a difference? Something local … something … what's local? Do the Swiss do wine?

Fritjof They do fondue.

Clare Doesn't quite scratch the same itch, does it? Jesus, the prices in this place.

Fritjof Have a good evening.

Clare Is your wife not with you? Again, not seducing … just smalltalk. Stay for another drink … stay for five minutes. I can't sleep … I can't … my brain is overflowing. If I order a bottle, I'll drink a bottle … so help a girl out?

Fritjof Sure.

Clare Is it past midnight?

Fritjof Yes.

Clare Oh, for fuck's sake. Sorry … I've forgotten your name.

Fritjof I didn't give you my …

Clare I'm just really bad with names.

Fritjof I haven't given you my name.

Clare No?

Fritjof No.

Clare Can I ask what it is?

Fritjof You can ask.

Clare *makes gesture that he should.*

Fritjof Fritjof.

Clare Excuse me?

Fritjof Fritjof.

Clare How are you saying that?

Fritjof You say it … Fritjof.

Clare How are you spelling that?

Fritjof F ... R ... I ... T ... Frit ... Jof ... J ... O ... F. Fritjof.

Clare And that's ... Scandi-something ... Scandiwegian?

Fritjof Swedish.

Clare Is that a common name?

Fritjof *shrugs*.

Clare Sorry ... sorry ... it's awful, isn't it? I'm being very English.

Fritjof Don't sweat it.

Clare I'm sure you'd have problems with my name. I've often found people have difficulty with ...

Fritjof What's your name?

Clare Clare. But I don't spell it with an 'i', which some people find confusing.

Fritjof It is a pleasure to meet you, Clare.

Clare I can put this on expenses. I'll put this on expenses.

Fritjof What business are you in?

Clare I'm a journalist.

Fritjof Good night.

Clare Wait ... what? Don't go!

Fritjof Talking to journalists makes me hate the world.

Clare I'm nice!

Fritjof I'm sure that you think so.

Clare Has it got that bad? (*Beat.*) Look ... wine ... free wine ... a glass ... that's it. No tricks ... no con. Where else have you got to be?

Fritjof *acquiesces.*

Clare Do we really get such a bad rap?

Fritjof Estate agents ... politicians ... journalists.

Clare And scientists?

Fritjof It depends on who you talk to.

Clare Are you a scientist?

Fritjof I am.

Clare I thought perhaps you didn't look like one.

Fritjof Um ... thanks, I guess.

Clare Where is everyone?

Fritjof It's a school night.

Clare Are you here for the throwing of the switch?

Fritjof Yes.

Clare The Large Hadron Collider.

Fritjof That's right.

Clare And how long have you worked for CERN?

Fritjof I don't.

Clare Oh.

Fritjof I am only visiting.

Clare Not part of the ...?

Fritjof No.

Clare Where do you ... what do you ...?

Fritjof I am a postdoctoral research associate ...

Clare Right.

Fritjof ... at the Institute of Particle and Nuclear Physics at the University of ...

Silence.

Clare Sorry ... at the University of ...?

Fritjof I sensed you glazing over, so I just kind of tailed off.

Clare Yeah ... I ... sorry. Go on. You're a research associate at the University of ... Oslo, is it?

Fritjof Oslo?

Clare Sorry ... I just assumed because you were Swedish ...

Fritjof Oslo is the capital of Norway.

Clare Oh. So ... then ... um ... Helsinki?

Fritjof The University of Edinburgh.

Clare Oh! My sister lives in Edinburgh!

Fritjof Whereabouts?

Clare I have no idea. We don't get on so we don't talk.

Fritjof Okay. Thank you for the drink, but I really should get some ...

Clare No! Don't ...! Don't go to your room ... don't ... please ... don't finish your drink and go to sleep. You have to help me.

Fritjof With what?

Clare I don't understand any of it.

Fritjof The Hadron Collider?

Clare Yes.

Fritjof Do you need to?

Clare A bit.

Fritjof You're writing an article on ...?

Clare Yes.

Fritjof ... the LHC ...?

Clare Yes.

Fritjof ... for tomorrow, I guess?

Clare Yes.

Fritjof And you thinking hitting on scientists in the hotel bar the night before ...?

Clare Not scientists. One scientist. You. And I'm not hitting on ...

Fritjof I know.

Clare Could you summarise in four words ... a sentence ...?

Fritjof It's a particle accelerator. I'm not going to do your homework for you.

Clare There's no need to be patronising.

Fritjof I apologise.

Clare You're a teacher ... you're a professor ...

Fritjof I'm a post-doctoral research ...

Clare So how would you describe it to an undergrad ... to someone interested in, but not au fait with ...?

Fritjof It's the largest machine ever built.

Clare And ...?

Fritjof Look ... I'm sorry. I'm not very interested in ...

Clare Oh ... just ... okay ... sure, but ...

Fritjof I'm not much of a hand-holder.

Clare Just a brief summation of the god-particle. That's all I ...

Fritjof *grimace.*

Fritjof 'The god-particle'.

Clare Is that not ...?

Fritjof You're not going to find God in a supercollider.

Scene 2 211

Clare Okay.

Fritjof If you put that in your article prepare to be flamed in the comments.

Clare Oh shit ... really?

Fritjof What was ...? Clare was it?

Clare Yes.

Fritjof That's right. No 'i'. What's your background, Clare? You have a science degree?

Clare Yes, but ... in biology. Not physics.

Fritjof But you write for a science journal or ...?

Clare I'm a correspondent for an online ... not online ... well, yes, online ... rather not the print edition ... for the online blog of ... edition of the ... for the science section of the ... online ... bloggery blog science blog ... (*Beat.*) I am a journalist. I am a science correspondent. I write for a London based broadsheet. I have been at the paper for two years now ... two and a half ... but I still feel very much a newbie. My job so far has involved cutting a pasting from press-releases ... churnalism, I guess ... cutting and pasting and reformatting in order to fit a pre-existing article-template. Though not my first proper reporting assignment ... it does feel like ... it feels like ... it requires actual words to be written by me ... it requires actual journalism. And I'm only here because the senior correspondent's mother has had some form of stroke-slash-paralysis and is unable to ... and I have a folder of ... folders of ... physics papers and cuttings from Wired and New Scientist ... I have an email from a professor at Imperial College that's supposed to explain ... supposed to ... I have pamphlets and PDF files from CERN's press department ... I have podcasts introduced by Professor Brian Cox ... and I can't ... I can't understand a fucking word of any of it. What I can grasp is that this is massive ... that this is important ... that this the biggest scientific endeavour since the moon-landing ... and I have been entrusted by one of the oldest established newspapers in the world to report on it ... the first draft of history ... and I'm going to fuck it up.

Fritjof   Clare.

Clare   Yes?

Fritjof   I'm going to bed.

Clare   Right.

Fritjof   Chop up the press-release ... there'll be another one tomorrow ... swap in some synonyms ... presto.

Clare   I want it to be good.

Fritjof   Yeah?

Clare   I want to be good at my job.

Fritjof   Well, that's different.

Clare   It'll have my name on it ... in perpetuity ... words out there ... bad words for all time ... with my name on it. The hideously permanent internet. I can blame CERN for that too.

Fritjof   You can blame CERN for the World Wide Web. It's not the same thing as the Internet.

Clare   Accurate yet unhelpful – like calling aubergines a fruit.

Fritjof   What would be helpful?

Clare   I don't ...

Fritjof   I'm offering.

Clare   Yeah?

Fritjof   What do you want to know?

Clare   Are they going to make a black hole?

Fritjof   Where did you hear that?

Clare   It's one of the fears, isn't it? It'll tear a hole in spacetime and the planet will be dragged into the void.

Fritjof I mean, there's that risk, yeah.

Clare What?!

Fritjof But it's not a big risk … about ten or fifteen percent.

Clare You're not serious. You're serious? You're not serious.

Fritjof The thing about the LHC … and this is an exclusive for your article if you like … CERN is actually the brainchild of an ancient illuminati cult seeking to bring about Armageddon. This 'science' is not about boring made up things such as quarks, neutrons and supersymmetry … that's all a big ruse to hide our true goal which is the opening of a hellmouth beneath Switzerland and ushering humanity into a new age of darkness.

Clare Many a true word said in jest.

Fritjof *laughs*.

Clare (*laughing*) Fuck you. Black holes – yes or no?

Fritjof Yes.

Clare Shitting hell.

Fritjof But we're talking about theoretical quantum black holes which would be so uncomprehendingly small as to be unable to interact with the rest of the universe … and it would collapse within a matter of milliseconds.

Clare Milliseconds?

Fritjof Well … yoctoseconds if you want to be accurate.

Clare What's a yoctosecond?

Fritjof It's the time it takes for a quark to emit a gluon. It's about one septillionth of a second.

Clare You're fucking with me now.

Fritjof It's all actual stuff.

Clare This black hole will collapse?

Fritjof Yes.

Clare You're sure?

Fritjof Fairly certain.

Clare And if it doesn't?

Fritjof You're asking if I think you'll spontaneously combust. It's not going to happen. And if it did ... well, I'd say 'go with the moment'.

Clare What are the chances that we are all going to die?

Fritjof One hundred per cent. But not because of a black hole, and certainly not because of the LHC. We won't be doing anything that isn't happening a billion times a day in the upper atmosphere. These particles are flying through space and colliding with each other all the time ... we're just creating an environment in which we can observe that naturally occurring event.

Clare Perhaps I should call my husband. I want to keep ... anything I talk about within the article ... I want to keep within ... you know ... the confines of human experience. Of everyday experience.

Fritjof No one is going to tear a hole in reality. But you should call your husband anyway.

Clare Why?

Fritjof Because it's nice to speak to the people you love.

Clare I shouldn't be drinking. We're trying to conceive.

Fritjof Because no one ever got pregnant drunk.

Clare Six units a week reduces a woman's fertility by around eighteen per cent. I haven't pissed on a stick today. He'll ask and I'll have to say I forgot ... that I don't know the Swiss word for pregnancy test ... that I've been drinking ... that I'm so full of physics and theories ... press-releases and information packs ... that there's no space left for babies. (*Beat.*) I was secretly hoping the world might actually end, then I wouldn't have to write up the science behind the reasons why it didn't. (*Beat.*) Have you fallen out with your wife?

Fritjof A man can be alone in a bar.

Clare Sure.

Fritjof How long have you been with your husband?

Clare The best part of ten years. He supported me through unpaid internships and barely-paid writing gigs … so I … um …

Fritjof You owe him?

Clare I'm just starting to get somewhere, you know? It's just starting to pay off. (*Beat.*) I guess something will have sunk in. And if not, I'll fudge the CERN press-release … hope I extract the salient points … talk of the god-particle and I'll just have to weather the below-the-line comments.

Fritjof Good luck with that.

Clare You put your name on something … you put your work into the public sphere … it's an open invitation for people to kick you in the tits.

Fritjof I could talk to Professor Higgs … I mean, he might not go for it … but I could mention it to him … and he might give you … I don't know … an exclusive quote or something.

Clare Are you talking about …?

Fritjof Peter Higgs.

Clare As in … Mister Boson?

Fritjof He's an Emeritus Professor at my university … part of the Institute for Particle and Nuclear Physics. He's a friend. His hotel room is next to mine.

Clare Well, that would be … that would be … yes … could you?

Fritjof Not now, obviously.

Clare No?

Fritjof Well ... no ... it's coming up to one o'clock and he's ...

Clare Asleep?

Fritjof ... seventy-nine years old. (*Beat.*) I'll ask him in the morning. When I see him. Over breakfast.

Clare Okay.

Fritjof Okay?

Clare Thank you. (*Pause.*) We could knock on his door. Lightly. He might be awake.

Fritjof In the morning.

Clare Okay. (*Beat.*) Do you want to get another bottle?

3.

Corridor.

Clare Are you awake, Professor Higgs?

Fritjof Shh.

Clare Wakey-wakey, Higgsy-wiggsy!

Fritjof Come on now ...

Clare I can't hear ... hang on ... is that the TV ...? Has he got the telly on?

Fritjof No, it's ... that's the air-conditioning ...

Clare The air-conditioning?

Fritjof ... or the heating.

Clare It's voices.

Fritjof It's not voices.

Clare It is.

Fritjof From upstairs, maybe?

Clare I should've brought a glass.

Fritjof A glass?

Clare A pint glass ... to hold against the door.

Fritjof It would be a litre.

Clare What?

Fritjof We're in Switzerland.

Clare This is the room?

Fritjof He's fast asleep.

Clare I'm going to knock.

Fritjof Don't knock.

Clare Just lightly.

Fritjof Not even lightly.

Clare I could ... I could ... push something over ... a water cooler ...

Fritjof What?

Clare Make some noise ... accidental ... wake him up ...

Fritjof I'm not going to wake him up.

Clare I bet he's excited. I bet he can't sleep. It's a big day for him tomorrow. It's like Christmas and birthday and ...

Fritjof Please ...

Clare Professor Higgs?

Fritjof Stop it.

Clare Professor Higgs?

Fritjof Come away.

Clare I'm going to start a small fire.

Fritjof Stop!

Clare Wake up, Peter Higgs! (*Listens.*) Nothing.

Fritjof Come away from ...

Clare Wake up, Peter Higgs!

Fritjof He's obviously sound asleep ...

Clare Wake up, Peter Higgs!

Fritjof Maybe he's taken something ... a sleeping pill.

Clare Are you going to stand there or ...?

Fritjof Wake up, Peter Higgs!

Clare Wake up, Peter Higgs! (*Listens.*) Still nothing.

Fritjof Wake up, Peter Higgs!

Clare Wake up, Peter Higgs!

4.

Office.

Herta This is your passport?

Fritjof It is.

Herta And this is yours?

Clare Can I have that back, please?

Herta You are in room 183?

Fritjof That is correct.

Herta And you are in room 250?

Clare Yes.

Herta What is the nature of your stay?

Clare The nature ...?

Herta You are here on business?

Clare Yes.

Herta You are not here on your hen party?

Clare No.

Herta You are not here on some jolly wheeze?

Clare I am here for work.

Herta Your behaviour is not professional.

Clare I would like my passport.

Fritjof We are sorry for any disturbance.

Herta What line of work are you in, Mr Karlsson?

Fritjof I am a physicist.

Herta We get a lot of physicists here.

Fritjof I can imagine.

Herta I have worked in many hotels, Mr Karlsson. Many hotels across Europe. Riga. Prague. Amsterdam. I know how to deal with rowdy behaviour. I know how to deal with the English.

Clare Excuse me?

Fritjof I am sure.

Clare I am sorry that we made a noise … we won't be …

Herta I am talking to Mr Karlsson.

Clare But …

Herta Mr Karlsson …

Clare Doctor Karlsson.

Herta Is that right? Is it Doctor Karlsson?

Fritjof It doesn't matter.

Herta Are you also a doctor?

Clare No.

Herta The collider brings us business. Our proximity to the collider … especially at this time … brings good business to this hotel. But you scientists do not own us.

Fritjof No.

Herta You cannot barrel up and down our corridors, whooping and yelling like the Rolling Stones.

Fritjof I understand that.

Herta We have other customers. We have other guests.

Fritjof Of course.

Herta They are sleeping.

Fritjof Yes.

Herta Perhaps you do not sleep. Perhaps you keep unusual hours in your lab. Perhaps you are like a nocturnal creature that lives underground. Are you a nocturnal creature, Doctor Karlsson?

Fritjof No.

Herta You are in room 250.

Clare I am.

Herta And you are in room 183.

Fritjof Correct.

Herta You are married?

Clare Not to each other.

Herta I ask you to keep the noise down.

Fritjof We will.

Herta Very good. (*Beat.*) We take security very seriously.

Fritjof Do you consider us a threat to security?

Clare For making a bit of noise?

Herta Tomorrow is a big day.

Clare So ... because of the LHC ... you're at an elevated security level?

Herta We have been advised to remain vigilant. (*Beat.*) Would you please empty your pockets.

Clare Excuse me?

Herta Please.

Clare I'm not sure you have the authority to ...

Herta Empty your pockets. Please. Thank you.

Clare On what authority do you ...?

Herta I am the manager of this hotel.

Clare But you're not the police.

Herta I am asking politely.

Clare And I am declining. Politely.

Herta I can call security if you wish.

Clare Do you have the authority to rifle through ...?

Herta I would like you to empty your pockets.

Clare I would like my passport back.

Herta I can ask you to leave.

Clare I am a journalist.

Herta Your threats are meaningless. We have a very favourable rating on TripAdvisor.

Clare I'm going back to my room.

Herta I can have you escorted from the grounds.

Clare You're ridiculous. (*Empties pockets.*) Room key. Gum. Bank card. Mobile phone. Not that it's any of your business.

Herta Thank you.

Clare There will be a letter of complaint.

Herta That is your right.

Clare I will publish it on my employer's website. 35 million unique users every month. I will also publish a fully referenced and hyper-linked version on my personal blog.

Herta As you wish.

Clare My social media presence reaches thousands.

Herta I am pleased for you. Sir?

Fritjof No.

Herta Will you empty your pockets, sir?

Fritjof No.

Herta Will you empty your pockets?

Fritjof No.

Herta Sir?

Clare What do you think we have? Do you think we're high? Do you think we have drugs?

Herta No one mentioned drugs.

Clare Do you think our clothes are lined with plastic explosives?

Herta No.

Clare Perhaps I'm wearing a wire. Do you think I'm wearing a wire?

Herta Why would you be wearing a wire?

Clare I don't know. You tell me. What have you done?

Herta Would you like me to call security?

Clare No one here is being threatened. What did you expect to find in my pockets? If you want gum, ask for gum.

Herta I do not want gum.

Clare What do you think you'll find in his?

Herta You were causing a disturbance. Do you deny this?

Fritjof No.

Herta Miss?

Clare No.

Herta It is reasonable to ask what you have in your pockets. (*Beat.*) You are turning on your machine tomorrow, yes?

Fritjof It is not my machine.

Herta But you are here for …?

Fritjof Yes, yes …

Clare … for the throwing of the switch.

Herta I like science.

Fritjof That is good to hear.

Herta I like Neil deGrasse Tyson. I like Carl Sagan.

Fritjof I like them too.

Herta But you are not out amongst the stars, Doctor Karlsson, you are underground in burrows and tunnels.

Fritjof I'm at a desk most of the time.

Herta You concern yourself with tiny things.

Fritjof With theoretical things.

Herta Is there much distance between the theoretical and the very small?

Fritjof I suppose not.

Herta I hope that while you're here you will enjoy the many sights of Geneva and its surrounds. You are staying long?

Fritjof No.

Herta You?

Clare No.

Herta That is a shame. Geneva really does have a lot to offer.

5.

Hotel room.

Clare The bar is closed. Can we order room service? Will they bring us some beer?

Fritjof Is that going to help with your article?

Clare I can write drunk. I'm at my most creative when drunk. I'm Hunter S Thompson. I'm Don Draper.

Fritjof There's always the minibar.

Clare The minibar is a trap.

Fritjof I thought you had an expense account?

Clare Let's crack that bitch open. I haven't had dinner.

Fritjof Neither have I.

Clare It's not good to skip meals.

Fritjof We should probably eat something.

Clare Are you hungry?

Fritjof No.

Clare I can't say that surprises me. If I was raised on a diet of meatballs and rye bread, I probably wouldn't be all that interested in food either.

Fritjof That's hardly representative of …

Clare Dude, I've eaten in Ikea.

Fritjof You should try gravlax.

Clare Is that raw salmon?

Fritjof Cured salmon. And dill.

Clare Dill is for fools. (*Beat.*) So what's in your pockets? You got to see the contents of mine. I understand not wanting to show her ... principle of the thing an' all ... invasion of privacy ...

Fritjof Why do you care?

Clare Because you were interestingly adamant about it.

Fritjof 'Interestingly adamant'?

Clare You woke up the journalist.

Fritjof I'm not going to empty my pockets.

Clare No?

Fritjof No.

Clare Well ... if you won't distract me, you're going to have to help me. Why is it called the God particle?

Fritjof It's not.

Clare Yes it is.

Fritjof It's really not.

Clare Then tell me why.

Fritjof There was a physicist ... Leon Lederman ... he was writing a book about the history of particle physics ... the history of the Higgs' boson. He wanted to call it the 'goddamn-particle', because no one could find the fucker ... but his publisher thought that might cause offence so they took out the 'damn'.

Clare He was probably working to a wordcount. (*Beat.*) I hate journalism. I hate press releases. I hate opinion pieces. You're either a parrot, a robot or a battery hen. I just wanted to go out into the world ... with a notebook ... investigate ... record some interviews on my phone and write something ... but this is just cold soup. I wanted to be Lois Lane ... or Katharine Hepburn in *His Girl Friday* ... I wanted to be *All the President's Men*. I still do. What I'm not built for is this. All that's required is that

I generate traffic. It's not about truth or story or making something. And I don't have opinions ... or rather the opinions I have are subject to change ... and that's no use to anyone ... my editor ... anyone.

Fritjof If an opinion isn't subject to change, you can hardly call it an opinion – it just becomes a lie you tell yourself. Something you repeat to keep your world from falling apart.

Clare Why is it so important that we find this boson?

Fritjof It's not.

Clare It's six billion pounds of important.

Fritjof The universe doesn't care if we know how it works.

Clare I see. You're one of those 'because the sun's going to expand and swallow the earth in four billion years ... everything is therefore meaningless' kind of people. Leave the Ladybird Book of Nihilism on the shelf and tell me something real.

Fritjof Light has no mass, but it does have momentum. The speed of light is the maximum speed that light can travel, but it can be slowed down. As it passes through atmospheres. As it passes through water. You could hold it in your hand. You could slow light down and hold it in your hand.

Clare *kisses him.*

Fritjof *no response.*

Clare I didn't ... I'm sorry ...

Fritjof There's no need to apologise.

Clare I didn't kiss you because you're smart.

Fritjof Okay.

Clare I'm not trying to make myself smarter by kissing you ... by association ... by osmosis ...

Fritjof Biology degree.

Clare Tick. I just … I just … it felt important to say that. I don't know why.

They kiss. These are the first new lips either of them have kissed in some years. It is awkward because their lips are expecting to kiss different mouths. But passion is soon remembered. There we go. That's it. Proper snogging now.

6.

Hotel room.

Both of them in a state of undress.

Fritjof Please don't apologise.

Clare It's just so …

Fritjof Probably for the best.

Clare … typical … of course … and gosh …

Fritjof Please don't be embarrassed.

Clare I'm not embarrassed.

Fritjof You have no need to be.

Clare Schoolgirls get embarrassed. They shouldn't, but they do.

Fritjof It was a bad idea.

Clare It's my body's way of saying 'no'.

Fritjof You have … everything you need?

Clare You can say 'tampon' – it's a perfectly good word.

Fritjof I know, but …

Clare … but …

Fritjof … but, yeah …

Clare I'm not one to be caught out. (*Pause.*) I do need to … I do need to apologise because … I have a limited vocabulary of action.

I am sorry for that. You've been kind ... you've been helpful ... sometimes that's how people say thank you ... how I say thank you ... or used to. Or we can call it a distraction ... procrastination ... a procrastination fuck. Jesus. So ... for that ... sorry.

Fritjof We stopped before anything really ...

Clare Well ... we were cock-blocked by womb-lining. It's the same thing, I suppose.

Fritjof I guess now you don't need that pregnancy test.

Clare I guess not.

Awkward silence.

Fritjof This isn't getting your article written.

Clare No.

Fritjof What are you going to do?

Clare Write something terrible. It doesn't matter. It'll just be lost in the noise. There must be a thousand pages a day uploaded to that website. One article of mediocre quality ... one beige, poorly researched soft turd of a piece amongst the rest ... who's going to notice? And if they do ... if those that know turn up to comment ... turn up to pick apart ... well, that's all ad-revenue. Why craft ... why refine ... why strive to be good ... when you'll never see the shark for the suckerfish? (*Beat.*) It's not that I want a child ... it's that I want a family ... I don't want to be alone ... and he's a little older ... if this is the last thing I write I want it to at least show some promise. (*Beat.*) He wants a child so much. And we've been trying. We've been trying ... for what feels like ... but my life is full ... my time is full ... do you understand? My days are full. I am full. To the brim. I've got books on how to declutter your life – hundreds of them. For him there's a space to be filled. (*Beat.*) Do you have kids?

Fritjof We talked about it.

Clare Do you think you ever will?

Fritjof Not now, no.

Clare How does your wife feel about that?

Fritjof Clare ... my wife died ...

Clare Oh ... I ... oh ...

Fritjof ... not quite a year ago.

Clare I am so ...

Fritjof Don't ... don't ... it's ... I'm okay. I've got support ... a support network. I've got friends and work colleagues. Everyone's been very kind. (*Beat.*) She loved this whole endeavour ... the Hadron Collider. The logistics of it. She was an engineer. We met when she was a postgraduate student. She was fascinated by the LHC as a ... as a building project. As construction. The tunnelling ... the earthworks.

Clare How did she die?

Fritjof *silence.*

Clare I shouldn't have ... I shouldn't have asked ...

Fritjof You can ask. I don't mind the asking. I just have to decide if I want to answer or not. (*Beat.*) That was the first ... yours are the first lips ... since my wife.

Clare Oh god ... I am so sorry.

Fritjof No ... it's fine ... it's good. Because there are bound to be other kisses ... other lips. I'm not an idiot, I'm young still. There will be other loves. It's less of a betrayal to throw it away – we both agree it was throwaway – than to burden any prospective future relationship with ...

Clare Yeah ... no ... of course.

Fritjof I grew up in a town called Kiruna ... in northern Sweden. It's a landscape of iron ore ... of mining and natural mineral resource. A mine towers over the town ... the excavated earth ... black and a heap ... like the corpse of a giant dragged from beneath the ground and left to calcify on the surface. You can take tours ... they conduct tours ... down into the pit ... there's a lift that takes you down ... and whenever I took her home ... whenever we visited ... we would take the lift and we would walk the miles of mineshaft. So much hollow ... so much empty ... you'd think the world was a honeycomb. (*Beat.*) Professor Higgs ... as a kindness ... offered to bring me with ... so of course I accepted ... of course. He wasn't to know that it would feel like a betrayal ... to be heading under the ground tomorrow ... into those hollows. It feels something like a betrayal.

Clare I'm sure she wouldn't ...

Fritjof Don't. Please. Thank you. (*Beat.*) She had hereditary angioedema ... it causes random swellings in the ... in the extremities, the face, the gastrointestinal tract ... in the ... in the airways ...

Clare Okay.

Fritjof ... she had to undergo surgery when ... but ...

Clare *takes his hand.*

Fritjof The LHC ... the vacuum of the collider ... is said to be the emptiest place in the solar system ... emptier than interplanetary space. That can't be right. (*Pause.*) I think we should call it a night. I think we should ...

Clare Yeah, sure ... of course ... here let me ...

Clare *starts gathering up* **Fritjof***'s clothes to pass to him. One item is unusually heavy.*

Clare Hmm.

Fritjof What is it?

Clare It's just ... nothing ... only ... this has a peculiar weight.

7.

Kitchen.

Fritjof I need a bigger pan. I really need a much bigger pan.

Clare　How many eggs?

Fritjof　I don't need eggs.

Clare　Yes, you need eggs.

Fritjof　I need corn-flour.

Clare　You can't make custard without breaking eggs.

Fritjof　I need corn-flour and water and I don't really need that much else.

Clare　Well that sounds delicious.

Fritjof　It's not meant to be delicious … it's meant to be illustrative.

Clare　When you say custard, you mean custard made from powdered custard?

Fritjof　Yeah.

Clare　I'm not sure this is the sort of establishment that'll keep a box of custard powder to hand – they serve their desserts on slate. Will it work if we make it from scratch?

Fritjof　I'm a theorist … you're asking the wrong guy.

Clare　Here's a pan. Now we need a whisk. Talk to me about custard.

Fritjof　Custard – as any fool knows – is a non-Newtonian liquid. Meaning that it doesn't act as water does. If you were to run at a lake of custard, the impact of your foot would cause the surface to momentarily increase in viscosity … momentarily solidify … so much so that it would support your weight as you peg it over to the other side. Stop or slow down and you would begin to sink into the crème anglaise and die a painful and gently vanilla-flavoured death. The Higgs field is custard. Photons – light – gathers no custard … has no mass. It skims across the Higgs' field as fast as any particle can – the speed limit of the universe – that's why that speed limit is known as the speed of light.

Clare　I've found a whisk. Check the fridges for eggs.

Fritjof So why don't all particles travel at that same speed? Why don't you and I … why don't these walls … this flooring …? Why isn't this hotel a cloud? Why isn't everything in the universe just a haze of unconnected particles tearing around at the very limit of light? Why does anything have weight? Why does mass exist? What is mass? What brings us together? We don't know. We guess some particles aren't travelling fast enough, so they get bogged down. But by what? Higgs' theoretical custard.

Clare I can't use that.

Fritjof No?

Clare As an analogy? No. Who the hell knows you can run across custard?

Fritjof There are people doing it all over YouTube.

Fritjof *opens a fridge.* **Clare** *opens a cupboard. In the fridge there is a large tub of fresh custard. In the cupboard is a large tub of powdered custard.*

Clare Jackpot.

Fritjof Same.

Clare Oh.

They prise the lids off their tubs.

Fritjof Powdered?

Clare Yeah. Yours?

Fritjof Fresh.

Clare Show me then.

Fritjof *brings his tub to the centre.* **Clare** *still holds hers.*

Fritjof Pass me a spoon?

Clare *does so.*

Fritjof (*stirs the custard*) Liquid … agreed?

Clare Agreed.

Fritjof The harder I hit this … the faster I am … the more energy … the more solid it will become. Okay?

Clare Okay.

Fritjof Okay.

Fritjof *lifts his hand and brings it down heavily on the surface of the custard. It's not the right kind of custard. His arm plunges deep into the tub.*

Clare *laughs.*

Fritjof *lobs some custard at her.* **Clare** *throws a handful of custard powder at him. They both laugh. He lobs some more. So does she.*

Custard fight!

8.

Office.

Herta The kitchen is off limits to guests.

Clare We understand that.

Fritjof We will pay for any costs.

Clare Absolutely.

Herta It is the inconsideration. For the property. For the chef. For the cleaning staff.

Fritjof We understand.

Herta If you understand you would not be here … in front of me … in this office.

Clare We understand now.

Herta Hindsight is a remarkable thing.

Fritjof You are within your rights to ask us to leave.

Herta I am.

Fritjof But … it is … it is 4 am …

Clare Is it 4 am?

Fritjof It is. We will pay for any costs. We will leave quietly in the morning.

Herta It is within my rights to call the police also.

Clare Oh come on …!

Fritjof There's no need for …

Herta I could suggest a charge of property damage.

Clare We didn't 'damage' anything.

Herta The custard is despoiled. It cannot be served now.

Fritjof Do you think the police will be interested in such a charge?

Herta Will you return to your rooms?

Fritjof Yes.

Herta Will you remain there?

Fritjof Yes.

Herta You will not be welcome back at this hotel. Do you understand that?

Fritjof We do.

Herta You are wrong if you believe that consequences cannot pass through hotel walls.

Fritjof Again, we apologise for any disturbance caused.

Herta Apologies are all very well, but if the price of such disturbance can be met with words alone then …

Clare Then …?

Herta *shrugs.*

Clare Hardly the end of the world, I think.

Herta And that is why the world is as it is.

Clare (*to* **Fritjof**) Do you have your wallet on you?

Fritjof Why?

Clare I only have a bank card. I'll pay you back.

Fritjof *hands over wallet.*

Clare *takes money from wallet and places it in front of* **Herta**.

Herta What is this?

Clare Two hundred Swiss Francs.

Herta What do you expect me to do with it?

Clare *shrugs.*

Herta *not impressed.*

Fritjof *puts the money back in his wallet.*

Herta It is too easy to throw around money and apologies. They often weigh the same.

Fritjof We didn't mean to insult you.

Herta I do not do this job because I like people, Doctor Karlsson. I do not enjoy this. I do not wish to interact with society. I want society to be tucked up asleep in their allotted rooms. A tick-box sheet of breakfast items hung on a door handle is all the human interaction I require. And yet … here I find myself presented with an opportunity. An opportunity for education. You must learn cost. Two hundred francs is seemingly nothing to you … an apology is seemingly nothing to you … a lifetime ban from this hotel also the same. I cannot say that I know you well, Doctor Karlsson, but there is one thing that I have seen that is a sticking point … and so to that I must return … so that you may understand consequence. Will you please empty your pockets?

Clare Oh my god.

Herta Doctor Karlsson?

Clare You don't have to do anything.

Fritjof *acquiesces. He pulls from his pocket the rectangle of glass. Daylight pours from it. Eerie and beautiful. Light fills the room. We never knew how dark it was before this light.*

9.

Hotel room.

Fritjof Light has no mass, but it does have momentum. The speed of light is the maximum speed that light can travel. But it can be slowed down. As it passes through atmospheres. As it passes through water. This ... this is Slow Glass. It is transparent ... light flows through it ... but at a greatly reduced speed. This piece ... it takes roughly ten years for light to pass through.

Clare It's not an iPad.

Fritjof No.

Clare She thought it was an iPad.

Fritjof She knows of iPads. She doesn't know of this. And so this unknowable thing ... which sits outside of her experience ... outside her frame of reference ... it is easier to replace it in her mind with something that she does know. It is always easier to believe what you already believe.

Clare It's heavy.

Fritjof Yes.

Clare It's cold. What is it made of?

Fritjof When you start closely packing atoms together ... at incredibly low temperatures ... in a vacuum ... matter can enter a pretty exotic state. As light travels through such a complex and dense material ... well, it slows down ... it takes on more physical properties. You could almost touch it ... almost hold it in your hands. Pick the light out of the air ... turn it over in your fingers ... mould it ... shape it ... make something new. In 1998 a team at

Harvard slowed light down to around 38 miles per hour. The speed of light is normally 186,000 miles per second. Within two years that same team managed to bring light to a full stop.

Clare A full stop?

Fritjof And then they restarted it again. There are practical applications ... in the fields of information storage ... quantum computing and the like ...

Clare This is daylight ... old daylight ... yesterdaylight ...?

Fritjof You hold in your hands ten years' worth of light. You're looking at the past.

Clare How did you get this?

Fritjof I knew someone working on a research team.

Clare At Harvard?

Fritjof No. This is from somewhere else. Somewhere less public. It was meant to be destroyed. Instead he sent it to me.

Clare Why isn't this stuff everywhere?

Fritjof Too expensive to manufacture ... difficult to apply to a practical purpose ... the Illuminati ... who knows?

Clare There's movement.

Fritjof Yeah.

Clare What am I looking at?

Fritjof I receive this message out of nowhere ... from an old friend ... a colleague. He'd fallen off the radar ... had lost contact. Friends drift apart, we all know this. And this message ... a letter ... well, a postcard in an envelope ... it simply says: 'I am sending you something'. No return address. No pleasantries. I don't even know how he knew where I lived. I mention it to my wife. She pulls a quizzical face ... I shrug my shoulders ... we have a little chuckle at the weirdness of it. The card goes in the recycling. A month later we receive a delivery ... UPS or ParcelForce, nothing odd ... she signs for this box. Not a big box, but it is heavy. No bigger than a three ream pack of A4, but the guy needs to use his trolley to get it from the van to the house. When I get home – I've been doing the weekly shop – it's about four o'clock in the afternoon but it's winter and Edinburgh, so you know: dark – I come into the front room ... and there is daylight. The brightest noonday sun. My wife is sat in the middle of the floor surrounded by these tiles ... these tiles of sunlight ... all fanned out in a spiral. She doesn't say anything ... she's just grinning ... that innocent 'let's fly a kite' grin that you can't hide ... that you can't stop yourself from smiling. I pick one of the tiles up and I'm looking at it ... I'm looking at it ... and it's wrong ... it's strange ... it's a landscape ... a window onto a landscape ... of mountains and trees and sky. I turn it over in my hands ... and it's Slow Glass. It's Slow Glass. I explain it to her ... I explain how light can be slowed down and stored ... how this theoretical material is now very much not theoretical but here ... in our front room. We spread it out ... link up the image ... like a jigsaw. We have some grout leftover ... because we'd not long done up the bathroom and she had become a dab-hand self-taught tiler. That night ... that same night ... we're covering one of the walls in our front room with these tiles of Slow Glass. It was living wallpaper. It was a portal to another dimension. Our best guess is that the view was of somewhere in Upstate New York ... the Appalachians ... oak, maple and spruce. Whatever the drizzle ... whatever the Scottish drizzle outside ... the flame of those Autumn North American colours filled our front room ... the bright blue sky ... the clearest days. And the wildlife ... the birds of prey ... the deer ... in our front room ... separated from us by a pane of glass and ten years. I remember we were sat on the sofa one night ... boxsetting our lives away ... and this ... this *immense* electrical storm broke out across the Slow Glass. Lightning without thunder. Sheets of rain. Trees bending in gales. And neither of us paying attention to the TV anymore ... just hands and fingers interlocked ... a head on a shoulder ... the smell of her ... the cocoa-butter on her skin ... her hair-products. I'm ... I'm sorry ... (*Beat.*) Even now ... just thinking about ... it brings back that arrhythmia of love ... that shimmer down one side of the heart ... this fucking phantom limb. (*Beat.*) No one takes pictures at funerals. No one hires a photographer.

I can't really remember the day ... it is all blurs and stabs. So now, when I see people ... friends ... family people ... I have to ask them 'were you there?' Because I don't know. And no one took a photograph. (*Beat.*) I functioned fairly well those first few weeks ... fed myself ... though I threw away a lot of off-milk. I needed to reset to 'shopping for one'. And then ... one day I came home and our house was dark. And our house was *never* dark. We had a wormhole in space and time on our living room wall. But the tiles were black. It never occurred to me that they would run out. Of course the light would end. I cried more on that day than on any other. I avoided the front room for a while ... ate in the kitchen ... I spent some nights at the Premier Inn down the road. Anything to get away from those spent tiles. But then ... with drink in my system ... one day I found myself reaching for my toolbox. The hammer smacked against the wall ... cracking the tiles ... breaking them ... a chip ... a splinter. I dug the claw-teeth into the grouting and pulled a section from the wall. The room filled with light again ... like a punch to the throat. The light ... from the rear side of the broken glass. I picked it up and held it to my eye. And there she was. There was Marie ... youthful and beautiful ... ten years younger. All those tiles ... all of those tiles ... the light of the past decade ... all of that love ... stored in those glass tiles. (*Beat.*) Here she comes. Coming home. She'll get some water from the kitchen and come back ... stand in front of the Slow Glass wall for a moment. She's looking at that landscape. It won't even occur to her that I could be watching from ten years in her future. Just light bouncing around the universe ... landing on this ... reflecting off that ... perhaps seen, probably not. (*Pause.*) Rosalind Russell.

Clare Excuse me?

Fritjof It was Rosalind Russell in *His Girl Friday*. The Hepburn film you're most probably thinking of is *Woman of the Year* ... opposite Spencer Tracy. Sorry. It's been bugging me ever since you said it.

Clare You knew what I was getting at.

Fritjof I suppose so. I didn't mean to ...

Clare It's fine.

Fritjof What time is it?

Clare It's late. Or early.

Fritjof Depending on how you look at it.

Clare You're from the north of Sweden?

Fritjof That's right.

Clare The northern lights.

Fritjof In the winter, yes.

Clare I've never seen them. I'd love to. They're on my list.

Fritjof They photograph better than they look. (*Beat.*) Kiruna … where I grew up … all that industry … all that tunnelling … it has literally undermined the town. To the extent that the ground is so thin, there's a real danger of collapse … of the city centre collapsing into the mines beneath. The ground is weak now. They are moving the town two miles to the East. Homes relocated … businesses … in case the ground opens up and swallows them all. Its entire centre is shifting. Will we even be able to call it the same place?

Clare You'll go down into the tunnels?

Fritjof Tomorrow?

Clare Well, later today.

Fritjof I suppose so.

Clare Will it still feel like a betrayal?

Fritjof *does not answer.*

Clare Do you want to know what I think? I think you cannot betray someone you've lost. Because you cannot go through the experience of losing someone and come out unchanged. They would have never known the you that underwent that process of grief. They never knew you as you are now, with that hurt in your heart. And that's okay. That's okay. The person that they knew died with them. (*Deep breath.*) Beneath Geneva, 100 metres down, is the greatest machine that humankind has ever built. And today we switch it on. A loop of 27km, a supercollider of such massive proportions that it has taken the combined effort and will of over 100 contributing countries ten years to build. Not only the greatest scientific endeavour of all time, but also the greatest single instance of international consensus this world has ever seen. When activated, subatomic particles will collide at close to the speed of light, generating temperatures 100,000 times hotter than the surface of the sun. And for what? The materially minded will ask 'what application will this science have? What significance for technology, human longevity or the military? How can this expense be justified? What do we hope to learn?' And I would answer: nothing. We simply hope to learn. TV's Professor Brian Cox said he was thrilled at the results and thought that the LHC was 'just amazing'. Black-hole boffin, Stephen Hawking, said something inspiring in his cool robot voice.

Fritjof That'll do.

Clare You think?

Fritjof Yeah.

Clare I want it to be good.

Fritjof Does it matter?

Clare I want it to matter.

Fritjof The only things that have meaning are those that we ascribe meaning to.

Clare I know. And some things fall apart before they even begin. And it's possible to feel loss for something you never wanted. And we'll all be forgotten, and the sun will swallow the earth and the universe will die. But you can't live your life like that, can you? Can you?

10.

Lobby.

Fritjof Good morning.

Clare Hi.

Fritjof Did you manage to sleep?

Clare I managed about an hour.

Fritjof Are you heading down to breakfast?

Clare I was just going to get some juice.

Fritjof How's the article coming along?

Clare There'll be quotes to add … a final update before publication … and my editor needs to sign it off.

Fritjof Formalities.

Clare And of course if something unexpected happens … the unspooling of space and time … a cascade of matter/anti-matter explosions … that sort of thing … then I'll have to take another pass at it.

Fritjof I haven't seen Professor Higgs yet this morning, so I haven't asked him for …

Clare Don't worry about it.

Fritjof Are you sure?

Clare It's fine. I don't think I need it.

Fritjof Okay.

Clare I've got my three hundred words.

Fritjof Yeah?

Clare I've been up since six.

Fritjof Oh, well done.

Clare Coffee is my friend.

Fritjof Are you happy with it?

Clare Yes. I think so. Yes.

Fritjof I can still get a quote …?

Clare There will be enough things said today. There will be a press release.

Fritjof If the world doesn't end.

Clare Yeah.

Fritjof So …

Clare It doesn't, though, does it?

Fritjof No.

Clare What if it's not there? You turn that machine on and there's no Higgs … and all you find is that you've given your life to asking the wrong question.

Fritjof Not finding it is just as interesting as finding it. Whatever happens, it'll be new.

Clare Doesn't it give you a sense of vertigo … these tiny, tiny things … so far removed from our day to day … and yet … they are everything?

Fritjof You asked me why it was called the 'god-particle' … I think there is a hope … that if we can reduce this enormous, chaotic, painful universe down to its constituent parts … if we can understand it at the most basic level … maybe … finally … we'll get a sense of 'why'. And is that not what we'd all ask if we met God? 'Why?'

Clare There's a bus picking up all the press …

Fritjof Right.

Clare … in front of the hotel in about half an hour. I need to brush my teeth and check out.

Fritjof You haven't brushed your teeth?

Clare I've not drunk any juice yet. I'm not an animal. (*Beat.*) Thank you.

She hugs him. A tight hug. One that says goodbye to an old friend.

Clare Well, you take care of yourself.

Fritjof You too.

Clare's *mobile phone rings. She looks at the screen.*

Fritjof Your husband?

Clare *nods.*

Fritjof *a little wave goodbye.*

Clare (*answers her phone*) Morning. Yeah … I'm just heading down to breakfast. Did you sleep well? I miss you. (*Exits.*)

Fritjof *alone, he pulls the pane of slow glass from his pocket, he looks at it, he doesn't need to look anymore, so he puts it away.*

Ravens

Tom Morton-Smith

Ravens

For Hester.

With thanks to Jack Bradley, Rose Cobbe, Annabelle Comyn and Jen Tan.

Ravens was first performed at the Hampstead Theatre, London, on 29 November 2019.

Guðmundur Þórarinsson	Gunnar Cauthery
Max Euwe	Simon Chandler
Fred Cramer/Lina Grumette	Buffy Davis
Lothar Schmid	Philip Desmeules
Bobby Fischer	Robert Emms
William Lombardy / Henry Kissinger	Solomon Israel
Iivo Nei	Beruce Khan
Regina Fischer	Emma Pallant
Boris Spassky	Ronan Raftery
Nikolai Krogius	Rebecca Scroggs
Efim Geller	Gyuri Sarossy
Sæmundur 'Sæmi-Rokk' Pálsson	Gary Shelford
Director	Annabelle Comyn
Designer	Jamie Vartan
Lighting Designer	Howard Harrison
Sound Designer	Philip Stewart
Video	Jack Phelan
Movement	Mike Ashcroft
Casting	Juliet Horsley

Characters

The Americans

Bobby Fischer, *challenger*
Fred Cramer, *manager*
Henry Kissinger, *foreign policy advisor*
Lina Grumette, *chess mother*
William Lombardy, *Fischer's second*
Regina Fischer, *communist*

The Soviets

Boris Spassky, *world champion*
Nikolai Krogius, *psychologist*
Efim Geller, *strategist*
Iivo Nei, *sparring partner*

Others

Guðmundur Þórarinsson, *organiser*
Max Euwe, *president of FIDE*
Lothar Schmid, *arbiter*
Sæmundur 'Sæmi-Rokk' Pálsson, *policeman*

Author's Notes

The play takes place in July and August 1972.

Included are the move lists for the twenty-one chess games of the championship – though it is not expected that each game be faithfully recreated. The games need not take the form of a literal chess game. Each bout should be represented by a different one-on-one contest – for example, arm wrestling, dueling pistols, fencing, boxing, drinking contest, rock-paper-scissors, dance-off, kendo, hungry hungry hippos, judo, food-fight and so on. The form of the contest matters less than the result.

A scoreboard showing the progress of the tournament is essential.

Act One

1.

The Loftleiðir Hotel, Reykjavík.

Efim *Geller,* **Nikolai** *Krogius and* **Iivo** *Nei are waiting.*

Efim   Stop.

Iivo   What?

Efim   Stop shaking your leg.

Iivo   I'm not shaking my …

Efim   You are.

Iivo   I can shake my leg if I want.

Efim   Why does a man shake his leg, Nikolai? Is it symptomatic of something?

Nikolai   A soothing ritual. Don't read too much into it.

Efim   Are you anxious, Iivo?

Iivo   Don't we have reason to be?

Efim   It's a weakness of character.

Nikolai   That goes a bit far.

Efim   It's what the American will think.

Nikolai   Is the coffee good?

Efim   Yes.

Guðmundur *Þórarinsson enters.*

Guðmundur   Is Mr Spassky … Comrade Spassky …? I thought he was …?

Nikolai   He's in the bathroom.

Guðmundur   Ah. We're still waiting on Mr Euwe and Mr Schmid …

Iivo And Mr Fischer.

Guðmundur Yes. Very good.

Efim Any word from …?

Guðmundur I think we should probably wait for …

Nikolai Of course.

Silence.

Guðmundur I'll just go and see if … (*Exits.*)

Iivo I'll take a cigarette.

Nikolai *passes him a cigarette.*

Efim What do you think?

Iivo Of what?

Efim The Western brands.

Iivo (*shrugs*) What else am I to smoke?

Nikolai They're better on the lungs.

Efim I'll stick with what I know.

Nikolai These are smoother.

Efim I like to feel what I'm smoking.

Iivo I prefer the taste.

Nikolai They'll give us the game.

Efim I'm not so sure.

Nikolai They don't have a choice.

Efim They're scared of the Americans.

Iivo The Chess Federation?

Efim The Icelanders.

Nikolai They're scared it might all fall apart.

Efim We should have insisted on a neutral location.

Iivo Reykjavík is neutral.

Efim There's an American military base not thirty miles from here.

Iivo There's no special love between Iceland and the US.

Efim They are allies.

Nikolai And we are trade partners – Iceland has a foot in both camps.

Boris *Spassky enters.*

Iivo We've got coffee.

Boris Is it good?

Iivo Makes you feel like part of the Muscovite art set.

Efim I've asked for tea.

Boris Can we arrange fresh orange juice?

Efim I'll call reception.

Boris No … I meant … I would like fresh orange juice before each of the games.

Nikolai Of course. Anything else?

Boris I don't think so.

Nikolai Can I get you an orange juice now?

Boris Coffee's fine.

Iivo Is Fischer sick?

Efim They may well say that.

Iivo Why would he forfeit the opening game? You can't win if you don't turn up.

Boris I'm not worried.

Iivo Why would he gift you an advantage?

Efim It's not about us, it's about the money. He is holding out for more.

Iivo It cannot simply be the money.

Nikolai He has asked for thirty per cent of the door ... on top of the percentage he gets for the broadcast rights.

Iivo And the prize pot.

Boris Nowhere does it say that only gentlemen can play chess.

Nikolai They will give us the game.

Efim They may not.

Iivo They'll hardly break their own rules.

Efim He acts like he's already won ... he acts like a champion.

Boris Champions don't act like this. I don't act like this.

Efim Still ... they are pandering to him.

Boris They simply want the game to go ahead.

Iivo How long is the flight from New York? Perhaps he is already in the air.

Nikolai If he were then they would know ... if they knew then they would say.

Efim In any other championship ...

Boris In any other championship it would be Russian against Russian ... it would be Petrosian versus Smyslov ... Taimanov versus Korchnoi ... it would be you versus me.

Iivo Taimanov is Ukrainian.

Efim It is the same thing ... Soviet versus Soviet ...

Nikolai Petrosian is from Georgia, I believe.

Iivo It is not the same.

Boris Even so ... even if it were myself versus ... I don't know ... the Danish champion ... Bent Larson ... no one would be as interested in a Dane overthrowing twenty-six years of Soviet chess dominance. Fischer is an American. It's a little bit of circus. I do not mind.

Guðmundur *re-enters with* **Max** *Euwe,* **Lothar** *Schmid and* **Fred** *Cramer.*

Max   Boris …

Boris   Max …

Nikolai   Max …

Max   Nikolai …

Boris   Lothar …

Lothar   Boris …

Iivo   Lothar …

Lothar   Iivo …

Max   Efim …

Efim   Max …

Max   Iivo …

Fred   Fred.

Boris   Boris.

Nikolai   Nikolai.

Efim   Efim.

Iivo   Iivo.

Lothar   Nikolai …

Nikolai   Lothar …

Efim   Lothar …

Lothar   Efim …

Guðmundur   Guðmundur Þórarinsson.

Boris Where is Bobby Fischer?

Max In New York.

Efim This is unacceptable.

Nikolai He is booked onto a plane?

Max No.

Boris How ill is he?

Max We have received a telegram …

Fred From a doctor.

Max … from a doctor.

Efim What kind of illness?

Fred That is a private matter.

Efim Does he have a cold? Is it scarlet fever? Is it the plague?

Fred We expect him to make a full recovery.

Efim When?

Fred In due time.

Efim Time is due! Time is past due!

Nikolai Excuse me, who are you?

Fred Fred Cramer.

Nikolai And you speak for Fischer?

Fred I do.

Max And he sends his apologies.

Fred You do not need to apologise when you are ill.

Boris When did you receive this telegram?

Fred Four o'clock this morning.

Boris May we see it?

Fred No.

Efim No?

Fred It is a private matter.

Nikolai Max ... have you seen this telegram?

Max I ...

Boris Max?

Max No.

Fred *disappointed.*

Max I won't lie. I haven't seen it.

Boris Lothar?

Lothar I haven't seen it either.

Fred It is a piece of paper with some words. I can tell you the words. Why do you need to see it?

Boris Because I am trying to work out whether it is Fischer that is lying or you.

Nikolai The President of the International Federation should see it. The referee ... the arbiter of the tournament ... should see it.

Lothar I would like to see it.

Fred There is no need.

Nikolai Then we do not believe that it exists.

Efim You are covering for him.

Guðmundur The priority above all else is the game.

Nikolai Perhaps we should start making our own demands.

Max It would be within your rights.

Nikolai It is within our rights to claim a forfeit.

Max That would be a shame.

Guðmundur No one wants that.

Efim We might want it.

Max He is ill.

Nikolai Then let us see the telegram.

Fred No.

Nikolai Then let us see your credentials ... some official warrant ... something signed by Fischer ... saying that you are authorised to speak for him.

Fred Are you serious ...?

Nikolai We do not know who this man is.

Fred My name is Fred Cramer.

Nikolai He claims to speak for Fischer ...

Fred I 'claim' ...?!

Nikolai If you do not speak for Fischer ... if you are not authorised by him ... if you are not in direct contact with Bobby Fischer ... then you have no authority in these discussions.

Efim And you should leave.

Nikolai Max ...?

Everyone looks to **Max**.

Max *capitulates.*

Fred *exits – furious.*

Max We must give Fischer time. If he is ill ...

Efim Then let him say that he is ill.

Lothar We must declare that he has forfeited the first game.

Guðmundur It is not the start that we had hoped for ...

Lothar ... but we would still, at least, have a tournament.

Iivo Is it better to declare the game lost, rather than forfeit?

Lothar The effect would be the same.

Max I do not like to declare the first game lost.

Lothar It would be a shame.

Guðmundur ... and not technically possible.

Max As President of the World Chess Federation ...

Guðmundur You can't declare a game lost before it has even begun ... if we claim the game forfeit, he may never come.

Efim Then Boris retains the title by default.

Boris It is not how I like to win.

Iivo Fischer is the one backing down, not you.

Max We must postpone the game.

Efim No.

Nikolai Absolutely not.

Efim There is no precedent for such a thing.

Nikolai The championship has already begun. You cannot postpone the first game.

Max The tournament may have started ... but the tournament is not the game. No pieces have been drawn ... no clock has been set ticking ... there have been no opening moves ...

Efim We attended an opening ceremony ... a ceremony to mark the beginning of the contest ... am I wrong?

Lothar You're not wrong.

Efim This man gave a speech.

Guðmundur It was my opening address.

Iivo His opening address.

Efim In front of the Prime Minister of Iceland.

Guðmundur And also the President.

Efim An official opening of the championship.

Max No clock has been started.

Efim Fischer is the challenger ... but he refuses to challenge. Why should the Federation support him?

Max We will draw the pieces in two days' time.

Nikolai The Soviet delegation does not agree with this postponement and the decisions taken by the Chess Federation's president.

Max Your objection has been noted.

Efim Boris?

Boris I want to play chess.

2.

A house in Douglaston, Queens.

Bobby *Fischer is on the phone. A* **Voice** *on the end of the line.*

Voice Is this Robert Fischer?

Bobby This is Bobby Fischer.

Voice This is Robert James Fischer?

Bobby Yes.

Voice Please hold for Doctor Kissinger.

Silence. **Henry** *Kissinger comes onto the line.*

Henry Hello, Bobby?

Bobby *no response.*

Henry Hello? Is there ...?

Bobby I'm here.

Henry Hello, Bobby.

Bobby Hello.

Henry Do you know who I am?

Bobby Yes.

Henry Do you know why I have called?

Bobby No.

Henry You don't know why I am calling?

Bobby I could take a guess.

Henry Why don't you take a guess then.

Bobby You think I should go to Reykjavík.

Henry I do think that, yes.

Bobby *silence.*

Henry You are having some second thoughts … is that fair to say, Bobby?

Bobby I don't know, sir.

Henry You don't know?

Bobby No, sir.

Henry Well, I think you are probably having some second thoughts. You have done well to get to this point. Do you not want to see it through?

Bobby You follow chess?

Henry I do.

Bobby Do you play?

Henry Enough to appreciate your skill. (*Beat.*) Do you like Communists, Bobby?

Bobby No, sir.

Henry Why don't you like Communists?

Bobby I don't know.

Henry You must have some idea.

Bobby They cheat.

Henry How do they cheat?

Bobby They work together.

Henry And that's cheating?

Bobby Yes, sir.

Henry And they've held the world championship since 1946.

Bobby Yes.

Henry That can't stand, can it, Bobby? Cheaters holding the world championship.

Bobby No.

Henry No. So what should we do about it, do you think? If an American player … such as yourself … were to knock them from their pedestal … that would be good, wouldn't it?

Bobby Yes.

Henry It would send out a powerful statement.

Bobby It would.

Henry What would that statement be?

Bobby Cheaters never prosper.

Henry 'Cheaters never prosper'. That's a good thing to tell the world, don't you think?

Bobby I was holding out for more money.

Henry Yes.

Bobby And they found more money.

Henry So I have heard.

Bobby The prize-pot has been doubled.

Henry But you haven't boarded that plane.

Bobby There are journalists outside. There are photographers. The phone has been tapped.

Henry I cannot speak to that. (*Beat.*) Are you scared?

Bobby No.

Henry Are you afraid?

Bobby No.

Henry What are you afraid of?

Bobby *no response.*

Henry To lead the world in chess is to claim a superiority of the intellect. This is a hill that they will die on. Wouldn't it be sweet to take it from them?

Bobby It would.

Henry Good. Well … I hope you will forgive me but I have other matters to attend.

Bobby Sure.

Henry The United States Government wishes you well and I wish you well.

Bobby Thank you, sir.

Henry The world is watching. You're a soldier now, Bobby.

3.

Laugardalshöll arena.

Boris, **Iivo**, **Efim** *and* **Nikolai** *wait backstage.*

Efim He'll offer you his hand palm down.

Boris What does that mean?

Efim It's an American thing.

Nikolai It's a dominance thing.

Efim If you miss the chance to initiate the handshake ... step forward when he proffers his hand ... on your left foot and into his personal space ... this should force him to lean back and you'll be able to manipulate his hand into a more standard upright position ... maybe even turn it fully over so you become the dominant party. If this doesn't work and he remains palm down, just grab him by the wrist ... place your hand on top of his. Though that might be considered a little aggressive. It's up to you.

Boris Are we certain he's even in the country?

Nikolai He's at the hotel.

Boris Our hotel?

Iivo He has a three room suite.

Boris Have you seen him?

Iivo No ... one of the Icelanders said.

Boris I thought they were giving him a house in the suburbs?

Nikolai Wasn't to his liking.

Boris I'm not going to grab him by his wrist.

Guðmundur *enters.*

Efim Okay ... they're ready.

The Russian team ready themselves to enter the arena.

Guðmundur Um ... if you could just ... wait ... one moment ...

Nikolai What is it?

Efim He's not here.

Guðmundur No ... we're still ... we'll hold the ceremony ... only ... it looks like it won't be Fischer drawing the pieces with you.

Efim I knew it.

Boris What does that mean?

Iivo Is he here? Is he in the building?

Guðmundur He's in Reykjavík.

Nikolai But he's not coming to the ceremony?

Guðmundur He's sent a substitute in his place ... his second ... William Lombardy.

Boris How is he allowed to do that?

Guðmundur There's no rule that says that he can't. The drawing ceremony is largely ... ceremonial. (*Beat.*) What should I ...? Will you ... will you go on?

Nikolai Could you give us a moment ...?

Guðmundur Guðmundur.

Nikolai Guðmundur. Thank you.

Guðmundur Of course. (*Exits.*)

Boris It's a direct and deliberate insult.

Iivo So rise above it and ...

Boris This isn't a schoolyard. He's not cussing out my mother. It's calculated. Am I wrong?

Efim No.

Iivo No ... but you should not take it as a ...

Boris *I* am not insulted ... he doesn't insult *me* ...

Efim He insults the Soviet people.

Boris To send an underling in his place ...

Nikolai And Father Lombardy at that.

Iivo Why is that significant?

Boris Because I've played Lombardy before ... and he beat me. Twelve years ago.

Nikolai You were cocky.

Boris And he was better. Then.

Efim What would you have us do?

Boris I don't know.

Efim Demand an apology ... demand a forfeit of the first game ... of the tournament?

Boris I do not know.

Efim Do we leave? Do you want us to leave?

Boris I want Fischer to be a human being.

Efim Do you want to call Moscow?

Boris No.

Nikolai We are too concerned with his motives. Whether he's a narcissist or a tactician ... it doesn't ultimately matter. He wants to elicit a reaction ... whether that's to gain an advantage or simply because he craves the attention ... either way we must be the adults in the room.

Iivo You should ask for an apology at least.

Nikolai But as a disappointed parent, not a fuming enemy.

Efim Boris ...?

Boris Fine.

Guðmundur *enters.*

Guðmundur Gentlemen ...? We are ready for you.

4.

Laugardalshöll arena.

The drawing ceremony.

An elevated stage. A wooden table and two chairs – one chair is wooden and upholstered in yellow, the other is a black leather swivel chair. A chessboard. A chess clock. Television cameras.

Max *and* **Lothar** *are onstage.* **Lothar** *holds a small bag.*

Boris *enters from one side.* **William** *Lombardy from the other. They meet in the middle and shake hands.* **Lothar** *opens the bag.* **Boris** *and* **William** *reach inside and draw a piece each. They reveal the colour of their pieces.* **Boris***' is white and* **William***'s is black.*

Much applause.

5.

Laugardalshöll arena.

The same elevated stage. **Bobby** *is inspecting the space.* **Fred** *and* **Guðmundur** *stand to one side.*

Bobby Brighter.

The lighting gets brighter.

Bobby Less.

The lighting dims.

Bobby Less.

The lighting dims again.

Bobby Brighter.

The lighting gets brighter.

Bobby Less.

The lighting dims fractionally.

Bobby Better.

Guðmundur Let's set the level there.

Bobby Brighter.

The lighting gets brighter.

Guðmundur There?

Bobby *nods*.

Guðmundur Okay … let's set it there.

Bobby The front row is too close. Remove the front two rows.

Guðmundur We have sold tickets for …

Bobby Move them back or take them out.

Guðmundur We'll see if we can move them back.

Bobby No … no … just get rid of them … breathing down my neck.

Fred You should be writing this down.

Guðmundur Everything meets with the pre-agreed specifications.

Fred Specifications can change.

Guðmundur Of course, but … this is … this is …

Bobby *swivels in his chair*.

Guðmundur Charles Eames for the Time Life building in New York. We had it flown out especially.

Fred It's a good-looking chair.

Guðmundur It is.

Bobby *swivels the full 360 degrees*.

Fred Bobby?

Bobby I like the chair. The cameras need to move back.

Guðmundur The cameras have been placed for optimal broadcast quality.

Bobby *inspects the pieces on the chessboard*.

Guðmundur *looks at his watch*.

Fred Are we keeping you up?

Guðmundur Not at all.

Bobby (*weighing one of the pieces in his hand*)   Lead weighted?

Guðmundur   Yes.

Bobby   The pieces are fine but I don't like the board ... too much pattern in the stone ... too many spots ... flecks.

Guðmundur   There have been weeks of consultation ... weeks to manufacture ...

Bobby   Have another one made.

Guðmundur   We cannot delay for the sake of the board!

Fred   No one is suggesting a delay.

Guðmundur   Requesting a new board is tantamount to ...!

Fred   How long would it take?

Guðmundur   I'm not a stonemason.

Fred   Perhaps you should talk to one.

Guðmundur   This was commissioned specifically.

Fred   Commission another.

Guðmundur   Now?!

Fred   Why not?

Guðmundur   It is two o'clock in the morning.

Fred   Do you require a break ... perhaps some coffee? Or do you want to speak to your stonemason?

Bobby   The table needs to be an inch lower.

Guðmundur   I need to make some calls.

GAME ONE

SPASSKY (white) vs FISCHER (black)

Nimzo-Indian

1.d4 Nf6 2.c4 e6 3.Nf3 d5 4.Nc3 Bb4 5.e3 0-0 6.Bd3 c5 7.0-0 Nc6 8.a3 Ba5 9.Ne2 dxc4 10.Bxc4 Bb6 11.dxc5 Qxd1 12.Rxd1 Bxc5

13.b4 Be7 14.Bb2 Bd7 15.Rac1 Rfd8 16.Ned4 Nxd4 17.Nxd4 Ba4
18.Bb3 Bxb3 19.Nxb3 Rxd1+ 20.Rxd1 Rc8 21.Kf1 Kf8 22.Ke2
Ne4 23.Rc1 Rxc1 24.Bxc1 f6 25.Na5 Nd6 26.Kd3 Bd8 27.Nc4
Bc7 28.Nxd6 Bxd6 29.b5 Bxh2 30.g3 h5 31.Ke2 h4 32.Kf3 Ke7
33.Kg2 hxg3 34.fxg3 Bxg3 35.Kxg3 Kd6 36.a4 Kd5 37.Ba3 Ke4
38.Bc5 a6 39.b6 f5 40.Kh4 f4 41.exf4 Kxf4 42.Kh5 Kf5 43.Be3
Ke4 44.Bf2 Kf5 45.Bh4 e5 46.Bg5 e4 47.Be3 Kf6 48.Kg4 Ke5
49.Kg5 Kd5 50.Kf5 a5 51.Bf2 g5 52.Kxg5 Kc4 53.Kf5 Kb4
54.Kxe4 Kxa4 55.Kd5 Kb5 56.Kd6

Bobby *resigns.* **Boris** *wins.*

BORIS SPASSKY (USSR)

1

ROBERT FISCHER (USA)

0

GAME TWO

FISCHER (white) vs SPASSKY (black)

Fischer *does not show.*

Forfeit. **Boris** *wins.*

BORIS SPASSKY (USSR)

2

ROBERT FISCHER (USA)

0

6.

The Loftleiðir Hotel, Reykjavík.

The restaurant is empty but for **Bobby** *and* **Lina** *Grumette.*

Bobby *is tucking into a big bowl of ice cream.*

Lina The way it is being reported ... dear me ...

Bobby What are they saying?

Lina Oh … unnecessary things.

Bobby Like?

Lina Enough for me to buy a plane ticket.

Bobby I haven't read them.

Lina Best that you don't.

Bobby Okay. (*Beat.*) What do they say?

Lina It's the darnedest thing … and strikes me as decidedly un-American …

Bobby What are they saying?

Lina Oh, ignore the press, Bobby. I am here now … that is all that matters.

Bobby You want to watch a movie?

Lina If that's what you want to do.

Bobby The hotel has a screening room.

Lina If that's what you need. (*Beat.*) You're like a son to me, Bobby.

Bobby What is it … Hollywood to Reykjavík … four thousand miles?

Lina Four and a half.

Bobby Must've been a long flight. (*Beat.*) Spassky says that I have insulted the Soviet people. Good. They're due a few insults. They should show respect.

Lina How are they not showing you respect?

Bobby I have twenty successive wins behind me. Grandmasters … former world champions …

Lina But not Spassky.

Bobby They do not want me to win.

Lina Why would any opponent want you to win?

Bobby Because I am the better player.

Lina You must prove it.

Bobby I don't have to prove anything.

Lina The World Championship must be won. It is not simply bestowed.

Bobby I am the better player.

Lina Not if you leave. Not if you pick up your ball and go home.

Bobby I will not run from Spassky ... I will play Spassky ... bring him here ... set up the board and pieces ... I will show him who is the world champion.

Lina Then why not play in the arena?

Bobby Because I might not win.

Lina Bobby ... my dearest, Bobby ... I believe in you.

Bobby Do you think I lack in confidence? Have you ever known me lack the confidence? The whole Soviet machine is an unfair advantage. They are in cahoots ... all of the Russian players. They throw games ... they go soft on each other ... they manipulate the rankings. A Russian plays a Russian and there's no fight ... no struggle ... because who wins and who loses is decided in the Kremlin long before the game actually begins.

Lina Then why partake in something so corrupt?

Bobby It is the World Championship. It is my title by rights.

Lina Not until you win it.

Bobby The lights are too bright. The audience is too close.

Lina You worry too much about that sort of thing.

Bobby Did you bring what I asked for?

Lina Yes. You want them now?

Bobby Yes.

Lina *gets a stack of comics out of her bag.*

Bobby *looks through the comics – Tarzan, Superman.*

Lina Are those the right ones?

Bobby *nods.*

Lina Tarzan.

Bobby Yes.

Lina Superman.

Bobby Yes.

Lina How long have we known each other, Bobby?

Bobby Since I was seventeen.

Lina Twelve years. A chess club is nothing without its resident wunderkind. You will miss it. You think you will not. You think the label 'child prodigy' patronises you. You will be judged as a man in this contest. Not as a curiosity … not as a savant. I wonder how much that scares you.

Bobby I am not scared.

Lina No?

Bobby No.

Lina Many would call you scared. Many would read your actions as those of a frightened child.

Bobby *furious.*

Lina Go ahead … stamp your feet … throw a tantrum. No one will see. No one will know but your Lina. The first game … you could have called a draw. Spassky would've accepted.

Bobby No.

Lina (*looks at the comics*) A lord raised by apes. An alien god raised by corn-belt yokels. (*Beat.*) How is your mother? She must be proud.

Bobby She doesn't matter. (*Beat.*) Do you know who is on his team?

Lina Who?

Bobby Nikolai Krogius … Iivo Nei … Efim Geller.

Lina I know Krogius. I know Geller.

Bobby Efim Geller is a Jew.

Lina What are you going to do?

Bobby I don't like the cameras. They make me feel sick.

Lina How so?

Bobby The closeness of them. I want to get on a plane.

Lina You want to run away.

Bobby It would be a boycott. It would be a protest.

Lina It would be running away.

Bobby I know Henry Kissinger.

Lina You do?

Bobby He calls me on the telephone.

Lina He wants you to win. All anyone wants is for you to do what you do best. Everyone is going out of their way to make you feel at home.

Bobby Homes can be dirty. Homes can be boring. I like hotels.

Lina The Russians won't want to win by default. The game has never been bigger. That you threw away the second game … it proves to them that you are not bluffing. You have never been in a stronger position.

Bobby I won't go back into that arena.

Lina The game is not the arena. *You* are the game.

Bobby *nods.*

Act One 273

Lina So you will stay?

Bobby *nods.*

Lina I want to hear you say it.

Bobby I will stay.

Lina Good. Have you finished your ice cream?

Bobby Yes. Thank you.

Lina Now ... tell me ... what movie should we watch?

7.

The Loftleiðir Hotel.

Boris, **Efim**, **Iivo** *and* **Nikolai** – *a chessboard in the middle of the room.*

Efim It's a broom-cupboard.

Nikolai It's not a broom-cupboard.

Efim Fischer wants to hold the World Championship in a broom-cupboard.

Iivo It's currently set up for table-tennis.

Nikolai The Federation has agreed in principle.

Efim His number one complaint is of the noise levels in the arena ... the distraction. This alternative room backs onto a main road! It's a joke.

Nikolai It's not about the noise ... it's about control.

Boris It makes no difference to me. I can play with frozen fingers and an empty stomach ... I can play in a cupboard.

Efim You shouldn't have to.

Nikolai He's trying to dispense with the ceremony ... the trappings of the occasion.

Efim I get that. How can we use it?

Nikolai We can keep him uncomfortable. Discomfort makes him petulant ... makes him bratty.

Efim You have the move list for the first game?

Iivo Of course. (*Finds his notebook.*)

Efim Set up move 29.

Boris We're in the middle of a game.

Efim *takes* **Iivo**'s *notebook and starts rearranging the pieces.*

Iivo At least let me make a note of ...

Efim You were going to lose.

Boris We'll play again later.

Efim Fischer's move ... Bishop to h2.

Boris His Bishop is trapped ... he can take two pawns only ...

Nikolai You were playing for the draw.

Iivo Maybe he wasn't expecting you to do that.

Efim It's more that he doesn't respect it.

Nikolai He's not interested in being forced into a stalemate.

Boris Is he purposefully throwing the game ...?

Efim He thinks winning on points is as bad as losing. He's looking for the knockout. Let's assume the mistake was planned.

Nikolai We can't assume anything.

Efim For the sake of argument. The 'mistake' was planned ... the forfeiture ... the cupboard ... it is all planned. So if we subvert his will ... if we demand to play the arena ... with cameras, with audience ... what has he gained? Distraction? Unnecessary negotiation? Deflection? Maybe he wants to exhaust us mentally with all his bullshit.

Boris It's working. (*To* **Iivo**.) Smoke a cigarette with me.

Iivo (*produces a pack of cigarettes*)   These ones have a little camel on the packet.

Boris *amused.*

Nikolai   You should go to bed.

Boris   I haven't eaten.

Nikolai   We'll order room-service.

Boris   I'm not hungry.

Nikolai   Go next door. Lie down. Order yourself some room service. Eat some food.

Efim   Bishop to h2. And the forfeit … in the forfeited game he was playing white … he would've opened with the advantage …

Iivo   He wants to …

Efim   It shouldn't matter what he *wants*. It's the moves … the moves not the man. His moves are stronger in the middle and end games … but his openings are predictable. Open with the Queen's pawn and he'll play a King's Indian defence. He thinks himself a radical, so beat him where he's most conservative.

Boris   What strategies have we got for King's Indian?

Nikolai   We can work on that.

Boris   I won't sleep.

Nikolai   Stare at the ceiling … watch television … have a bath. Turn off your chess brain.

Boris   I might go for a swim.

Nikolai   Good. Do it. We'll crunch strategy and let you know what results.

Boris *nods and exits.*

Silence.

Iivo   Have you ever played table-tennis?

Nikolai It is not a serious pursuit.

Efim 'Ping-pong'.

Iivo (*to* **Efim**) They have a table downstairs – if you fancy a game?

Efim I think I'll leave it to the Chinese.

Iivo Why do they invest in table-tennis of all things?

Nikolai They want to be seen as swift, precise, skilled ... and the best propaganda for that is to lead the world in table-tennis. Russia has marked as its territory chess, ballet and circus. Chess is the intellect ... ballet the art ... and circus is gymnastic, physical prowess. This is how we choose to lead – in brain, heart and body.

Iivo Chess doesn't strike me as an especially Soviet game. If the pawns would take their own castles ... overthrow their bishops ... drag the king and queen to the cellar and shoot them in the face, then maybe ...

Efim Iivo ...

Iivo What? I'd say the same at home.

Efim But of course you would, Comrade.

Iivo And the Americans? What do they invest in?

Nikolai Hollywood. They are the world leaders in escapism. They are the kings of Fantasy Island. I think we are happy enough to cede that territory. Boris isn't playing a grandmaster; he's facing a movie-star. (*Beat.*) Fischer is testing his boundaries ... like a tiger in a new enclosure ... like a horse in a field ... but he's not getting the pushback he expected ... the fence isn't electrified after all ... the checks and balances of the Chess Federation are, in the end, hollow threats.

Efim He's waiting for someone to say 'no'.

Iivo So we say 'no'. We say 'play in the arena in the proper manner'.

Nikolai And be seen as the rigid, inflexible, Politburo automatons they already believe us to be? He's a 'maverick' ... a freewheeling, rule-breaking, Easy Rider. If we win by enforcing the rules, we lose.

Iivo (*starts resetting the board*) I have some ideas on how we should approach a King's Indian ...

Nikolai Why don't you go and join Boris? He's exhausted. Keep him from drowning.

Efim We can handle this.

Iivo If you think that's where I'll be of most use. Why don't I just show you ...?

Efim You're a sparring partner, not a strategist. Leave this to us.

Iivo *nods, exits.*

Efim *and* **Nikolai** *sit down at the board and are quickly immersed in strategy.*

8.

Laugardalshöll arena.

The back room.

The table, chairs and board have been reset here.

Guðmundur *is up a ladder. He is wrapping a blanket around a small CCTV camera mounted high in a corner.*

Lothar *paces around the room.*

Guðmundur Can you hear that?

Lothar No.

Guðmundur Good.

Lothar I couldn't hear it before.

Guðmundur What does it look like?

Lothar Like you've wrapped a camera in a blanket.

Guðmundur I need to check the feed … make sure it's not obscuring … do you think he will notice?

Lothar Are you trying to camouflage …?

Guðmundur No, just dampen any sound … or perhaps … the magnetic-field. Should I wrap the camera in plastic?

Lothar Would that do anything?

Guðmundur I am not a scientist.

Lothar Neither is Fischer.

Guðmundur Tinfoil?

Boris *enters.* **Lothar** *shakes his hand.*

Boris We are all set?

Lothar I hope so.

Guðmundur The clock is due to start at 5pm.

Boris Thank you.

Guðmundur *takes his ladder and goes.* **Boris** *looks up at the CCTV camera.*

Lothar There are a thousand people in the arena. We have set up a screen. And one in the press lounge.

Boris *waves at the camera.*

Lothar It is not broadcasting yet.

Boris *sits at the table.*

Lothar *opens a window. The noise of traffic and children playing bleeds in from outside.*

Lothar Does that bother you?

Boris *shakes his head.*

Lothar Thank you.

Boris I wonder what you will concede to him next? Perhaps I will have to come dressed as a clown.

Silence.

Lothar How are you finding your hotel?

Bobby *enters.* **Lothar** *proffers a hand.* **Bobby** *ignores him. He looks up at the camera.*

Bobby 'Removed' – do you understand the word?

Lothar Yes, but …

Bobby I want the cameras removed.

Lothar As per your request, there is only one remaining camera …

Bobby That was not my 'request' … I asked for *no* cameras …

Lothar … and so we compromise with one.

Bobby You tell me the cameras are removed … they are not removed … therefore you are a liar and I cannot deal with you.

Lothar It is out of your eye-line … it is hidden from …

Bobby I can hear it … I can feel it …

Lothar There is no discernible … detectable … difference in the decibel level of …

Bobby Your machines are faulty … if they cannot detect what I can clearly hear … what use are they?

Lothar I am telling you that there is no difference between the cameras being present and not.

Bobby When electricity runs through a wire an electromagnetic field is created.

Lothar I really don't think …

Bobby Do you deny this?

Lothar   Perhaps if Comrade Spassky was complaining of something similar ...

Bobby   That is not likely.

Lothar   We are not removing the camera.

Bobby   I call bullshit. I call corruption. The Chess Federation is a Communist front.

Lothar   We have commitments ... we have contracts ... broadcast rights ... television ...

Bobby   I do not care about television. I am the reason people are watching.

Lothar   I thought you wanted the money?

Bobby   I want what is mine. I want what is due.

Lothar   Deals have been made. I am not going to renege on ... it is not making any noise ... no noise at all ...

Bobby   Shut up.

Lothar   Bobby ...

Bobby *spits on* **Lothar**.

Lothar *shocked, wipes the saliva from his face.*

Boris *stands.*

Lothar *motions for* **Boris** *to sit.*

Bobby   Don't look at him ... look at me.

Lothar   Bobby ... please ...

Boris   This is insane.

Lothar   ... one second ... please ...

Boris   I am returning to my hotel. When I return ... *if* I return ... it will be to the arena as agreed and as is proper.

Lothar   There is no need for ...

Bobby If you move the game back into the arena, I will take a hammer and smash the board to pieces!

Lothar Gentlemen ... please! Boris ... you made a promise ... to play in this room. Bobby ... you must be kind. No one wants another forfeited game ... sit ... come and sit ... Boris ... will you sit?

Boris *sits.*

Lothar Bobby ... sit ... please ...

Lothar *leads* **Bobby** *to the table. He sits.*

Guðmundur *enters.*

Guðmundur Are we ready to begin?

Lothar Gentlemen?

Guðmundur Whenever you are ready.

GAME THREE

SPASSKY (white) vs FISCHER (black)

Modern Benoni

1.d4 Nf6 2.c4 e6 3.Nf3 c5 4.d5 exd5 5.cxd5 d6 6.Nc3 g6 7.Nd2 Nbd7 8.e4 Bg7 9.Be2 0-0 10.0-0 Re8 11.Qc2 Nh5 12.Bxh5 gxh5 13.Nc4 Ne5 14.Ne3 Qh4 15.Bd2 Ng4 16.Nxg4 hxg4 17.Bf4 Qf6 18.g3 Bd7 19.a4 b6 20.Rfe1 a6 21.Re2 b5 22.Rae1 Qg6 23.b3 Re7 24.Qd3 Rb8 25.axb5 axb5 26.b4 c4 27.Qd2 Rbe8 28.Re3 h5 29.R3e2 Kh7 30.Re3 Kg8 31.R3e2 Bxc3 32.Qxc3 Rxe4 33.Rxe4 Rxe4 34.Rxe4 Qxe4 35.Bh6 Qg6 36.Bc1 Qb1 37.Kf1 Bf5 38.Ke2 Qe4+ 39.Qe3 Qc2+ 40.Qd2 Qb3 41.Qd4 Bd3+

Boris *resigns.* **Bobby** *wins.*

BORIS SPASSKY (USSR)

2

ROBERT FISCHER (USA)

1

9.

The Loftleiðir Hotel.

Efim, **Nikolai** *and* **Iivo** *around a chessboard.*

Iivo Boris opens with d4.

Efim Fischer plays Knight f6 … and we think we're in for a King's Indian opening … because … because that's what Fischer plays … has always played … and Boris is prepared … has practiced for this …

Iivo Boris follows with his pawn to c4.

Efim But Fischer doesn't want to do that … he plays e6 …

Iivo Boris responds with Knight f3 …

Efim … and we're no longer in King's Indian … we're playing Modern Benoni.

Iivo It's not in Fisher's top ten.

Efim It's not in his repertoire.

Nikolai He gets a reputation for playing King's Indian … spends his entire career playing King's Indian … his opponent studies King's Indian … so when he reaches the World Championship he plays Modern Benoni … a sequence of moves he's never been known to play before … a once in a career manoeuvre. Bobby Fischer has been playing this game his entire life.

Iivo People don't think that far in advance.

Nikolai Maybe *you* don't.

Efim We have to throw out all of our books … our notes … everything we thought we understood about him as a player …

Iivo Look at move eleven … Knight to h5 … no one plays like that.

Efim He's hugging the sides … he attacks the centre from the sides.

Nikolai One of the first things we learn is that to dominate the game you must control the four central squares ...

Efim He's not just breaking the rules ... any fool child can do that ... he has spent his life mastering technique in order to now disassemble it. He's won. If we play him at the board ... he's won.

Iivo Boris is still leading by two games to one.

Nikolai It only takes one bad game.

Efim We need to get him back in the arena.

Boris *enters.*

Boris I know I played poorly.

Nikolai I wouldn't say that.

Boris It's as though we are playing by different rules.

Iivo The knight is still the knight ... the rook is still the rook ...

Boris He is at war with us.

Nikolai Maybe.

Boris I am not a soldier.

Nikolai No one's asking you to be.

Boris Have you spoken to the Kremlin recently? (*Beat.*) He yelled at Lothar Schmid ... he spat at him ... he told him to shut up.

Iivo When was this?

Boris Before the game. I should've walked ... I should've stood up and left ... a letter to the federation and the first flight to Moscow.

Nikolai Why didn't you?

Boris I wanted to play.

Iivo You can't claim a forfeit now.

Boris I don't want to claim a forfeit.

Efim This is such a fucking debacle.

Boris Put this board away. I can't look at it. (*Beat.*) He's a boy really … and all boys need boundaries … but the poor little fucker is brilliant, so we're all too scared to tell him 'no'. I doubt he even knows what he represents … what *this* represents … the whole thing … he is America … I am Russia … but I am a poor emissary for Communism. I am not even a Party member.

Nikolai And you think Fischer is a good example of Americanism?

Efim He is ruthless … self-obsessed … paranoid …

Boris I can only represent myself.

Nikolai You do not get to choose what you represent.

Boris So I am to be paraded around like Gagarin … Nureyev … Pavlichenko …?

Nikolai You think you won't be put on a stamp if you win? Pavlichenko … she and her rifle had to claim 309 Nazi scalps for that honour. You need only claim one American.

Boris I am not a political man. I have no desire to be a political man.

Efim The times we live in don't allow for that.

Boris I'm still ahead.

Efim Yes.

Boris Two games out of three.

Efim No one's saying you're not doing well.

Boris I'm done accommodating his theatrics.

Nikolai Sure. We get the cameras back … get the front rows reinstated …

Boris The cameras aren't part of the game.

Nikolai They really are.

Boris I don't want to win by tricks.

Efim There are no prizes for sportsmanship.

Nikolai Do you think he won't be trying to keep you off balance?

Boris Perhaps we should kidnap his dog … threaten to wring its neck … that'll distract him.

Nikolai I'm not saying that.

Iivo I don't think I'd be okay with killing a dog.

Efim No one's asking you to.

Nikolai What you want from him … an honest game … he will not give it to you.

Boris Then why am I even playing him at all?

Nikolai Because his dishonest game cannot be seen to win.

Iivo What breed is it?

Efim What?

Iivo His dog. What breed? If we're going to kill it …

Boris Why would that make a difference?

Iivo I'm not sure.

Nikolai He doesn't have a dog!

Efim I'll draft a letter to Lothar Schmid. Plain … but forceful … put the tournament back in the arena … return to the conventions of championship play.

Iivo They may not go for it.

Efim Of course they will.

Iivo They want to keep Fischer onside.

Boris Stop it … stop it … this is nonsense.

Nikolai Boris …

Boris I am not going to buy into Fischer's self-created mythos. He is a man-baby with a startling aptitude – nothing more. He is so intimidated by the whole thing that he hides in his hotel room. Yet he is also so monumentally arrogant that he demands to relocate the World Championship to a broom-cupboard … and we cave … FIDE cave. He demands that we treat him as some special case. No. No games but chess. Understood?

10.

In the countryside outside of Reykjavík.

Bobby *is chasing a sheep. Sæmundur* (**Sæmi-Rokk**) *Pálsson, a policeman, is watching.*

Bobby They can run fast … faster than you think …!

Sæmi-Rokk And jump.

Bobby Yes!

Sæmi-Rokk Good at jumping. Good at landing.

Bobby Stupid animals.

Sæmi-Rokk I don't think so.

Bobby They are. They are stupid.

Sæmi-Rokk Not as smart as pigs or dogs maybe …

Bobby One turns left; they all turn left.

Sæmi-Rokk Safety in numbers.

Bobby *shrugs*.

Sæmi-Rokk You want to go back to the hotel?

Bobby No.

Sæmi-Rokk It is getting late.

Bobby What time is it?

Sæmi-Rokk Nearly one.

Bobby In the morning?

Sæmi-Rokk Yes.

Bobby The sun is up.

Sæmi-Rokk Barely.

Bobby This country is a joke.

Sæmi-Rokk We are not responsible for the sun. Your jumper is too thin.

Bobby I will run around if I am cold.

Sæmi-Rokk I have a coat in my car.

Bobby You are not my mother.

Sæmi-Rokk You want me to leave?

Bobby I did not ask for a bodyguard.

Sæmi-Rokk I am not that.

Bobby I did not request a security detail.

Sæmi-Rokk I am just here to be of help.

Bobby Who are you working for?

Sæmi-Rokk Reykjavík Police.

Bobby Yes, but … who else?

Sæmi-Rokk No one else.

Bobby The Chess Federation?

Sæmi-Rokk No.

Bobby FBI … CIA … KGB …?

Sæmi-Rokk You think I am a spy?

Bobby You could be. Why not?

Sæmi-Rokk I don't own a tuxedo.

Bobby What is your name again?

Sæmi-Rokk Sæmundur Pálsson. Everyone calls me Sæmi-Rokk.

Bobby Why?

Sæmi-Rokk I am a good dancer.

Bobby Sammy. Okay, Sammy. You play chess?

Sæmi-Rokk Yes, but ...

Bobby But ...?

Sæmi-Rokk I'm not going to play you.

Bobby But you do play?

Sæmi-Rokk It is not my game. I know the rules, sure ... I am Icelandic ... the winters are long ... six months of the year is dark. When we're not having sex or making music, we play chess. It passes the time. But no ... I was never any good.

Bobby No?

Sæmi-Rokk No.

Bobby What is your game?

Sæmi-Rokk Handball. I was goalkeeper in the national team.

Bobby We don't have handball in New York. We have baseball ... football ...

Sæmi-Rokk Handball is like football ... but with hands.

Bobby We use our hands in football.

Sæmi-Rokk Well, that makes no sense.

Bobby What else?

Sæmi-Rokk I do judo.

Bobby Judo?

Sæmi-Rokk I am a gold medal winner in the Icelandic championship.

Bobby Show me some.

Sæmi-Rokk I'm not going to do that.

Bobby Show me some judo.

Sæmi-Rokk No.

Bobby Throw me on the ground.

Sæmi-Rokk What if I broke your arm … your fingers … how would you play? The Icelandic economy would collapse. I would be charged with treason.

Bobby I could refuse to play until you demonstrated some judo.

Sæmi-Rokk You would not do that.

Bobby No?

Sæmi-Rokk I cannot tell if you are joking. (*Takes up a judo stance.*) Stand here … like this … hands here and here … okay?

Bobby Okay.

Sæmi-Rokk Ready?

Bobby Yes.

Sæmi-Rokk I am going to throw you to the ground.

Bobby Do it already!

Sæmi-Rokk I can't.

Bobby Do it!

Sæmi-Rokk (*sweeps **Bobby**'s legs from under him and deposits him on the ground*) There you go … judo.

Bobby You use these moves on criminals?

Sæmi-Rokk I could do.

Bobby Have you though?

Sæmi-Rokk We shouldn't be chasing sheep.

Bobby Do you like movies?

Sæmi-Rokk I do. I like James Bond ... *Thunderball* ... *On Her Majesty's Secret Service* ...

Bobby Not for me.

Sæmi-Rokk That is a shame.

Bobby *Planet of the Apes.*

Sæmi-Rokk Those are good films.

Bobby We are going to be friends.

Sæmi-Rokk Okay.

Bobby Bobby and Sammy.

Sæmi-Rokk If you like.

Bobby Can I ask you something ... as a friend?

Sæmi-Rokk Of course.

Bobby Do you think I've broken him?

Sæmi-Rokk Spassky?

Bobby Of course Boris Spassky – who else?

Sæmi-Rokk I thought perhaps you meant the sheep?

Bobby *laughs – much to his surprise.*

Sæmi-Rokk I could not say if he is broken, but you definitively won that last game.

Bobby Yeah ... I don't care about that.

Sæmi-Rokk You do not play to win?

Bobby No.

Sæmi-Rokk That will come as a surprise to ... everyone ... the entire chess community.

Bobby (*scoffs*) 'Community'.

Sæmi-Rokk For someone who is not trying to win, you seem to be doing very well for yourself.

Bobby I play so that I don't lose.

Sæmi-Rokk Is that different?

Bobby Yes.

Sæmi-Rokk It is subtle.

Bobby It is a distinct difference.

Sæmi-Rokk Okay.

Bobby Winning is fine ... very nice ... good. But losing is a devastation. I play so that I don't lose. And I don't lose when the other guy is toast. The moment when you break someone ... when you break their ego ... I like that. You see their confidence wither. You take their bravado from them ... their mask ... and you see them for the nothing they are ... and they see it too ... they see themselves for the first time. Play me at chess and I will reveal your true self. (*Beat.*) The only Bond movie I've seen is *From Russia with Love.*

Sæmi-Rokk It is a good one. You like it because of the chess?

Bobby I didn't say that I liked it. The chess scene is wrong. They based the board on Spassky versus Bronstein, Leningrad 1960. Only they removed pawns on c5 and d4 ... which might have been better for the camera ... better for the shot ... but it made a nonsense of the game.

Sæmi-Rokk Are you all the same ... playing not to lose?

Bobby Are who all the same?

Sæmi-Rokk Chess players.

Bobby I am not one of them. They don't matter.

Sæmi-Rokk You are not a chess player?

Bobby Not in the way that they are. It is a cabal. They do not respect me.

Sæmi-Rokk You are playing the world championship ... you are the hero of chess.

Bobby No. Had I been a musical prodigy ... with violin or piano ... they would respect the work. They would respect the hours. Had I been proficient at football ... at baseball ... that would be best ... that would be welcome ... because it would confirm that the poor man is the working man ... the physical man ... the grunt labour. But chess is a sport of the brain ... of the intellect ... and these assholes like to equate intellect with education. So a poor boy from Brooklyn must be dismissed as a savant ... a freak ... a curiosity. A horse who counts out to ten with his hoof. A parrot that greets you 'good morning'. Parade me like the dog-faced boy. Parade me like the gimps and the geeks and the bearded lady. 'Remarkable', they say, 'Extraordinary'. But never as an equal. Never as a brother. So it is not enough to beat them. It is not enough to be counted among them. You must destroy them. There is no room in their world for you. So you must supersede their world. You must be so far above them that their world is nothing but dirt in the grooves of your shoe. Fuck them. Fuck their established structure. (*Beat.*) I'm going to get that sheep.

Sæmi-Rokk Okay.

Bobby Are you going to help?

Sæmi-Rokk Okay.

GAME FOUR

FISCHER (white) vs SPASSKY (black)

Sicilian Sozin

1.e4 c5 2.Nf3 d6 3.d4 cxd4 4.Nxd4 Nf6 5.Nc3 Nc6 6.Bc4 e6 7.Bb3 Be7 8.Be3 0-0 9.0-0 a6 10.f4 Nxd4 11.Bxd4 b5 12.a3 Bb7 13.Qd3 a5 14.e5 dxe5 15.fxe5 Nd7 16.Nxb5 Nc5 17.Bxc5 Bxc5+ 18.Kh1 Qg5 19.Qe2 Rad8 20.Rad1 Rxd1 21.Rxd1 h5 22.Nd6 Ba8 23.Bc4 h4 24.h3 Be3 25.Qg4 Qxe5 26.Qxh4 g5 27.Qg4 Bc5 28.Nb5 Kg7 29.Nd4 Rh8 30.Nf3 Bxf3 31.Qxf3 Bd6 32.Qc3 Qxc3 33.bxc3 Be5 34.Rd7 Kf6 35.Kg1 Bxc3 36.Be2 Be5 37.Kf1 Rc8 38.Bh5 Rc7 39.Rxc7 Bxc7 40.a4 Ke7 41.Ke2 f5 42.Kd3 Be5 43.c4 Kd6 44.Bf7 Bg3 45.c5+

Draw.

BORIS SPASSKY (USSR)

2.5

ROBERT FISCHER (USA)

1.5

GAME FIVE

SPASSKY (white) vs FISCHER (black)

Nimzo-Indian

1.d4 Nf6 2.c4 e6 3.Nc3 Bb4 4.Nf3 c5 5.e3 Nc6 6.Bd3 Bxc3+
7.bxc3 d6 8.e4 e5 9.d5 Ne7 10.Nh4 h6 11.f4 Ng6 12.Nxg6 fxg6
13.fxe5 dxe5 14.Be3 b6 15.0-0 0-0 16.a4 a5 17.Rb1 Bd7 18.Rb2
Rb8 19.Rbf2 Qe7 20.Bc2 g5 21.Bd2 Qe8 22.Be1 Qg6 23.Qd3 Nh5
24.Rxf8+ Rxf8 25.Rxf8+ Kxf8 26.Bd1 Nf4 27.Qc2 Bxa4

Boris *resigns.* **Bobby** *wins.*

BORIS SPASSKY (USSR)

2.5

ROBERT FISCHER (USA)

2.5

GAME SIX

FISCHER (white) vs SPASSKY (black)

Queen's Gambit Declined, Tartakower

1.c4 e6 2.Nf3 d5 3.d4 Nf6 4.Nc3 Be7 5.Bg5 0-0 6.e3 h6 7.Bh4
b6 8.cxd5 Nxd5 9.Bxe7 Qxe7 10.Nxd5 exd5 11.Rc1 Be6 12.Qa4
c5 13.Qa3 Rc8 14.Bb5 a6 15.dxc5 bxc5 16.0-0 Ra7 17.Be2 Nd7
18.Nd4 Qf8 19.Nxe6 fxe6 20.e4 d4 21.f4 Qe7 22.e5 Rb8 23.Bc4
Kh8 24.Qh3 Nf8 25.b3 a5 26.f5 exf5 27.Rxf5 Nh7 28.Rcf1 Qd8
29.Qg3 Re7 30.h4 Rbb7 31.e6 Rbc7 32.Qe5 Qe8 33.a4 Qd8

34.R1f2 Qe8 35.R2f3 Qd8 36.Bd3 Qe8 37.Qe4 Nf6 38.Rxf6 gxf6 39.Rxf6 Kg8 40.Bc4 Kh8 41.Qf4

Boris *resigns.* **Bobby** *wins.* **Boris** *applauds.*

BORIS SPASSKY (USSR)

2.5

ROBERT FISCHER (USA)

3.5

11.

Laugardalshöll arena.

The elevated stage.

The arena is empty.

A large wooden crate has been delivered.

***Max** and* **Guðmundur** *inspect it.*

Max   When did it arrive?

Guðmundur   An hour ago.

Max   Who placed the order?

Guðmundur   The Russians.

Max   Has Fischer got wind of this?

Guðmundur   I don't know.

Max *heavy sigh.*

Guðmundur   With all the concessions afforded to …

Max   Can we get this open?

Guðmundur   Efim Geller has gone in search of a crowbar. (*Beat.*) There is no rule that says that they can't …

Max   I know the rulebook. I am the rulebook.

Guðmundur If we send it away, the Russians might …

Max The Russians won't do anything.

Guðmundur They have threatened to withdraw from the chess federation …

Max That won't happen.

Guðmundur Hmm.

Max What?

Guðmundur Nothing … it's just … when the Americans threaten the same …

Max The threats are not equally weighted. The Americans have never won the championship – so they lose nothing if they walk. The Soviets, however, are invested to the tune of twenty-six years and ten titles. They can threaten and pout as much as they like but they know and I know that to denounce the federation would invalidate … or worse *diminish* … the titles they historically hold. So no, I do not need to consider the Russians' *feelings* … and yes, I will bend rules to accommodate the Americans … because to the world Bobby Fischer is already the champion. For America to walk and Fischer to not claim his crown, well … that would rather diminish *us*.

Guðmundur I just worry for our neutrality … our impartiality …

Max Yes, yes … all very nice … as everyone abandons us … as the televisions are turned off … once they have all gone home … in our insignificance … our neutrality will be a soothing cup of cocoa.

Fred *enters.*

Fred This is outrageous.

Max Mr Cramer …

Fred This is a direct violation of our agreement … we must be consulted on any change to the set up … especially regards to the staging area …

Max There is nothing to say that a player cannot request an alternative ...

Fred It is unacceptable that Mister Fischer has no right of veto to any alteration to any item within the arena.

Max This is Comrade Spassky's space as much as it is Fischer's. We have changed the board at Bobby's request ... we have made alterations to the table ... to the proximity of the pot-plants ...

Fred ... and the Russians could have rejected any of those if they so wished.

Max Fred ... please ... don't demean yourself.

Efim *and* **Iivo** *enter.* **Efim** *is carrying a crowbar.*

Max Are these games really necessary?

Efim Comrade Spassky has requested a new chair.

Iivo He finds his current one too restrictive.

Max (*to Fred*) Do you have any objections to Spassky replacing his chair?

Fred I will have to consult with my team.

Efim *and* **Iivo** *break open the crate.*

Efim I am sure Mister Fischer will find no cause for complaint.

The new chair revealed. It is exactly the same make and model as **Fischer***'s swivel-chair.*

Fred What is this?

Efim Spassky's new chair.

Fred It's a replica ...

Efim It's the same design.

Fred We object.

Iivo It's the same chair.

Fred We object!

Iivo What possible objection could you …?

Fred There is no way he will stand for it.

Iivo … could he possibly have to us using the exact same type of …?

Fred Max …

Efim If it's good enough for the Americans, it's good enough for us.

Fred You think you are so clever … so smart. It's an obvious attempt to …

Iivo … to what?

Efim If anything it's a flattery.

Fred How am I supposed to sell this to him?

Iivo Comrade Spassky admired the chair. He admired its swivel.

Efim We are within our rights and within championship norms to replace our chair should we so desire. And we do. We do desire it.

Fred This is a blatant attempt to unsettle …

Iivo After all Fischer has done!

Max Honestly, Fred, no. What would you have me do? (*Beat.*) The longer you leave it before you tell him …

Fred *nods.*

Efim *grins.*

Fred You needn't look so smug, you piece of shit.

Fred *heads to the exit, but at the last moment, decides to turn and rush the stage. He grabs onto the new chair and seeks to drag it from the arena. He is physically restrained by* **Guðmundur**, **Iivo** *and* **Max**.

12.

Naval Air Station Keflavik.

A US airbase thirty miles Southwest of Reykjavík.

A bowling alley.

Bobby, **Sæmi-Rokk** *and* **William** *Lombardy are bowling.*

A table with burgers, fries and milkshakes. **William** *has a pocket chessboard set up and is playing a game against himself in between throws.*

William ... and Benjamin Franklin responds: 'I see that my king is in check, but I won't defend him. Had he been a good king such as yours then he would deserve the protection of his subjects ... but no ... this king is a tyrant and has cost them more than he is worth. Take him, if you please ... I can do without him ... and I will fight out the rest of the game as a republic.'

Sæmi-Rokk If you start changing the rules then you are no longer playing the same game.

William The game is manmade ... the rules are manmade ... and can be unmade or remade as man sees fit.

Sæmi-Rokk But there must be agreement.

William If there are rules then there is ambiguity ... if there is ambiguity then we need interpretation.

Sæmi-Rokk So speaks a man of God.

William What gave it away?

Sæmi-Rokk The dog collar.

William I was joking.

Sæmi-Rokk So was I.

William Right.

Bobby Talk about something else.

Sæmi-Rokk Sorry.

Bobby *bowls.*

William Bobby and I don't necessarily agree on religious matters. For example, I – as a Roman Catholic – believe in papal infallibility and transubstantiation. Bobby – as a member of Southern California's Worldwide Church of God – believes that Jesus will return to us perched on the back of a nuclear warhead.

Sæmi-Rokk (*to Bobby*)   You believe this?

Bobby   I find it interesting.

Sæmi-Rokk *bowls.*

William   We try not to talk about religion.

Sæmi-Rokk   When is this supposed to happen … Jesus … the second coming … nuclear apocalypse?

Bobby   1975.

William   Three years to go. Tick tock tick tock. I guess we'll just have to wait and see.

Bobby *steps up to the lane.*

Sæmi-Rokk   Oh … Bobby … I think it's Father Lombardy's turn …

William *shakes his head to say: it doesn't matter.*

Bobby *bowls.*

Sæmi-Rokk *bowls.*

William *steps up to the lane.*

Bobby (*studying William's chessboard*)   That's a mistake.

William   Hmm?

Bobby   You're sacrificing your pawn to no good advantage.

William   I'm trying something. Leave me alone. (*Bowls.*) Are you a religious man, Mr Palsson?

Sæmi-Rokk (*shrugs*)   I'm a Protestant if I am anything.

Bobby (*the chessboard*)   If you put pressure on the black rook you'll force your opponent into a mistake.

William   I am playing against myself.

Bobby Then you're going to lose. (*Bowls.*)

Bobby *is not very good at bowling.*

Sæmi-Rokk Here ... let me show you ... (*Takes a bowling ball and takes up a stance at the lane.*) It's all about your approach and position ... you want your front foot in line with that central dot ... two inches back from the foul line ... approach from about five steps back ... keep your centre of gravity low and ...

Bobby It doesn't matter.

Sæmi-Rokk What doesn't?

Bobby Approach ... stance ... position ...

Sæmi-Rokk I'm just showing you ... if you want to avoid the gutter ...

Bobby I don't care about the gutter.

Sæmi-Rokk ... if you want to strike the pins ...

Bobby I throw this heavy ball to exercise my arm ... so that I am in better physical shape ... so that I am physically exercised ... so that I may raise my heart rate ... so that I may sleep deeper ... so that I can play better chess. I'm not interested in strikes or spares or gutters ... I am not interested in the pins at all. I'm done. Drive me to the hotel.

William We're supposed to be analysing Spassky's openings.

Bobby It doesn't matter.

William You've had a good run, but Boris knows how to win a tournament.

Bobby No. I sit with him at the table and you can see ... it's gone ... in his eyes ... it's gone. I've broken him. But you're right in that I'm not quite finished ... I still need to humiliate him.

William At least let's discuss strategy for five minutes.

Bobby Bill – you play like a house. What have you got to teach me?

William Unlike you I've actually won against Boris Spassky.

Bobby Do you think you'd win against him today?

William *he knows he wouldn't.*

Bobby Sammy – let's go.

William I am your second ... your support ... use me ... bounce ideas off me ... I am a resource ... and I am the closest you have to an equal in the American game. Spassky likes to sacrifice ... he likes to throw away a piece to no discernible advantage ... just to derail his opponent ... you know this ... so let's talk about it ... let's talk about how not to be distracted ...

Bobby I doubt he'll be in a state to deploy psychology.

William A few days ago, you were cowering in your room like a frightened child.

Bobby (*furious*) I am not a child!

William Oh so it's some 'master strategy'? That nonsense may fly in the papers, but not with those who know you ... those of us who see your hands shake.

Bobby I don't believe in psychology – I believe in good moves.

William Then show me.

Bobby (*picks up a bishop from* **William**'s *board*) What is this piece called?

William Excuse me?

Bobby What is this piece called?

William It's a bishop.

Bobby How does it move?

William You know how it moves.

Bobby Tell me.

William Diagonally.

Bobby (*picks another piece from the board*) And this?

William A rook.

Bobby And how does it move?

William *stubborn silence.*

Bobby (*throws pieces at* **William**) If you're going to treat me like a novice, treat me like a fucking novice.

William Calm down.

Bobby Suck my dick.

Sæmi-Rokk The man's a priest …

William It's alright …

Bobby … then he's a puppet. Puppets and vampires … feeding off my energy … scratching around for that reflected glory … junkies twitching for it … or it's fingers in all things … levers and strings … are you my shadow-man … reporting to your elders … your cabal … whose familiar are you? You're a joke. I've made you, William Lombardy. I've fucking made you.

Silence.

William Mr Palsson …?

Sæmi-Rokk Yes, Father.

William Will you ensure he takes a bath tonight?

Bobby Stop it.

William Lay out a fresh suit and a clean shirt for tomorrow.

Bobby I told you to stop it.

William Encourage him to put a brush through his hair. He is representing America on the world stage.

Bobby I only represent myself.

William It's laughable if you believe that.

Bobby *upends the table.*

William *calm.*

Bobby *fuming*.

Sæmi-Rokk *begins to tidy*.

William Why don't you wait for Bobby in the car, Mr Palsson?

Sæmi-Rokk *exits*.

William There was a time when I beat you at every game … week in week out … we'd sit down at the board … Jack Collins' house … and I would trounce you. We came up together … those quiet rooms in the clubs in the brownstones … the old Jewish men in the parks. You were twelve years old … I was eighteen. Those old men … they played you for the curiosity … for the novelty. Did I ever play you for the novelty?

Bobby No.

William No, I did not. And though I won those games … I never toyed with you … I never patronised you … I never treated you as a child. And then one day you simply 'got good' and I haven't beaten you since.

Bobby I know it.

William He dines out on that now … 'Jack Collins: Svengali of Chess' … mentor to Lombardy and Fischer … but honestly, we were both well beyond his ability before we put one foot through his door. I bet you my last dime he's loving this … watching you on TV … the coverage in the Times … 'the man who taught Bobby Fischer' … 'taught him everything he knows' …

Bobby *scoffs*.

William We all have our teachers. You were one of mine. I think I can say I was one of yours. So let's put away this bullshit, please. You may well win … you may well argue that you have already won … but if you think that 'good moves' alone will humiliate him, you have not paid enough attention to your opponent. He applauded his own defeat. He stood at the end of the sixth game and applauded the beauty of what you had given him. To defeat Spassky … *truly* defeat him … you must make it ugly … you must make the sight of the board repulsive to him ... you must take what he loves and ruin it. Is that what you want?

Bobby Yes.

William Good ... because it is what your country requires. Collegial sportsmanship and fair play will win you handshakes and backslaps ... but slaughter him ... offer up his eviscerated corpse to the gods of war, and you will be held aloft ... anointed and revered. Your countrymen will see themselves reflected in you. Everything they want to believe about their exceptionalism ... their superiority ... the *rightness* of their ideology ... will be confirmed.

Bobby When I win it will be *my* victory ... not America's.

William You can't extricate yourself from what you represent.

Bobby What I *represent* is that I am the greatest ranked chessplayer that has ever lived. The concentration is mine ... the work is mine ... the stamina is mine. I came to the chessboard on my own ... found the problems in the back-pages of newspapers by myself. Lots of people ... Jack Collins ... you ... Lina ... even Spassky ... will claim mentorship ... will claim some possession of my achievements ... but the greatest games I have ever won were against Bobby Fischer. And you tell me that people want to siphon off my energy ... my *lifeforce* ... for the pathetic coincidence that we happen to share a nationality? I did not decide the borders ... I did not issue the passports ... I do not recognise any kind of fellowship with you or with anyone.

William I am proud ... is that wrong of me? We are all so very proud of you.

Bobby Your pride is an insult. Reflected glory is theft. The Russians cheat. They have a hundred men in the Kremlin sweating and calculating and feeding back Spassky's moves. My moves are my own. My successes are my own. I will defeat him because I choose to ... and it will be a blow to their collectivism ... to their *communalism* ... good ... because I detest it. It will not be America that bloodies the Soviets' nose ... this is not America versus Russia ... this is Bobby Fischer versus all you fucks.

Fred *enters – nervous.*

William Yes?

Fred They have ...

William Yes?

Fred They have replaced Spassky's chair.

William *and* **Fred** *look at* **Bobby** *– bracing themselves for his response.*

Fischer *laughs and laughs and laughs.*

GAME SEVEN

SPASSKY (white) vs FISCHER (black)

Sicilian Najdof

Draw

1.e4 c5 2.Nf3 d6 3.d4 cxd4 4.Nxd4 Nf6 5.Nc3 a6 6.Bg5 e6 7.f4 Qb6 8.Qd2 Qxb2 9.Nb3 Qa3 10.Bd3 Be7 11.0-0 h6 12.Bh4 Nxe4 13.Nxe4 Bxh4 14.f5 exf5 15.Bb5+ axb5 16.Nxd6+ Kf8 17.Nxc8 Nc6 18.Nd6 Rd8 19.Nxb5 Qe7 20.Qf4 g6 21.a4 Bg5 22.Qc4 Be3+ 23.Kh1 f4 24.g3 g5 25.Rae1 Qb4 26.Qxb4+ Nxb4 27.Re2 Kg7 28.Na5 b6 29.Nc4 Nd5 30.Ncd6 Bc5 31.Nb7 Rc8 32.c4 Ne3 33.Rf3 Nxc4 34.gxf4 g4 35.Rd3 h5 36.h3 Na5 37.N7d6 Bxd6 38.Nxd6 Rc1+ 39.Kg2 Nc4 40.Ne8+ Kg6 41.h4 f6 42.Re6 Rc2+ 43.Kg1 Kf5 44.Ng7+ Kxf4 45.Rd4+ Kg3 46.Nf5+ Kf3 47.Ree4 Rc1+ 48.Kh2 Rc2+ 49.Kg1

In an upset, the game is a draw. It is as good as a victory for **Boris**. **Bobby** *however is stunned. He is left alone on the stage as doubt creeps in.*

BORIS SPASSKY (USSR)

3

ROBERT FISCHER (USA)

4

Act Two

1.

A bar in central Reykjavík.

Max *is nursing a drink.*

Guðmundur *approaches, drink in hand.*

Guðmundur Can I join you?

Max Sure.

Guðmundur If you need some peace ... I'd hate to interrupt a quiet moment ...

Max Nonsense. Sit down.

Guðmundur This is a bit of a risk, isn't it?

Max What is?

Guðmundur Drinking in a pro-Fischer bar. If the Russians see you ... bang goes your air of impartiality.

Max I hadn't noticed.

Guðmundur There's a poster with his face right on the door.

Max I'll finish this and then find a Spassky bar and drink the same. Just to be fair.

Guðmundur Good idea.

Max The chessboard is still not right. Two weeks into the tournament and we're still negotiating the chessboard.

Guðmundur What's wrong with it?

Max The shading of the squares ... not enough definition ... too light or too dark, I forget which. Worse than the marble board, he says.

Guðmundur This is the wooden board?

Max Yep.

Guðmundur What are you going to do?

Max Do? Nothing.

Guðmundur Are we going ahead?

Max Oh … yes … yes … Spassky put his foot down … any alteration to the equipment must be approved by both sides …

Guðmundur And Fischer agreed?

Max Nothing's certain until he's sat at the board … and even then … (*Shrugs.*) He's lashing out … blaming his tools … blaming Spassky's new chair … anything but himself. (*Beat.*) The system we have … the rules and the conventions of the International Chess Federation … there's an assumption at the heart of our system that we would always be dealing with reasonable men. The norms and customs of championship play never accounted for bullies and madmen.

Guðmundur He is an outlier … a once in a generation player …

Max It is in the event of outliers that we have such safeguards. He is popular … and that makes chess popular … and my god aren't we delighted. Take away the cameras … take away the circus … take away his charisma … and would we bend? No. There were too many exceptions made … too many rules circumvented or bent all out of shape … just so that we could proceed. I should have claimed the first game forfeit. We should not have tolerated his requests … even if it meant defaulting the championship to the Soviets. The fallout would have been great … the investment lost … the profile squandered … the *embarrassment* … but, after it all, we would have maintained our integrity. We have long been a dying interest … niche … exclusive and exclusionary … for the sake of some attention … for the sake of column inches and relevance we've let this arsehole crap all over us.

Guðmundur Chess will survive Bobby Fischer.

Max And all the arseholes of the future will be able to cite him as precedent. How will we enforce laws we've so publicly allowed to be broken?

Guðmundur Spassky could still win.

Max Would it matter now?

Guðmundur So ... should we void it all ... start again ...?

Max To what end?

Guðmundur To restore faith.

Max Faith doesn't break, it dies ... and what is dead remains dead. Trust, however ... we can rebuild trust ... but that takes time and repentance.

Guðmundur He is our Muhammad Ali ... our James Dean ... the membership books of clubs across the whole world are full of fresh ink ... new names ...

Max And so we should allow him free rein ... declare Bobby Fischer untouchable?

Guðmundur He is a genius.

Max It is a stupid term. 'Geniuses' do not appear fully formed like a star in the night sky ... no ... they are more the tallest sunflower in the field. We are bound by laws and strictures ... canes and wires ... but for some reason allow men like him to grow like weeds. Why do we believe 'genius' to be so fragile that we cannot ask it to behave? Urgh ... oh ... I am drunk.

Guðmundur You still have to find a pro-Spassky bar.

Max No, I have to find my hotel. And there ... there you are ... my bias laid bare.

Guðmundur No one expected the rules would ever need to be enforced ... we have never seen a player like him before.

Max Which is exactly why I should have enforced them! And now those chessclubs you speak of are filling up with aspiring Bobby Fischers ... a generation of them ... god help us.

GAME EIGHT

FISCHER (white) vs SPASSKY (black)

English Symmetrical

Black resigns

1.c4 c5 2.Nc3 Nc6 3.Nf3 Nf6 4.g3 g6 5.Bg2 Bg7 6.0-0 0-0 7.d4 cxd4 8.Nxd4 Nxd4 9.Qxd4 d6 10.Bg5 Be6 11.Qf4 Qa5 12.Rac1 Rab8 13.b3 Rfc8 14.Qd2 a6 15.Be3 b5 16.Ba7 bxc4 17.Bxb8 Rxb8 18.bxc4 Bxc4 19.Rfd1 Nd7 20.Nd5 Qxd2 21.Nxe7+ Kf8 22.Rxd2 Kxe7 23.Rxc4 Rb1+ 24.Bf1 Nc5 25.Kg2 a5 26.e4 Ba1 27.f4 f6 28.Re2 Ke6 29.Rec2 Bb2 30.Be2 h5 31.Rd2 Ba3 32.f5+ gxf5 33.exf5+ Ke5 34.Rcd4 Kxf5 35.Rd5+ Ke6 36.Rxd6+ Ke7 37.Rc6

Boris *resigns,* **Bobby** *wins.*

BORIS SPASSKY (USSR)

3

ROBERT FISCHER (USA)

5

GAME NINE

SPASSKY (white) vs FISCHER (black)

Queen's Gambit Declined, Semi Tarrasch

Draw

1.d4 Nf6 2.c4 e6 3.Nf3 d5 4.Nc3 c5 5.cxd5 Nxd5 6.e4 Nxc3 7.bxc3 cxd4 8.cxd4 Nc6 9.Bc4 b5 10.Bd3 Bb4+ 11.Bd2 Bxd2+ 12.Qxd2 a6 13.a4 0-0 14.Qc3 Bb7 15.axb5 axb5 16.0-0 Qb6 17.Rab1 b4 18.Qd2 Nxd4 19.Nxd4 Qxd4 20.Rxb4 Qd7 21.Qe3 Rfd8 22.Rfb1 Qxd3 23.Qxd3 Rxd3 24.Rxb7 g5 25.Rb8+ Rxb8 26.Rxb8+ Kg7 27.f3 Rd2 28.h4 h6 29.hxg5

BORIS SPASSKY (USSR)

3.5

ROBERT FISCHER (USA)

5.5

GAME TEN

FISCHER (white) vs SPASSKY (black)

Ruy Lopez Breyer

Black resigns

1.e4 e5 2.Nf3 Nc6 3.Bb5 a6 4.Ba4 Nf6 5.0-0 Be7 6.Re1 b5 7.Bb3 d6 8.c3 0-0 9.h3 Nb8 10.d4 Nbd7 11.Nbd2 Bb7 12.Bc2 Re8 13.b4 Bf8 14.a4 Nb6 15.a5 Nbd7 16.Bb2 Qb8 17.Rb1 c5 18.bxc5 dxc5 19.dxe5 Nxe5 20.Nxe5 Qxe5 21.c4 Qf4 22.Bxf6 Qxf6 23.cxb5 Red8 24.Qc1 Qc3 25.Nf3 Qxa5 26.Bb3 axb5 27.Qf4 Rd7 28.Ne5 Qc7 29.Rbd1 Re7 30.Bxf7+ Rxf7 31.Qxf7+ Qxf7 32.Nxf7 Bxe4 33.Rxe4 Kxf7 34.Rd7+ Kf6 35.Rb7 Ra1+ 36.Kh2 Bd6+ 37.g3 b4 38.Kg2 h5 39.Rb6 Rd1 40.Kf3 Kf7 41.Ke2 Rd5 42.f4 g6 43.g4 hxg4 44.hxg4 g5 45.f5 Be5 46.Rb5 Kf6 47.Rexb4 Bd4 48.Rb6+ Ke5 49.Kf3 Rd8 50.Rb8 Rd7 51.R4b7 Rd6 52.Rb6 Rd7 53.Rg6 Kd5 54.Rxg5 Be5 55.f6 Kd4 56.Rb1

Boris *resigns,* **Bobby** *wins.*

BORIS SPASSKY (USSR)

3.5

ROBERT FISCHER (USA)

6.5

2.

The Loftleiðir Hotel, Reykjavík.

Boris *is alone in a darkened room. A half-drunk glass of orange juice in front of him. He stares at the glass of juice.*

Nikolai *enters.*

Nikolai You're supposed to be sleeping.

Boris I'm too tired.

Nikolai If you want to join us in the bar …

Boris I don't think so.

Nikolai We've revisited each of the games … we have some notes … on your moves … on Fischer's …

Boris And your conclusion?

Nikolai Come for a drink … see for yourself.

Boris Does this juice taste odd to you?

Nikolai Is it not fresh?

Boris Taste it.

Nikolai *does so.*

Boris Well?

Nikolai It tastes of orange juice.

Boris *not satisfied.*

Nikolai What do you want me to say?

Boris Is there any juice in the minibar?

Nikolai Come and have a drink … it'll help you relax.

Boris I don't want to relax. I want to compare this juice with the juice from the minibar.

Nikolai Boris …

Boris What?

Nikolai You're exhausted.

Boris I can't sleep.

Nikolai We need to talk about your performance. You can barely sit up straight.

Boris I agree.

Nikolai Great.

Boris But I don't think sleep will help. (*Opens a juice from the minibar and hands it to* **Nikolai**.)

Nikolai Do you need to see a doctor?

Boris Drink it.

Nikolai *does so*.

Boris And now the other ...

Nikolai *sips the original glass of juice*.

Boris Well?

Nikolai *shrugs*.

Boris How does it taste?

Nikolai What do you want me to ...?

Boris Just ... have an opinion.

Nikolai This one's sour.

Boris It is.

Nikolai You want me to complain to the hotel?

Boris I brought this one back from the arena.

Nikolai So it's been at room temperature for five hours.

Boris It was sour before. Why do you think I brought it back here?

Nikolai I honestly have no idea.

Boris I'm fine at the hotel ... I'm awake ... I'm alert ... psychologically prepped ... but when I sit at the board ... I'm lethargic ... sluggish ... I can't focus ...

Nikolai ... and you're blaming the caterers?

Boris Don't make light of this.

Nikolai I'm not. You asked for fresh juice. But we are in Iceland. How fresh can the oranges be?

Boris Do we trust the Americans not to spike my food?

Nikolai *has no answer.*

Boris Could I be playing better? Yes. Could I have been better prepared? Maybe. Would you expect the reigning world champion to struggle as I have these last few games? No. And I don't think that's me being arrogant.

Nikolai I can't watch out for their dirty tricks … I'm not equipped to recognize them.

Boris I think they're poisoning me.

Nikolai Bobby Fischer doesn't want to beat you poisoned … what kind of victory is that?

Boris It needn't come from Fischer. I wouldn't put it past Lombardy. I wouldn't put it past their crook of a president.

Nikolai You shouldn't have been so belligerent back in Moscow … you should have accepted the offer of an interpreter … a fixer …

Boris I wasn't going to welcome the KGB on to my team.

Nikolai *sigh.*

Boris What?

Nikolai You think the KGB are just going to stay at home … because you asked? (*Beat.*) Moscow has concerns. They've studied footage of you playing and want to sweep the arena for radiation … they're talking about maybe the Americans have used hypnosis … parapsychology …

Boris Mind-control?

Nikolai … subconscious coercion … I don't know …

Boris Is that even possible?

Nikolai *non-committal.*

Boris Is that your opinion as a psychologist?

Nikolai I'm guessing there's an element of projection here … 'We always see our own mistakes in our opponent.'

Boris I only ever wanted to play chess.

Nikolai That last game …

Boris It was as though I had the flu.

Nikolai He was aggressive … he played aggressively … and that effects rational thought. If you're forced to only think defensively … (*Beat.*) So maybe that's it … not poison or radiation or psy-ops.

Boris I played against Misha Tal … Tbilisi, 1965 … and Tal is friends with Wolf Messing …

Nikolai The psychic?

Boris Mesmerist … telepathist … whatever he calls himself. I didn't know he was in the audience until after the game. I made mistakes … moves a novice wouldn't make. I froze for minutes at a time … as though my brain had short-circuited.

Nikolai Do you think you were influenced by …?

Boris I was not in control of myself at that board.

Nikolai And you feel that same way now?

Boris Yes … something similar, at least.

Silence.

Nikolai I don't know how you screen an audience for telepaths.

Boris You are making fun of me.

Nikolai I think you are looking for excuses. (*Beat.*) The Sports Committee have asked me to fly home.

Boris When?

Nikolai Now. Today.

Boris Absolutely not. Why?

Act Two   315

Nikolai   Because you're not winning. Because he is ahead by three games. And they want to know why.

Boris   I can pull it back.

Nikolai   You should be doing better than you are.

Boris   No. You can't go. Tell them I need you here.

Nikolai   Fine.

Boris   Send them this juice. Bottle it up ... diplomatic bag it back to Moscow ... test it in a lab ...

Nikolai   ... and then what? If they find sedatives ... isotopes ... voodoo ... what do you think would happen?

Boris   We would have proof!

Nikolai   So? It wouldn't matter. How they win doesn't matter. Cheating and lying and subterfuge is just a sideshow ... only really of interest to geeks and obsessives. The vast majority of people see it as all part of the larger game. The Cold War is still a war. Soft Power is still power. You're out here playing by the rules ... they're out here playing to the crowd. (*Beat.*) I will send a sample of this to Moscow ... but it won't be your silver bullet. Be careful. You get a lot of leeway ... a lot of freedom ... as world champion.

Boris   I've never been super political ...

Nikolai   ... and the fact that that's permitted speaks volumes. You may not want to engage with this ... all of this ... the time you were born into ... the politics of the day ... you may consider yourself above such things ... as an artist-grandmaster ... as a world champion ... but, fucking hell, Boris ... try to be aware of your context.

Boris   What should I be doing ... as a 'Good Soviet' ... as a 'Good Russian'? Should I speak of the glory of the Motherland? The weakness of the Western ways-of-life? Or maybe I should highlight the paranoia ... the fear we all live with ... the famines we try to forget? Or maybe I should mention the insane waste of resource that is our tit-for-tat pissing contest of a space race

... of an arms race? Perhaps I should talk of Baba Yaga and her grandson, the Devil, and how they squat hunched over in the Politburo ... at the ears of our leaders ... with their fingers in our lives and their nails at our throats.

Nikolai You are going to lose the World Championship. To an American. Russian chess dominance will come to an end. Because of you. All of the perks and the freedoms that you currently enjoy ... all of the dispensations and the blind-eyes ... they'll be gone ... and you'll be back under the same scrutiny as the rest of us. I hope you're ready.

GAME ELEVEN
SPASSKY (white) vs FISCHER (black)
Sicilian Najdorf
Black resigns

1.e4 c5 2.Nf3 d6 3.d4 cxd4 4.Nxd4 Nf6 5.Nc3 a6 6.Bg5 e6 7.f4 Qb6 8.Qd2 Qxb2 9.Nb3 Qa3 10.Bxf6 gxf6 11.Be2 h5 12.0-0 Nc6 13.Kh1 Bd7 14.Nb1 Qb4 15.Qe3 d5 16.exd5 Ne7 17.c4 Nf5 18.Qd3 h4 19.Bg4 Nd6 20.N1d2 f5 21.a3 Qb6 22.c5 Qb5 23.Qc3 fxg4 24.a4 h3 25.axb5 hxg2+ 26.Kxg2 Rh3 27.Qf6 Nf5 28.c6 Bc8 29.dxe6 fxe6 30.Rfe1 Be7 31.Rxe6

Bobby *resigns,* **Boris** *wins. It is shocking – a comeback.*

BORIS SPASSKY (USSR)

4.5

ROBERT FISCHER (USA)

6.5

3.

The Loftleiðir Hotel – **Bobby***'s hotel room.*

Bobby *is on the telephone to* **Henry***.*

Celebratory noises bleed in from elsewhere in the hotel.

Henry Bobby …?

Bobby Wait.

Henry Bobby … are you there?

Bobby I'm here.

Henry What's happening, Bobby?

Bobby Can you hear that?

Henry I don't …

Bobby Noise.

Henry I can't hear anything, Bobby.

Bobby Listen. (*Beat.*) The Russians.

Henry What are they doing?

Bobby Cheering, I think … singing …

Henry A celebration?

Bobby They're taunting me … to keep me from my sleep.

Henry It's his first win for three weeks … it's to be expected. (*Beat.*) Everyone over here speaks very fondly of you. You are doing good things and we are proud. The American people want you to do well. You mustn't lose heart, Bobby … not over losing a single game.

Bobby He was lucky and I wasn't paying attention. He distracted me.

Henry How did he distract you?

Bobby I don't know … I don't know … but he must have done.

Henry You are still ahead.

Bobby They don't play fairly … they're arrogant and they don't show respect.

Henry And that is why it is important that you bring them down a peg or two. Would you like that? To bring them down a peg?

You are ahead by a good margin. I have every faith that you will continue to lead and deliver a conclusive and devastating blow.

Bobby   My mother's a Communist. Did you know that?

Henry (*long pause*)   Yes, I did know that, Bobby.

Bobby   She sent me to Moscow when I was fifteen ... hoping that I'd get bitten by the 'red bug'. But I'm not so feeble-minded. I saw through them. I wanted to play Botvinnik ... I wanted to play Smyslov ... but I was told that they were unavailable. Grown men too scared to face me. I played Petrosian ... you know Petrosian? He bored me to tears. The lesser players ... they were lining up to play me ... to be beaten by me ... delighting in it like some pervert masochists. It was a joke. And when we were done I asked them ... the Moscow Central Chess Club ... 'where's my money?' 'You're a guest ... we don't pay fees to guests!' They're herd animals ... clumping together ... relying on others to pick up after their mistakes ... to clean the gravel from their grazes ... to wipe their shitty asses. Not one of them could survive alone.

Henry   You have your own team, Bobby. Father Lombardy ...

Bobby   He's a joke.

Henry   And I am here ... on the phone ... talking to you. And you have the American people ... they are your team. They have a great investment in you, Bobby ... a great investment in your doing well.

Bobby   I didn't ask for it and I don't want it.

Henry   You are not alone in this. (*Pause.*) Who won ... between you and Petrosian?

Bobby   Why?

Henry   I am curious.

Bobby   He did ... most of the time.

Henry   Then I'm sure you must have learnt something. (*Beat.*) Do you know what my job is, Bobby?

Bobby You work for President Nixon.

Henry I *advise* President Nixon. Do you know on what matters I advise him?

Bobby *shrugs.*

Henry Bobby … are you there?

Bobby I shrugged.

Henry This is a telephone call, Bobby … I can't see it if you shrug. (*Beat.*) My job is mostly concerned with foreign affairs … with America's standing in the world … our *engagement* with other governments and regimes. War. We are fighting a war right now. Do you know how the Vietnamese fight a war?

Bobby No.

Henry They exhaust us … they have us chasing after false targets. A guerrilla soldier wins when he does not lose. A conventional army loses when it does not win. Are you a guerrilla, Bobby?

Bobby *no response.*

Henry In all things there are rules that are written and rules that are not. A written rule is easier to bend or break because language is fallible … language is translatable … mutable. The words themselves hardly matter. But I always advise against breaking the *unwritten* rules … because breaking them can cause far more damage. Fairness … justice … betrayal – these are the rules I am talking about. Better to keep them moving … keep them undefined … never pin them down. Always be aggrieved.

Bobby Have you got what you wanted?

Henry How do you mean?

Bobby In your life.

Henry The problem is … is that I want a great deal.

Bobby There's an episode of Star Trek … the crew find this woman … her spaceship crashed on this planet years before …

everyone aboard died but her ... a child ... her injuries were great ... and the aliens tried to put her back together ... tried to stitch her back together ... but they'd never seen a human before ... didn't know what one should look like ... didn't know what should go where. So she was a mangled, monstrous thing. How can you build something ... feel something ... *live* something ... if you've never seen it ... if you don't know what it's supposed to look like?

Henry   I know you will do your country proud.

Bobby   People say that like it should mean something. But I don't think I like America very much, Mister Kissinger.

Henry   Is that so, Bobby?

Bobby   It is.

Henry   Can I ask why?

Bobby   It's built on death. Nothing is earned ... everything is taken. Taken from the red man and built on the labour of the black ... and the working class whites buy into it ... keep the system as it is ... sustained by the false hope of the American Dream ... that uncashable IOU ... told that they are the best, shining example to the world ... even as they're forced to sit in their own shit.

Henry   I don't think that is fair, Bobby.

Bobby   Are you a Jew, Mister Kissinger?

Henry   By birth, yes ... though I am sure there are those within the community who would disown me if they could. I am as Jewish as you are, Bobby.

Bobby   I'm not even circumcised. (*Beat.*) Does your job cover ivory?

Henry   Ivory?

Bobby   The international trade in ivory.

Henry   No ... that would be the United States Fish and Wildlife Service. Why do you ask?

Bobby   I want you to do something about the elephants.

Henry The elephants?

Bobby Yes.

Henry What's wrong with the elephants, Bobby?

Bobby They are being hunted to extinction.

Henry Yes. It's a ... I'm sure it's a bad situation.

Bobby It's because an elephant's trunk reminds them of an uncircumcised penis.

Henry The Jews want to wipe out elephants because a trunk looks like a penis?

Bobby Yes.

Henry *laughs, long and hard.*

Bobby Don't laugh at me. Stop laughing at me. I'm serious.

Henry Oh, Bobby Bobby Bobby ... you're American but not American ... Jewish but not Jewish ... what does that leave?

Bobby *silence.*

Henry Bobby ...?

Bobby *silence.*

Henry Are you there ...?

Bobby *doesn't respond.*

The sound of Russian drinking songs fills the hotel.

GAME TWELVE
FISCHER (white) vs SPASSKY (black)
Queen's Gambit Declined, Orthodox
Draw

1.c4 e6 2.Nf3 d5 3.d4 Nf6 4.Nc3 Be7 5.Bg5 h6 6.Bh4 0-0 7.e3
Nbd7 8.Rc1 c6 9.Bd3 dxc4 10.Bxc4 b5 11.Bd3 a6 12.a4 bxa4
13.Nxa4 Qa5 14.Nd2 Bb4 15.Nc3 c5 16.Nb3 Qd8 17.0-0 cxd4
18.Nxd4 Bb7 19.Be4 Qb8 20.Bg3 Qa7 21.Nc6 Bxc6 22.Bxc6 Rac8

23.Na4 Rfd8 24.Bf3 a5 25.Rc6 Rxc6 26.Bxc6 Rc8 27.Bf3 Qa6 28.h3 Qb5 29.Be2 Qc6 30.Bf3 Qb5 31.b3 Be7 32.Be2 Qb4 33.Ba6 Rc6 34.Bd3 Nc5 35.Qf3 Rc8 36.Nxc5 Bxc5 37.Rc1 Rd8 38.Bc4 Qd2 39.Rf1 Bb4 40.Bc7 Rd7 41.Qc6 Qc2 42.Be5 Rd2 43.Qa8+ Kh7 44.Bxf6 gxf6 45.Qf3 f5 46.g4 Qe4 47.Kg2 Kg6 48.Rc1 Ba3 49.Ra1 Bb4 50.Rc1 Be7 51.gxf5+ exf5 52.Re1 Rxf2+ 53.Kxf2 Bh4+ 54.Ke2 Qxf3+ 55.Kxf3 Bxe1

BORIS SPASSKY (USSR)

5

ROBERT FISCHER (USA)

7

GAME THIRTEEN
SPASSKY (white) vs FISCHER (black)
Alekhine's Defence
White resigns

1.e4 Nf6 2.e5 Nd5 3.d4 d6 4.Nf3 g6 5.Bc4 Nb6 6.Bb3 Bg7 7.Nbd2 0-0 8.h3 a5 9.a4 dxe5 10.dxe5 Na6 11.0-0 Nc5 12.Qe2 Qe8 13.Ne4 Nbxa4 14.Bxa4 Nxa4 15.Re1 Nb6 16.Bd2 a4 17.Bg5 h6 18.Bh4 Bf5 19.g4 Be6 20.Nd4 Bc4 21.Qd2 Qd7 22.Rad1 Rfe8 23.f4 Bd5 24.Nc5 Qc8 25.Qc3 e6 26.Kh2 Nd7 27.Nd3 c5 28.Nb5 Qc6 29.Nd6 Qxd6 30.exd6 Bxc3 31.bxc3 f6 32.g5 hxg5 33.fxg5 f5 34.Bg3 Kf7 35.Ne5+ Nxe5 36.Bxe5 b5 37.Rf1 Rh8 38.Bf6 a3 39.Rf4 a2 40.c4 Bxc4 41.d7 Bd5 42.Kg3 Ra3+ 43.c3 Rha8 44.Rh4 e5 45.Rh7+ Ke6 46.Re7+ Kd6 47.Rxe5 Rxc3+ 48.Kf2 Rc2+ 49.Ke1 Kxd7 50.Rexd5+ Kc6 51.Rd6+ Kb7 52.Rd7+ Ka6 53.R7d2 Rxd2 54.Kxd2 b4 55.h4 Kb5 56.h5 c4 57.Ra1 gxh5 58.g6 h4 59.g7 h3 60.Be7 Rg8 61.Bf8 h2 62.Kc2 Kc6 63.Rd1 b3+ 64.Kc3 h1=Q 65.Rxh1 Kd5 66.Kb2 f4 67.Rd1+ Ke4 68.Rc1 Kd3 69.Rd1+ Ke2 70.Rc1 f3 71.Bc5 Rxg7 72.Rxc4 Rd7 73.Re4+ Kf1 74.Bd4 f2

Boris *resigns,* **Bobby** *wins.*

BORIS SPASSKY (USSR)

5

ROBERT FISCHER (USA)

8

4.

Laugardalshöll arena.

Iivo, Efim, Fred and Guðmundur are on the elevated stage. Boris watches to one side.

The lighting rig is lowered. Guðmundur inspects each lamp.

Fred I don't know what you expect to find.

Guðmundur And I don't know what I'm looking for.

Efim There will be some device ... some machinery or electronics that should not be there.

Iivo Something that doesn't look right.

Efim There are frequencies that can cause nausea ... can disrupt concentration ... can incapacitate ...

Fred Are they joking ... are you joking with this?

Iivo What do you mean?

Fred That's rich ... that's really rich ... don't give me this 'frequencies' bunk ... what do you take us for? When your own people sit in the front row blowing on whistles ...!

Iivo Who's blowing on whistles?

Fred Don't try to deny it.

Guðmundur A couple of Icelanders ... members of the audience ... reported a Russian man sitting in the front row with a thin metal tube in his mouth. Anytime an official walked past he would retract the tube back into his mouth. We tried to follow it up, but we couldn't find him after the game.

Iivo How did they know he was Russian?

Guðmundur They overheard him talking.

Efim We know nothing of this.

Fred Of course you would say that.

Iivo During which game?

Fred Excuse me?

Iivo During which game was this supposed to have happened?

Fred The tenth.

Iivo I didn't hear a whistle.

Fred Because the pitch was so high that it was inaudible.

Iivo Then what would be the point in blowing it?!

Fred Fischer suffers from hyperacusis.

Iivo I don't know what that is.

Fred It means he doesn't like whistles.

Efim He won the tenth.

Fred What?

Efim Fischer won the tenth game.

Fred So?

Efim So the whistle ... if there was a whistle ... which I doubt ... didn't make the blindest bit of difference anyway.

Fred That's not the point and you know it.

Guðmundur Am I looking for a transmitter or a speaker or ...?

Iivo Something that emits radiation.

Guðmundur And what does a 'radiation emitter' look like?

Efim Like it doesn't belong in a lighting rig.

Guðmundur Wouldn't such a device effect the audience as well?

Fred That's fair, isn't it? Shouldn't people be vomiting in the aisles?

Guðmundur Or at least complaining of headaches or stomach-upsets or …?

Efim We don't know how advanced this technology is … how directional … how *controlled* …

Fred This is some Buck-Rogers-bullshit. You're trying to imagine into existence a technology to suit your paranoia …

Iivo Searching this rig is in your interest just as much as it is in ours.

Fred If your side had planted anything … then yes, I'm sure you would lead me directly to it and show me how it works.

Guðmundur If the Russians were really cheating, you'd think they would have won a few more games by now.

The Soviets are not amused.

Guðmundur Sorry.

Efim You're going too slowly. (*Starts inspecting the lamps himself.*)

Guðmundur Wait! I've … I think I've …

Efim What is it?

Guðmundur (*inspecting a lamp*) There's … hang on … there's something in here.

Everybody gathers round as **Guðmundur** *opens up the lamp.*

Guðmundur Hang on … nearly there … nearly got it … two of them …

Efim What are they?

Guðmundur Bugs.

Efim I knew it.

Guðmundur Not *bugs* ... not *spy-bugs*. They're flies ... look ... two of them.

Efim What?

Guðmundur Two dead flies.

Iivo *starts laughing.* **Guðmundur** *laughs as well.* **Fred** *joins in.*

Efim Keep looking.

Iivo Efim ... please ...

Efim Keep looking!

Boris, *quiet until now, strides over to the two chairs on the stage. He pulls at* **Fischer***'s chair and upends it.*

Fred Hey! Woah! You can't ... you can't ...

Guðmundur Mister Spassky ... Comrade Spassky ... please ...

Boris Open this up.

Guðmundur No ... we can't tamper with ...

Boris Open up the chair! Take it apart!

Fred What are you doing?!

Boris Fischer is getting external help ... a radio receiver ... a miniature computer ... something ... there is something in his chair and it reeks of corruption.

Guðmundur Please ... there's no need for –

Fred It is the responsibility of the Icelandic Chess Federation to ensure that there is no tampering with –

Guðmundur Yes ... yes ... of course ... Comrade Spassky ... Boris ...

Fred We will not tolerate Soviet interference with our *American* chairs.

Guðmundur We can't pull it apart without any suggestion of ... without probable cause ... please.

Efim X-ray it.

Guðmundur What?

Efim You have x-ray machines on this little island, don't you? X-ray it.

Boris Yes!

Guðmundur Come on now ... this is ridiculous ...

Boris X-ray Fischer's chair or the entire Soviet team walks.

5.

In the countryside outside of Reykjavík.

Sæmi-Rokk *and* **Bobby**.

Sæmi-Rokk Raven-Flóki ... Hrafna-Flóki ... Flóki Vilgerðarson ... he was the first of the Norsemen to set sail for Iceland. Oh there had been rumours ... fables ... but Raven-Flóki was the first to seek it. He set sail from Horgaland, Norway ... sailed to Shetland and the Faroes ... before striking out west. He took with him two ravens. Ravens, as you'll know, are not seabirds – they will not land on water like gulls. Once the Faroes were behind him, Hrafna-Flóki released the first of the ravens. The bird flew straight up into the sky, and ... seeing nothing but the Faroes far behind them ... flew backwards from the stern for the safety of those islands. Days passed before Flóki thought to release the second raven. It flew upwards, and ... seeing no land at all ... circled a few times before returning to the boat. Flóki and his men continued on. More days passed before he thought to release it again ... it flew up from the boat ... but it didn't return ... no, it flew north-westerly ... straight on from the prow. Raven-Flóki steered his ship in the direction of his raven, knowing that it must've sighted land. Flóki and his men disembarked at what we now call Reykjavík ... a place where butter dripped from every blade of grass ... or so they said. I would like to have seen that Reykjavík ... this one is wet and grey and smells of fish. (*Beat.*) What you do not know ... and what I can see ... as I watch you eating your burgers and fries ... swimming in the hotel pool ... on the stage with Spassky ... what you do not know is that you are a raven. Where you go, the world is going to follow.

Bobby　I am not a leader.

Sæmi-Rokk　Maybe not a politician or a general or a guru ... but you set precedence. You make space for others to act as you act ... to think as you think.

Bobby　I am not responsible for anyone but myself.

Sæmi-Rokk　No. And neither is the raven.

Bobby　I'm not interested in that.

Sæmi-Rokk　Of course you are not.

Bobby　Ravens are scavengers.

Sæmi-Rokk　Yes they are.

Bobby　I am not a scavenger.

Sæmi-Rokk　No.

Bobby　I am the top of the food-chain.

Sæmi-Rokk　Why does that matter? (*Pause.*) I am a policeman. I am a judo champion. If there is a domestic disturbance ... if there is a scuffle in a bar ... a fist-fight ... a punch-up ... I am there. And it always calms down when I arrive. If the uniform isn't enough ... if my height and build isn't enough ... then the reputation is. Sometimes a tough guy ... drunk ... tries his luck ... throws a punch ... it is easily dealt with. Whatever the situation is, I can usually calm it. Judo hold or a night in the cells. These men have a constant need to jostle for the top in any situation ... I've never felt the need myself. All it takes is for a bigger dog to turn up. I am a big dog. I have become an expert in the insecurities of men.

Bobby　You think I need a big boy to come and put me in my place? I've had my nose broken and my pocket change taken. I got over it.

Sæmi-Rokk　I think you worry that there are no bigger dogs than you ... and what would that mean? If you are the biggest dog and the world is *even then* still chaos, then it means we are all fucked. And this is where we find the paranoia ... the conspiracies ... the accusations of unfairness ... as if somehow you are being victimised even as you ascend to the throne. You have everything you say you want ... everything you have set out to achieve ... but you do not seem content. You seem horrified at a world that would glorify you.

Bobby Careful, Sammy.

Silence.

Sæmi-Rokk There's going to be a new James Bond.

Bobby Is that so?

Sæmi-Rokk Yes.

Bobby Who?

Sæmi-Rokk Roger Moore.

Bobby I don't know who that is.

Sæmi-Rokk Neither do I. (*Beat.*) I'm driving back into town. I can give you a lift or you can walk back alone. Which is it to be?

GAME FOURTEEN
FISCHER (white) vs SPASSKY (black)
Queen's Gambit Declined, Harrwitz
Draw

1.c4 e6 2.Nf3 d5 3.d4 Nf6 4.Nc3 Be7 5.Bf4 0-0 6.e3 c5 7.dxc5 Nc6 8.cxd5 exd5 9.Be2 Bxc5 10.0-0 Be6 11.Rc1 Rc8 12.a3 h6 13.Bg3 Bb6 14.Ne5 Ne7 15.Na4 Ne4 16.Rxc8 Bxc8 17.Nf3 Bd7 18.Be5 Bxa4 19.Qxa4 Nc6 20.Bf4 Qf6 21.Bb5 Qxb2 22.Bxc6 Nc3 23.Qb4 Qxb4 24.axb4 bxc6 25.Be5 Nb5 26.Rc1 Rc8 27.Nd4 f6 28.Bxf6 Bxd4 29.Bxd4 Nxd4 30.exd4 Rb8 31.Rxc6 Rxb4 32.Kf1 Rxd4 33.Ra6 Kf7 34.Rxa7+ Kf6 35.Rd7 h5 36.Ke2 g5 37.Ke3 Re4+ 38.Kd3 Ke6 39.Rg7 Kf6 40.Rd7 Ke6

BORIS SPASSKY (USSR)
5.5

ROBERT FISCHER (USA)

8.5

GAME FIFTEEN
SPASSKY (white) vs FISCHER (black)
Sicilian Najdorf
Draw

1.e4 c5 2.Nf3 d6 3.d4 cxd4 4.Nxd4 Nf6 5.Nc3 a6 6.Bg5 e6 7.f4 Be7 8.Qf3 Qc7 9.0-0-0 Nbd7 10.Bd3 b5 11.Rhe1 Bb7 12.Qg3 0-0-0 13.Bxf6 Nxf6 14.Qxg7 Rdf8 15.Qg3 b4 16.Na4 Rhg8 17.Qf2 Nd7 18.Kb1 Kb8 19.c3 Nc5 20.Bc2 bxc3 21.Nxc3 Bf6 22.g3 h5 23.e5 dxe5 24.fxe5 Bh8 25.Nf3 Rd8 26.Rxd8+ Rxd8 27.Ng5 Bxe5 28.Qxf7 Rd7 29.Qxh5 Bxc3 30.bxc3 Qb6+ 31.Kc1 Qa5 32.Qh8+ Ka7 33.a4 Nd3+ 34.Bxd3 Rxd3 35.Kc2 Rd5 36.Re4 Rd8 37.Qg7 Qf5 38.Kb3 Qd5+ 39.Ka3 Qd2 40.Rb4 Qc1+ 41.Rb2 Qa1+ 42.Ra2 Qc1+ 43.Rb2 Qa1+

BORIS SPASSKY (USSR)

6

ROBERT FISCHER (USA)

9

GAME SIXTEEN
FISCHER (white) vs SPASSKY (black)
Ruy Lopez Exchange
Draw

1.e4 e5 2.Nf3 Nc6 3.Bb5 a6 4.Bxc6 dxc6 5.0-0 f6 6.d4 Bg4 7.dxe5 Qxd1 8.Rxd1 fxe5 9.Rd3 Bd6 10.Nbd2 Nf6 11.Nc4 Nxe4 12.Ncxe5 Bxf3 13.Nxf3 0-0 14.Be3 b5 15.c4 Rab8 16.Rc1 bxc4 17.Rd4 Rfe8 18.Nd2 Nxd2 19.Rxd2 Re4 20.g3 Be5 21.Rcc2 Kf7 22.Kg2 Rxb2 23.Kf3 c3 24.Kxe4 cxd2 25.Rxd2 Rb5 26.Rc2 Bd6 27.Rxc6 Ra5 28.Bf4 Ra4+ 29.Kf3 Ra3+ 30.Ke4 Rxa2 31.Bxd6 cxd6 32.Rxd6 Rxf2 33.Rxa6 Rxh2 34.Kf3 Rd2 35.Ra7+ Kf6 36.Ra6+ Ke7 37.Ra7+ Rd7 38.Ra2 Ke6 39.Kg2 Re7 40.Kh3 Kf6

41.Ra6+ Re6 42.Ra5 h6 43.Ra2 Kf5 44.Rf2+ Kg5 45.Rf7 g6
46.Rf4 h5 47.Rf3 Rf6 48.Ra3 Re6 49.Rf3 Re4 50.Ra3 Kh6 51.Ra6
Re5 52.Kh4 Re4+ 53.Kh3 Re7 54.Kh4 Re5 55.Rb6 Kg7 56.Rb4
Kh6 57.Rb6 Re1 58.Kh3 Rh1+ 59.Kg2 Ra1 60.Kh3 Ra4

BORIS SPASSKY (USSR)

6.5

ROBERT FISCHER (USA)

9.5

6.

The Loftleiðir Hotel – a hotel room.

Efim *and* **Nikolai**. **Nikolai** *is holding an x-ray.*

Nikolai   I'm not about to accuse the Americans of espionage.

Efim   Why not ... if they're guilty of it?

Nikolai   This makes things worse, not better ... do you understand that?

Efim   We are in the right and they are in the wrong.

Nikolai (*pointing to something on the x-ray*)   You can't even tell me what this object does.

Efim   I'm not a spy ... I don't know spy-craft. I'm not familiar with gadgets and technology ... of what is or what is not possible in the realms and worlds of espionage ... telephones in shoe-heels ... tracking devices in cigarette packets ... but this is quite clearly ... *something*.

Nikolai   Unless I have been briefed to do so, I won't start hurling around accusations. This is an international stage covered by the international press.

Efim   There is no bad time to expose a cheat ... a fraud ... a hypocrite.

Nikolai Boris may have said that he didn't want to be chaperoned, but do you honestly think that there is no KGB presence in Reykjavík right now? These rooms are bugged ... our movements tracked ... our dealings with the Americans recorded ... because of course they are!

Efim You think this could be us?

Nikolai We cannot be certain of anything. We have more immediate concerns.

Efim This cannot be allowed.

Nikolai I wish I had your certainty. I wish that *whatever this is* fitted so neatly within my worldview that there was no room left for doubt ... that I could be confident in chucking around words like 'cheat' and 'liar' and 'betrayal' without concern for consequence or fallout.

Efim The Americans have acted in a way that is not true to the spirit of the game. They have cheated. The tournament is void. This is incontrovertible proof.

Nikolai We are in the midst of a stand-off involving ICBMs and Doomsday devices ... and you keep adding straw to the camel's back. Enough of this.

Boris *enters.*

Nikolai You look like hell. What have you eaten today?

Boris Cluck cluck cluck, mother hen.

Efim Do you want me to order you some room service?

Boris No.

Nikolai He's concerned his food is being tampered with.

Efim Are you being serious?

Nikolai Specifically his orange juice. I had a sample sent back to Russia ... it came back clean. There were no unusual traces ... just juice ... just orange juice ... a bit of pulp. The Sports Committee is satisfied.

Efim He looks fine ... you look fine.

Boris It was making me lethargic.

Efim It's to be expected at this stage of the competition. The opening flurry is well behind us ... and there is always a natural plateau. Now it becomes about endurance ... fitness ... but I would be concerned if he wasn't feeling a little run down.

Boris Have we heard back about the x-rays?

Nikolai FIDE want to scan the chair for a second time before any decision is made.

Efim I'm pretty confident that they'll find the proof we ...

Boris (*exhausted, to* **Nikolai**) Are you on top of this?

Nikolai I am.

Boris Then I don't need the details.

Nikolai You have to eat something.

Boris I need to keep my head clear.

Efim I'll order the food, if you're that worried ... no one will know that it's meant for you.

Boris That's a good idea ... had you not just said it out loud for the lamp and the light fittings to hear. (*Beat.*) Sorry. (*Beat.*) Where's Iivo? He should be back by now.

Nikolai You don't have to be here for this.

Efim It is better to present a united front.

Boris I am sure there is a reasonable explanation.

Efim He has brought this on himself.

Boris Don't.

Efim This isn't the time for naivety.

Boris I'm hardly going to condemn a man without first hearing his ...

Nikolai You want to believe the best of him …

Boris I want honesty.

Efim I understand that … but this could be useful.

Boris How …?

Nikolai The American press has been speculating about your possible defection. Even if it's just the same template for any high-profile Soviet abroad … you should consider …

Boris Let them say what they want.

Efim Even if it fits a narrative … if one were looking for a narrative … as to why you are performing so poorly?

Nikolai We all have to go home after this … and we all have families.

Boris You want to sacrifice Iivo to dispel some half-hearted lies?

Efim He made his choices. And if you benefit … (*Shrugs.*)

Iivo *enters.*

Iivo What are you all doing in my room?

Nikolai Iivo …

Iivo What is this? Have the autopsies come back on those two flies?

Nikolai Take a seat.

Efim Where have you been?

Iivo Just for a walk … along the front … along the sea fortifications … down by the …

Nikolai We know you've been meeting with the Americans.

A deathly silence falls on the room.

Efim Okay … I'm going to lay out what we think … what we believe to be true … how we understand the situation to be … and then you'll have a chance to either refute or deny anything that you deem to be false.

Iivo I'm not entirely sure what I'm supposed to have done.

Efim Then let me tell you. Robert Byrne ... the American chess player ... Grandmaster ...

Nikolai He won the US Championship this year, I believe.

Efim Did he? Good for him. He's in Reykjavík currently ... I've seen him around ... we've all seen him. I don't think he's officially attached to Fischer's team ... he's just here of his own volition. And you have been meeting with him ... between games ...

Iivo I can see how things must look ...

Boris Don't wriggle ... don't squirm ... own it and we can move on.

Iivo Boris, I ... this can all be easily explained.

Boris So explain it.

Iivo *nothing.*

Boris We all know each other ... the chess playing fraternity ... we all play each other ... and friendships can form over chessboards despite barriers of language or politics ... so two friends meeting ... having a conversation ... sharing a cigarette or a cup of coffee ... like opposing border guards at Checkpoint Charlie ... that can be overlooked ...

Iivo Boris ... I have never ... and I would never ... betray you ...

Boris Please. Don't insult me.

Efim One coffee ... one dinner ... maybe dinner and a film ... but between every single game ...?

Silence.

Iivo We're writing a book.

Silence.

Efim What?

Nikolai You're writing a book?

Iivo Yes.

Efim A chess book?

Iivo It's not a ... a ... detective novel! He approached me ... he said he had an idea for a book. There are millions of people across the globe itching for an insight into Spassky ... into Fischer ... so why not write a book? We only ever discuss the games just gone ... never the next game ... never the tactics for the following game. I would want to read such a book ... people all over the world would want to read it ... someone's going to write it ... so why not me?

Boris You should have told us.

Iivo But you'd have made me stop! Wouldn't you?

Nikolai Yes.

Boris I fought for you ... for your place on this team ... against advice ... against the wishes of our superiors ... and you steal from me ... carve bits off and hawk them on the open market.

Iivo I haven't sold you out.

Efim It's not a question of personal loyalty ... if you're passing secrets to the Americans ...

Iivo It's not like we're discussing atomic research ... it's not like I'm funnelling state secrets ...

Efim So you say.

Iivo I ... I'm *not* ... does it need to be said?

Nikolai This is a lot more serious than I think you realise.

Efim If *we* can find out about it ... if the three of us are troubled ... how do you think it'll look to the Kremlin?

Nikolai Are you going to defect?

Iivo I wasn't thinking of ... I wasn't thinking ...

Boris No, you weren't.

Nikolai We get to travel the world ... we get to smoke Western brand cigarettes ... go to the cinema ... see places and ways of living our fellow countrymen do not ... we get to dip our toe in the West ... and it can be very beguiling ... we are high risk and high value ... do you understand that?

Iivo I am not being groomed by the West and I don't want to defect. I don't want to defect. I am loyal. (*Beat.*) Boris?

Boris *no response.*

Iivo What happens now?

Nikolai We've informed the Sports Committee of your decision to fly home. They'll be expecting you on a flight this evening.

Efim The ticket's been booked and your suitcase has been packed.

Boris Thank you, Iivo. Goodbye.

GAME SEVENTEEN
SPASSKY (white) vs FISCHER (black)
Pirc Defense
Draw

1.e4 d6 2.d4 g6 3.Nc3 Nf6 4.f4 Bg7 5.Nf3 c5 6.dxc5 Qa5 7.Bd3 Qxc5 8.Qe2 0-0 9.Be3 Qa5 10.0-0 Bg4 11.Rad1 Nc6 12.Bc4 Nh5 13.Bb3 Bxc3 14.bxc3 Qxc3 15.f5 Nf6 16.h3 Bxf3 17.Qxf3 Na5 18.Rd3 Qc7 19.Bh6 Nxb3 20.cxb3 Qc5+ 21.Kh1 Qe5 22.Bxf8 Rxf8 23.Re3 Rc8 24.fxg6 hxg6 25.Qf4 Qxf4 26.Rxf4 Nd7 27.Rf2 Ne5 28.Kh2 Rc1 29.Ree2 Nc6 30.Rc2 Re1 31.Rfe2 Ra1 32.Kg3 Kg7 33.Rcd2 Rf1 34.Rf2 Re1 35.Rfe2 Rf1 36.Re3 a6 37.Rc3 Re1 38.Rc4 Rf1 39.Rdc2 Ra1 40.Rf2 Re1 41.Rfc2 g5 42.Rc1 Re2 43.R1c2 Re1 44.Rc1 Re2 45.R1c2

BORIS SPASSKY (USSR)

ROBERT FISCHER (USA)

10

GAME EIGHTEEN
FISCHER (white) vs SPASSKY (black)
Sicilian Rauzer
Draw

1.e4 c5 2.Nf3 d6 3.Nc3 Nc6 4.d4 cxd4 5.Nxd4 Nf6 6.Bg5 e6 7.Qd2 a6 8.0-0-0 Bd7 9.f4 Be7 10.Nf3 b5 11.Bxf6 gxf6 12.Bd3 Qa5 13.Kb1 b4 14.Ne2 Qc5 15.f5 a5 16.Nf4 a4 17.Rc1 Rb8 18.c3 b3 19.a3 Ne5 20.Rhf1 Nc4 21.Bxc4 Qxc4 22.Rce1 Kd8 23.Ka1 Rb5 24.Nd4 Ra5 25.Nd3 Kc7 26.Nb4 h5 27.g3 Re5 28.Nd3 Rb8 29.Qe2 Ra5 30.fxe6 fxe6 31.Rf2 e5 32.Nf5 Bxf5 33.Rxf5 d5 34.exd5 Qxd5 35.Nb4 Qd7 36.Rxh5 Bxb4 37.cxb4 Rd5 38.Rc1+ Kb7 39.Qe4 Rc8 40.Rb1 Kb6 41.Rh7 Rd4 42.Qg6 Qc6 43.Rf7 Rd6 44.Qh6 Qf3 45.Qh7 Qc6 46.Qh6 Qf3 47.Qh7 Qc6

BORIS SPASSKY (USSR)

7.5

ROBERT FISCHER (USA)

10.5

GAME NINETEEN
SPASSKY (white) vs FISCHER (black)
Alekhine's Defence
Draw

1.e4 Nf6 2.e5 Nd5 3.d4 d6 4.Nf3 Bg4 5.Be2 e6 6.0-0 Be7 7.h3 Bh5 8.c4 Nb6 9.Nc3 0-0 10.Be3 d5 11.c5 Bxf3 12.Bxf3 Nc4 13.b3 Nxe3 14.fxe3 b6 15.e4 c6 16.b4 bxc5 17.bxc5 Qa5 18.Nxd5 Bg5 19.Bh5 cxd5 20.Bxf7+ Rxf7 21.Rxf7 Qd2 22.Qxd2 Bxd2 23.Raf1 Nc6 24.exd5 exd5 25.Rd7 Be3+ 26.Kh1 Bxd4 27.e6 Be5 28.Rxd5 Re8 29.Re1 Rxe6 30.Rd6 Kf7 31.Rxc6 Rxc6 32.Rxe5 Kf6 33.Rd5 Ke6 34.Rh5 h6 35.Kh2 Ra6 36.c6 Rxc6 37.Ra5 a6 38.Kg3 Kf6 39.Kf3 Rc3+ 40.Kf2 Rc2+

BORIS SPASSKY (USSR)

8

ROBERT FISCHER (USA)

11

GAME TWENTY
FISCHER (white) vs SPASSKY (black)
Sicilian Rauzer
Draw

1.e4 c5 2.Nf3 Nc6 3.d4 cxd4 4.Nxd4 Nf6 5.Nc3 d6 6.Bg5 e6
7.Qd2 a6 8.0-0-0 Bd7 9.f4 Be7 10.Be2 0-0 11.Bf3 h6 12.Bh4
Nxe4 13.Bxe7 Nxd2 14.Bxd8 Nxf3 15.Nxf3 Rfxd8 16.Rxd6 Kf8
17.Rhd1 Ke7 18.Na4 Be8 19.Rxd8 Rxd8 20.Nc5 Rb8 21.Rd3 a5
22.Rb3 b5 23.a3 a4 24.Rc3 Rd8 25.Nd3 f6 26.Rc5 Rb8 27.Rc3
g5 28.g3 Kd6 29.Nc5 g4 30.Ne4+ Ke7 31.Ne1 Rd8 32.Nd3 Rd4
33.Nef2 h5 34.Rc5 Rd5 35.Rc3 Nd4 36.Rc7+ Rd7 37.Rxd7+ Bxd7
38.Ne1 e5 39.fxe5 fxe5 40.Kd2 Bf5 41.Nd1 Kd6 42.Ne3 Be6
43.Kd3 Bf7 44.Kc3 Kc6 45.Kd3 Kc5 46.Ke4 Kd6 47.Kd3 Bg6+
48.Kc3 Kc5 49.Nd3+ Kd6 50.Ne1 Kc6 51.Kd2 Kc5 52.Nd3+ Kd6
53.Ne1 Ne6 54.Kc3 Nd4

BORIS SPASSKY (USSR)

8.5

ROBERT FISCHER (USA)

11.5

7.

Laugardalshöll arena.

Guðmundur, *under the supervision of* **Lothar**, *is dismantling the chairs.*

Max is inspecting two sets of x-rays.

Nikolai *and* **Efim** *stand to one side.*

Guðmundur There is nothing here.

Efim What does that mean?

Guðmundur It means ... that there is nothing here.

Max The first x-ray clearly shows a *something* ... that a *something* was present.

Lothar But the second x-ray does not.

Guðmundur Whatever it is ... or was ... is not here now.

Efim That proves ...

Lothar What does it prove?

Efim ... that whatever was there has been removed ... some device ... a micro-computer ... a radio-transmitter ...

Max But without anything in our hands ...

Efim The Americans have cheated.

Max (*to* **Nikolai**) Do you agree?

Nikolai Efim's opinions do not reflect the official position of the Russian team.

Lothar Is there anything to suggest what might have been present?

Guðmundur No. Nothing.

Lothar Then what else can we do?

Efim Void it! Void it all! This entire tournament ... Fischer's mind games ... his lateness ... his idiot demands ... the fuss over the lighting and the cameras ... arbitrary delays ... talk of chemical substances ... suspicions of spiked food and drink ... and no one can rule out mesmerism ... psychic attack. I have known Boris for many years and I have never seen him so struck ... so depleted ... during a game. We demand that the arena be closed off ...

Nikolai Stop.

Efim   ... and a thorough investigation launched into ...

Nikolai   Efim ... stop.

Efim   You are not the only one who can speak to Moscow.

Lothar   The arena has been swept repeatedly ... for bugs ... for devices. We have had Soviets in here with Geiger Counters ... Americans with decibel meters ... we have x-rayed the chair multiple times ... hospital resources are being used and ... and honestly ... it is probably for the best that we have not found anything suspicious.

Efim   Those x-rays are suspicious.

Lothar   A mistake ... an error ... a screwdriver left behind during manufacture ... who's to say?

Max   It doesn't matter. And I would as soon believe that you Soviets had planted something just to cast suspicion on your opponents.

Lothar   There have been so many accusations that the idea of truth has lost all shape and meaning. But we have to believe that the chess ... that the *game* ... remains one of perfect information. If we were to discover after it all that we have given over our lives to what turns out to be an *imperfect* one ... then ... then what even is the world? (*Beat.*) What a fucking mess.

Max   Nikolai ... if there's nothing else?

Nikolai *shakes his head.*

Max   Very well. Gentlemen.

Max, **Lothar** *and* **Guðmundur** *exit.*

Efim   Do the x-rays count for nothing?

Nikolai   Enough.

Efim   Something was in his chair.

Nikolai   Yes. And then something wasn't. And that's all we know.

Efim   It cannot stand!

Nikolai Why not?

Efim It is not the way that things should be done.

Nikolai Oh my god … an international sporting tournament is being used to further the agendas of nation states! I'm *shocked*! You should probably get on the phone to the Olympic Committee. I have FIFA's number round here somewhere.

Efim So we do nothing?

Nikolai We are the cover under which our nation's security services work … we are the public face … the veneer. We should do what is expected of us … and nothing more. (*Beat.*) I'll inform the Sports Committee. Pass it back up the chain. It is enough.

Efim We should rerun the entire thing.

Nikolai They would only cheat again … in some other way … or we would cheat this time … or we would accuse them of cheating … and they would accuse us. Let us pretend to live in a black and white world … I am not sure that we can cope with anything more complex.

Efim It was not a Soviet device.

Nikolai All the spaces … all the doubts … all the uncertainties we encounter in our lives … we fill them with what we want to be true. So go ahead. Believe what you need to believe.

Efim I believe that … stripped of undue outside influence … that Boris can still win this tournament.

Nikolai We are due to play game twenty-one in a best of twenty-four championship. There is maybe one game – maybe two – before the gravity of Fischer's advantage pulls it to a close. Do you seriously believe that Boris can win three times on the trot from his current position?

Silence.

Efim We have a game to prepare for.

8.

The Loftleiðir Hotel – **Bobby***'s hotel room.*

Bobby *and his mother,* **Regina** *Fischer.*

Regina *is in disguise – a horrendous blond wig and sunglasses.*

Bobby What's wrong with your hair?

Regina It's a wig.

Bobby Why are you wearing a wig?

Regina I didn't want to be recognised.

Bobby Who would recognise you?

Regina This hotel is crawling with journalists.

Bobby I don't see why they would be interested in you.

Regina I didn't want to cause you any trouble.

Bobby You don't look like you.

Regina Shall I take it off?

Bobby Yes.

Regina (*removes her wig and sunglasses*) Hello, Bobby.

Bobby Hello, mother.

Regina So.

Bobby Do you want money?

Regina No, I don't want money.

Bobby Reflected glory?

Regina No.

Bobby Then what?

Regina To see your face.

Bobby Turn on a television. (*Beat.*) I don't understand why you are here.

Regina I don't want to distract you from the tournament ...

Bobby You won't.

Regina ... but this ... this is everything we've ever worked for. It felt wrong not to be near you ... not to share this moment with you.

Bobby Two hundred and fifty thousand dollars.

Regina Excuse me?

Bobby Two hundred and fifty thousand dollars.

Regina Is that how much ...?

Bobby It's how much I'm getting.

Regina For playing?

Bobby For winning.

Regina Well.

Bobby You were wrong. Chess makes money.

Regina I only wanted what was best for you.

Bobby What was best for me was that I played chess. So you were wrong.

Regina They said you were sick ... that you were delayed in New York because you were ill.

Bobby I am the fittest I have ever been.

Regina Sickness doesn't have to be in the body.

Bobby You think I'm a nutbar.

Regina No.

Bobby You think I'm a froot loop.

Regina I have struggled ... I can see you struggle ...

Bobby I am not you.

Regina No.

Bobby They'll take your money ... that's all they want ... when you should spend it on food ... on clothes ... they'll take your money and tell you you're sick ... make up brain diseases ... invent disorders ... they call you crazy so they can take your money. Psychiatry ... it's a racket ... and we all know who runs it. Filling your head ... telling you to be one way ... telling you it's better than the way you are ... well the way I am is that I am the world champion! Top player. Top of the heap. So what do they know ... what do they know?

Regina No one ever tried to put an idea in your head.

Bobby Psychiatrists should be paying me ... working on my brain would be a privilege ... best of all time ... best of all time ...

Silence.

Regina You're ahead. That's good.

Bobby It is.

Regina Near the end.

Bobby Yes.

Regina Would it distract you were I to be in the audience?

Bobby Yes.

Regina Let me see your teeth.

Bobby No.

Regina Your breath stinks. Let me see your teeth.

Bobby *opens his mouth for her.*

Regina Where are your fillings?

Bobby I don't have any.

Regina You had a number of fillings.

Bobby I had them removed.

Regina Why, Bobby?

Bobby I don't want people putting things in my head.

Regina Your teeth will fall out … they'll rot.

Bobby It doesn't matter.

Regina I want you to do well. Haven't I always wanted you to do well?

Bobby Best of all time.

Regina So you say.

Bobby Best. Of. All. Time. (*Beat.*) I am not a child.

Regina No.

Bobby I do not want you here.

Regina You have made that clear. You have always made that clear. And haven't I always done as you've asked? When you were sixteen … I moved out … I left the apartment to yourself and your sister … at your request. I gave you what you wanted … such a special talent … haven't I given you everything you ever wanted? I have not seen you for ten years … I have stayed away for ten years … because that is what you asked of me. Are you not happy? You could have been anything … why have you chosen to be this?

Bobby I am the best.

Regina Let me enjoy this moment. Let me see my son achieve what he always wanted to achieve. Let me see my son happy.

Bobby I don't know what that's supposed to look like … I've never seen it before … I've never known it … how am I supposed to put it together from broken bits? (*Beat.*) There are Communists in this hotel.

Regina I am sure there are.

Bobby Go and knock on their door. They may want you. There are Jews there too. You will feel right at home.

Regina *doesn't leave.*

Bobby They tried to tell me that chess wasn't chess. They tried to tell me about Freud ... about Oedipus ... that taking the king was killing the father ... a father-murder-fantasy game. The queen ... the powerful ... the mother. I tried to tell them the king wasn't a king ... it was just a piece of often-wood that could move one square in any direction. The bishop used to be an elephant ... a messenger ... a jester ... a madman. And a castle can't move. I can play both black and white. I can hold in my mind both halves of the game at once ... and keep them separate ... so that my black-self doesn't know what my white-self is planning. You can only truly know someone when you destroy them ... like a cannibal takes the strength of his opponent in the eating ... and that is what I do when I am at the chessboard ... but increasingly everything is so bland ... because I am at the top now ... so who is there left to destroy?

Regina *comforts him, kissing him gently on the forehead.*

Bobby Get your hands off me – they're dirty. You're dirty. A filthy dirty pig. Jew.

Regina (*steps away*) I am glad you are doing well, Bobby. I wish only the best for you. I hope you get what you need.

Bobby What I *need* is what is due me. What I need is for the universe to be a single star. What I need is for everyone to blink out of existence when I exit a room. I want no before and no after. I want to ascend above the stink and sweat ... the body odour and athlete's foot ... the pimples and boils of other people. I want my mind in space ... a clear white space ... beyond this cheap, physical world with its history and people ... its politics and compromise ... its lies and deceptions. I want to tear down this world ... burn down this world ... so that all that remains is Bobby Fischer. That is what it means to win. I want to win.

GAME TWENTY-ONE
SPASSKY (white) vs FISCHER (black)
Sicilian Taimanov
White resigns

1.e4 c5 2.Nf3 e6 3.d4 cxd4 4.Nxd4 a6 5.Nc3 Nc6 6.Be3 Nf6 7.Bd3 d5 8.exd5 exd5 9.0-0 Bd6 10.Nxc6 bxc6 11.Bd4 0-0 12.Qf3 Be6 13.Rfe1 c5 14.Bxf6 Qxf6 15.Qxf6 gxf6 16.Rad1 Rfd8 17.Be2 Rab8 18.b3 c4 19.Nxd5 Bxd5 20.Rxd5 Bxh2+ 21.Kxh2 Rxd5 22.Bxc4 Rd2 23.Bxa6 Rxc2 24.Re2 Rxe2 25.Bxe2 Rd8 26.a4 Rd2 27.Bc4 Ra2 28.Kg3 Kf8 29.Kf3 Ke7 30.g4 f5 31.gxf5 f6 32.Bg8 h6 33.Kg3 Kd6 34.Kf3 Ra1 35.Kg2 Ke5 36.Be6 Kf4 37.Bd7 Rb1 38.Be6 Rb2 39.Bc4 Ra2 40.Be6 h5 41.Bd7

BORIS SPASSKY (USSR)

8.5

ROBERT FISCHER (USA)

12.5

Bobby *wins. He is triumphant.*

9.

Bessastaðir – the President of Iceland's official residence.

A grand end of tournament party – black tie, loud music, dancing.

A laurel wreath is placed around **Bobby***'s neck. A cheque giving ceremony. Champagne and standing ovations. Music. Dancing.*

Bobby *is closely examining his winner's cheque.*

Boris *approaches.*

Boris   I just wanted to take the opportunity to congratulate you.

Bobby (*points to the name on the cheque*)   Robert James Fischer.

Boris   It was my honour to play against you.

Bobby   Your team spread rumours ... that I poisoned your orange juice ... that I hypnotised you ... that I had teams of lackeys and minions feeding chess moves to me via ear-piece. I didn't hypnotise you. I didn't do any of that. If anyone cheated, you cheated. And what did it get you? Nothing. A whole bag of nothing. A whole suitcase. (*Points again to the cheque.*) Robert James Fischer.

Boris If my side interfered with the game, I was unaware of it. If there was any kind of interference, it was obviously ineffective. (*Beat.*) Don't leave that behind ... your wreath ... bay leaves. My wife still cooks with the leaves from mine. (*Beat.*) I suppose I should say something grand ... something to mark the occasion. I was at the table ... you were at the table ... there is what I know and there is what you know ... somewhere amongst all of that is the truth.

Bobby Cheating is not winning.

Boris It is also not losing.

Bobby No. (*Beat.*) There were some good games.

Boris There were. I hope to play you again someday.

Bobby If the money is right. (*Beat.*) How old are you?

Boris What ...?

Bobby How old are you?

Boris I'm thirty-five.

Bobby There's six years between us.

Boris Is that important?

Bobby I am your better.

Boris So says the base of the trophy.

Bobby I am not a child.

Boris I never said you were. (*Beat.*) You want to say we met as equals? Yes, we met as equals. You want to say you outplayed me? Yes, you outplayed me. You want to say you are my better? I am not going to stop you. I am proud to have played you, Bobby Fischer. I am proud to have played those beautiful games. But I am also tired. It is a lot to carry. I daresay your American burdens will be somewhat different to the expectations I've shouldered ... but there is some relief for me in all of this. Let me give you some advice … from one world champion to another. It will be hard for you. You will feel like a god. You will feel unstoppable. When you want something for so long … when you define yourself by the wanting of it … it can be disarming to finally … to finally achieve … do you understand? You think it will solve all your problems … but often it only magnifies them. It will bring you friends who are not your friends … lovers without love … and you will have no control over how other people see you … how the world sees you. And that will infuriate you like nothing else before. (*Beat.*) I must drink more champagne.

Bobby I beat you.

Boris You did.

Bobby I won.

Boris Well done.

Bobby Best of all time.

10.

The Loftleidir Hotel – foyer.

Nikolai *and* **Efim** *wait with their suitcases – they look tired, beaten.*

Nikolai I'm going to get some air.

Efim It's raining.

Nikolai Then I'll take an umbrella.

Efim It's that sort of preparation and forethought that has so far been lacking on this trip.

Nikolai Is that our defence then? Our strategy? Is that we will tell them? That Boris was underprepared?

Efim He thought he could play honestly. His views on bourgeois sportsmanship scuppered us. His trust in the sport was naïve.

Boris *enters with a suitcase.*

Nikolai Our car should be here in …

Boris Just put me on the plane. The details don't matter.

Nikolai There are going to be questions asked …

Boris Then let them be asked back home. We have a three-hour flight to Copenhagen … and from Copenhagen then on to Moscow … let me have my time … these last few moments outside the state machinery.

Sæmi-Rokk *enters – a box in his hands.*

Nikolai I think our taxi is here. Efim?

Efim *and* **Nikolai** *exit with their suitcases.*

Sæmi-Rokk Mister Fischer wanted me to send his regards.

Boris Did he?

Sæmi-Rokk He wanted me to give you this … a token … it's nothing …

Boris *opens the box – inside is a camera.*

Sæmi-Rokk It's a camera.

Boris Why has he given me a camera?

Sæmi-Rokk People give him gifts … gifts he doesn't need or want.

Boris Thank you. Thank him.

Sæmi-Rokk Of course.

Boris You'll stay in contact with him … now the championship is over?

Sæmi-Rokk He is my friend. You'll be glad to get home.

Boris I haven't walked those streets … entered those rooms … those Russian rooms … those Soviet rooms … the Moscow Central Chess Club … having lost a title before. I can't see the next move. I don't know what it looks like. I first learnt this damn game when I was four years old ... born in Leningrad ... a child of war. We were evacuated ... taken to an orphanage ... myself and my older brother. There was a chessboard and some of the children knew the rules. We would sometimes hear news from home ... things people had seen ... done ... rumours and trauma. We had friends there still ... family ... neighbours. Unburied bodies in the streets ... limbs ... rubble ... hunger. People did desperate things to survive ... animalistic things. How can a child process *chaos* on such a scale? Chess was an escape ... a simple universe ... simple in its movements ... yet still it contains infinities. And I stayed there for a while ... hiding in that world of kings, knights and rooks. I stayed there for a long time. Stayed there through Stalin ... through Khruschev ... through Brezhnev. But it seems that chaos has found me again ... and I ... and I ... (*Beat.*) I should be cursing his name. I should hate him. In a long match such as this ... a player can travel very deep inside himself ... into dark unlit depths ... and when it's all done ... you come to the surface very fast. Every time after a tournament ... if I win or lose ... I become so incredibly depressed. People seem alien to me ... friends seem like strangers ... because no one knows me like he does ... no one has struggled with me ... wrestled with me ... on such a fundamental level. It's ridiculous but I miss him already.

End.